By the very nature of its conception, the history of The Parachute Regiment is not centuries old. Formed in 1940, it has packed in an enormous amount over the last seventy-five years and I have been enormously privileged to have been involved with the Regiment for over half of this time; indeed, I am now beginning to see the grandsons of those Paras I first came across when I became Colonel-in-Chief in 1977 joining their "family regiment". The officers and soldiers I have met over the years are fiercely proud of the Regiment in which they serve, and rightly so. I have always found them to have the infectious optimism, unstoppable energy and drive that Field Marshal Montgomery spoke of. You will see that evidenced again and again in this book.

There is no doubt that an oral history such as this is hugely important. To my mind, there is no better way to obtain an understanding of the realities and challenges of warfare and military operations than by listening to those who have lived through them. The officers and soldiers of The Parachute Regiment have always been at the forefront of the action, or at the point where the toughest decisions have to be made. So, it is vital that those making history should at the very least be able to set out their part in it.

I very much suspect that you will be as hugely impressed as I am by the professionalism, initiative, courage and humour of the men who wear the red beret. Their recent history, set out in these pages, makes me immensely proud to serve as their Colonel-in-Chief.

Also by Max Arthur

*The Busby Babes: Men of Magic*

*Above All, Courage: First Hand Accounts from the
Falklands Front Line*

*Northern Ireland: Soldiers Talking*

*Men of the Red Beret*

*Lost Voices of the Royal Air Force*

*Lost Voices of the Royal Navy*

*When This Bloody War is Over: Soldier's Songs of the
First World War*

*Symbol of Courage: A History of the Victoria Cross*

*Forgotten Voices of the Great War*

*Forgotten Voices of the Second World War*

*Last Post: The Final Word From Our First World
War Soldiers*

*Lost Voices of the Edwardians*

*Faces of World War One*

*Dambusters: A Landmark Oral History*

*The Road Home: The Aftermath of the Great War Told
by the Men and Women Who Survived It*

*Fighters Against Fascism: British Heroes of the
Spanish Civil War*

*The Last of the Few: The Battle of Britain in the
Words of the Pilots Who Won It*

*The Silent Day: A Landmark Oral History of D-Day
on the Home Front*

*Churchill: The Life*

# The Paras

*From The Falklands to Afghanistan
in their own words*

## MAX ARTHUR

HODDER &
STOUGHTON

First published in Great Britain in 2017 by Hodder & Stoughton
An Hachette UK company

1

Copyright © Max Arthur 2017

A CIP catalogue record for this title is
available from the British Library

Hardback ISBN 9781444787580
Trade paperback ISBN 9781444787573
eBook ISBN 9781444787559

Typeset in Sabon MT by Palimpsest Book Production Ltd,
Falkirk, Stirlingshire

Printed and bound by Clays Ltd, St Ives plc

Hodder & Stoughton policy is to use papers that are natural, renewable and
recyclable products and made from wood grown in sustainable forests.
The logging and manufacturing processes are expected to conform to
the environmental regulations of the country of origin.

Hodder & Stoughton Ltd
Carmelite House
50 Victoria Embankment
London EC4Y 0DZ

www.hodder.co.uk

This book is dedicated to all who have served or were attached to the Airborne Forces and in particular those who stand proud in Valhalla.

*Unus pro omnibus, omnes pro uno.*

# CONTENTS

# THE PEGASUS ETHOS

As British Airborne soldiers we place the mission, and our comrades, before ourselves. Our bravery is founded upon determination, endurance, and selflessness. We are supremely disciplined and that discipline is primarily self-imposed. We take pride in being part of an elite, and we understand our responsibility to strive for the highest standards of achievement, turnout and attitude. We wear Pegasus with humility, recognising our obligation never to demean or diminish the value of others. We are a compassionate friend, but a ferocious enemy. In battle, in barracks, and at home, we always do the right thing.

# PREFACE

*The Paras: The Falklands to Today* is based on interviews with those who have served or are still serving with the Parachute Regiment in 1, 2, 3, 4 or 10 Para, as well as men of the Pathfinder Platoon. It also contains interviews with members of the Royal Army Medical Corps who have worked closely and saved so many soldiers of the Parachute Regiment.

Like *Men of the Red Beret*, written in 1987, I have not set out to write the history of the Regiment; rather I have sought to capture something of the spirit of these men and those who have served alongside them. The majority of the accounts have come from personal interviews or from accounts sent to me, then edited and returned to be checked. Wherever possible, the historical accuracy of these accounts has been verified, but errors of time, places and names may still be present. Apart from the occasional interlinking sentence or minor grammatical changes, these accounts are entirely in their own words. The rank given at the start of each of account is the one held at the time. For reasons of security, a small number have only their rank and not their name before their account.

There is a brief historical outline to all the operations in which the Regiment has been deployed and what follows are personal accounts beginning with the Falklands Campaign and ending in the long-fought war in Afghanistan. Each account is a chapter in itself, a chapter in the life of the person who related it. I have arranged these accounts within the context of the operation in which he or she was involved and because these are personal accounts, not cold history, the order will undoubtedly be imperfect. Many go into great detail, while others select the most affecting moments.

Throughout the writing of this book it has been my privilege to meet so many brave men of the Parachute Regiment and I believe that their words not only provide a unique chronicle of an elite force in action, but also illustrate their inimitable and indomitable character, as well as their remarkable humour in the grimmest of circumstances.

These are their words – I have been but a catalyst.

Max Arthur
London
September 2017

*Further information can be found on www.paradata.org.uk or www.army.mod.uk/infantry/regiments.*

# INTRODUCTION

War and conflict has an enduring nature but a changing character, unique to each period of warfare. Since the publication of *Men of the Red Beret* in 1990 (on the occasion on the fiftieth anniversary of Churchill's call on 22 June 1940 for 5,000 parachute troops), much has changed: there are now five domains of war: cyber and space have been added to the land, sea and air environments. The weapons have changed, but at its heart, war remains a clash of wills, where sheer bloody-mindedness to prevail – or die trying – remains as relevant today as it was at the pass of Thermopylae with a few hundred Spartans.

Airborne Forces may not lie in a direct lineage from Leonidas, but many within this particular brotherhood would believe that they are. I believe them, for they are of the same unshakeable spirit and warrior culture. It is primary group cohesion that keeps men fighting long after they should. This was evident in those who fought at Arnhem. The United States Liaison Officer with 1st Airborne Division said, 'I saw men who were hungry, exhausted, hopelessly outnumbered, men who by all the rules of war should have gladly surrendered to have it all over with, who were shelled until they were hopeless psychopaths; and through it all they laughed, sang and died, and kept fighting.' That remains true today. A key variable will always be 'how will people fight' and 'how well will people fight'. The concept of group success potentially at an individual's expense is largely alien in modern society. It is not for those who via the challenges of Pre-Parachute Selection – P Company – serve in Airborne

Forces. Success of the group is more important than the individual.

Many of the more recent campaigns, such as Iraq and Afghanistan, were fought in an arena where the absence of a clear mission and end state meant that it was hard to find a purpose for which the Toms (privates) might willingly sacrifice themselves for an uncertain mission and unifying purpose. That unifying purpose became each other. As always, 'matehood' meant that Airborne Forces fought for what they have always fought for – each other. No one wanted to let their 'mucker' on their left or right flank down. None did.

The period since 1990 has been a period of intense operational tempo. Airborne Forces continued to provide support to Northern Ireland almost to the end of the normalisation period in 2007. Other campaigns and deployments took Operation Banner's place. Kosovo, Macedonia, Sierra Leone, Iraq and Afghanistan have provided the backdrop to the be-medalled chest we see on the current generation. This book tells the tale of these medalled men with the same fortitude, good humour and resilience that was the mark of the men who came before.

What has not changed is the quality of the soldier. The Airborne soldier has never been bewildered for long in a fight with our enemies where our collective experiences have given us 'riotous excursions with privileged glimpses into the human heart'. When the time came for deployment on each occasion, we never feared the enemy. Every Tom, NCO and officer feared only that he might somehow disappoint those who preceded him. It never happened.

We serve in an elite that has always stood shoulder to shoulder with each other with a clear understanding that our job is to fight, and to fight well. If you think you are second best, you are. Airborne Forces have never suffered from that lack of self-confidence: 'knowledge dispels fear' as the motto of the Parachute Training School tells us, and each red-bereted member has always had the knowledge that he is part of a brand of excellence.

This excellence is reflected in the honours and awards given to the men of Airborne Forces. *Men of the Red Beret* concluded with the award of two Victoria Crosses for Lieutenant Colonel H. Jones of 2 Para and Sergeant Ian Mackay of 3 Para in the Falklands campaign. The modern generation of Airborne soldiers took up the baton, and that 'golden thread' continues in this volume with the award of the nation's highest honour 'for gallantry' to Corporal Bryan Budd and Lance Corporal Josh Leakey. Neither would see himself as a man apart; merely part of that extraordinary 'band of brothers' that is marked by those who wear the red beret. Every man remains, in Montgomery's famous words, 'an emperor'.

I was privileged to serve in this modern era of the Airborne soldier for thirty-three years. It was too short, for every day with these men of action and thought was an honour. In the formalities of military hierarchies, they often saluted me; it is now my time to salute them. I gladly do so.

*Major General Chip Chapman, 2017*

# 1

# THE FALKLANDS
# 1982

## Operation Corporate

On 2 April 1982, Argentina invaded Port Stanley, the capital of the Falkland Islands Dependencies. With only about eighty marines for defence, the islands and South Georgia were quickly overrun. A British Task Force was rapidly gathered to retake the islands. At this time, the 3rd Battalion was the spearhead battalion, and they were attached to 3 Commando Brigade Royal Marines, leaving the UK on 9 April on SS *Canberra*. The 2nd Battalion were also stood to, and departed on 26 April on MV *Norland*. During the long voyage south, both battalions carried out intensive training.

On the night of 21 May, 3 Commando Brigade Royal Marines went ashore at Ajax Bay. The 2nd Battalion established itself on Sussex Mountain, protecting the south of the bridgehead without opposition, and the 3rd Battalion landed in the north, near Port San Carlos. On 26 May, the 2nd Battalion was ordered to move south and engage the Argentinians on the Darwin/ Goose Green Peninsula. The attack began during the early hours of 28 May with naval and artillery support. At daylight, however, it was held up by strong enemy defensive positions near Darwin, and the CO and adjutant were killed trying to take out a machine-gun post. The assault continued and by last light the whole peninsula, less the Goose Green Settlement, was taken. Negotiations with the Argentinians produced their surrender the next day. It is estimated over 1,200 Argentinian prisoners were taken and fifty-six killed.

Mount Longdon was attacked by the 3rd Battalion during the night of 11 June. The enemy were well dug in and prepared and it was only after ten hours of fighting that the 3rd Battalion secured the objective. They then held it for forty-eight hours under intense and accurate artillery fire.

On the night of 13 June, the 2nd Battalion passed behind the 3rd Battalion and attacked Wireless Ridge. This again was secured by first light and shortly afterwards, the enemy resistance collapsed. Both battalions followed up and were the first troops to enter Port Stanley. In all, forty-two men of the airborne forces were killed in the Campaign, including three personnel on attachment.

## Goose Green

*Major John Crosland, 2 Para*

After we had been on the *Norland* for four or five days, I got the Toms together and told them what my thoughts were – that we were going to war! The reason I felt that was that Margaret, who is a very determined lady, had set the ground rules very early on. She had said she wouldn't negotiate until the Argentinians had left, and having been involved in the Iranian Embassy siege in London in 1980, I knew her thinking, because she'd set the ground rules there.

We had about three weeks before landing, in which we could concentrate on one solid objective – training for war. We'd never had a period like this since Borneo, which was fourteen years ago. I could really concentrate the Toms' minds, because there were no outside imbuggerancies like duties and guards and everything else.

Fortunately, I'd given a lot of thought to the psychological preparation and battlefield stress, based around Lord Moran's book, *The Anatomy of Courage*. I'd also had previous experience in Northern Ireland and with the SAS in Oman.

Northern Ireland had its very violent periods and some prolonged operations, but none with the full orchestration of war. There were shooting engagements, but you can't compare those to a full-scale battle. The Toms in my company hadn't heard the noise of a sustained battle, or felt the intense loneliness and fear that results from such an experience. I was fortunate to have had that experience, so spent a lot of time talking to my company, to the officers and NCOs, taking them through a scenario which was to prove close to the reality of the battles that were to come.

The one thing I had to impress on my soldiers was that the Northern Ireland image of a casualty halting an operation wasn't going to happen in the Falklands. We had an objective to take, so whoever got bowled over had to administer their own first aid and look after themselves. Then, once we'd secured our objective, we'd come back and sort out the casualties. So, for ten days, the highly professional medical people in the FSTs (Field Surgical Teams) put the Toms through an intensive medical cadre on life-saving, first aid, gunshot wounds, tears, rips and all the rest of it.

At the end of it, they could take blood, put in drips and repair all manner of wounds very efficiently. Because I'd instilled in them that we were going to war, they didn't play at it – they were totally committed. This was going to be the most frightening thing they had ever come across in their lives, but they'd have to get over that and get on and do their job. In their training, I'd tried to instil in them the need to be aggressive, because I don't think people understand the amount of violence that's got to be generated to impress your point of view on somebody who's equally keen to impress his view on you.

The opposition would be a regular army with conscripts, so if we made our presence felt initially, they might just crack. This proved correct, because at Goose Green we not only beat them physically, but psychologically. So from then on (although there were severe battles in the mountains), they never counter-attacked, yet they had the troops, ammunition and logistics. In the first encounter at Goose Green, we'd given them what's called a classic Parachute Regiment punch-up – a gutter fight – but then our blokes are bloody good at that, probably the best in the world. Some of the rumours about the Argentinians being ill-equipped, underfed and lacking ammunition were just not true. I mean, our blokes were amazed at what we found around the place. With our calibre of blokes in those positions, it would have been Crete all over again, and we would have wiped anyone out.

We landed on 21 May, and had five or six days of bad weather until we moved off from Sussex Mountains towards Goose Green. Our first scheduled attack on Goose Green was cancelled. We moved off again on the 26th/27th towards Camilla Creek House. On that march down, which was a four- or five-hour trog, we were carrying a lot of weight on our backs, but at least the Toms were on the move. There were various shell holes on the way, and I remember some of the younger ones asking what they were. I said, 'Well, they're not moles!'

What I was trying to get them to do was to look for signs. I'd seen shell holes before and pointed out some that were fresh and had obviously been made that night, because there was ice on the others. The blokes then started to become attuned to what to look for and what the signs meant. I also told them to listen carefully so they would tune their ears to the incoming artillery fire. They could hear the guns firing and the whistle – and they were all going down a bit bloody quick. So I explained that the shots that they'd just heard were well over to our east, but it was the first time they'd heard it, and as it was coming vaguely towards them, they were obviously very wary. So I really had to orchestrate their ears.

The one thing I stressed was, 'You will get artillery and mortar fire against you, but you've got to maintain your momentum – I may not be there – you may lose your section commanders or senior soldiers, but someone's got to keep it going. That's what it's all about. You may be on your own, isolated and feeling afraid – but you must keep thinking, because if you don't think, you'll get killed.'

We stayed at Camilla Creek House for a while. While we were there, a breach of security happened when, for some inexplicable reason, the BBC World Service told the world and his wife where we were. That involved four hundred of the enemy being flown in and positions being turned round to meet our likely advance. A fairly stressful time, especially as H (Lieutenant Colonel H. Jones) had already told us that we were going into action against odds of two to one; these were already sporting odds, so we didn't need them increased!

We were fairly well forward of our own defensive position and well in range of enemy artillery and their air recce, facing a garrison which was fairly well equipped. H had an O Group and I got back to give my orders just after last light. I sat facing my company O Group, three young platoon commanders: the eldest could only have been in the army for a year and a bit, and the youngest had only been with me since January of that year, so for them it was a big occasion. My three platoon sergeants were not that experienced either, so it was not the best time to start giving out orders or talking about hundreds of the enemy. But one had to be fairly blunt about things. I told them that the training we had done before was all part of the great maxim that in peace we were training for war. We had trained aggressively and realistically and now we were at war.

I went through our battle plan of what I wanted them to do: how we were going to get on with it; how they would do their job in controlling their platoons and sections; how I would keep the direction with the forward observation officer. I then talked about keeping the supporting fire moving ahead, casualty procedure and prisoners of war. We'd been put on the west side to blockbust down towards Boca House. H's plan was for a six-phase day/night or night/day silent/noisy attack. H knew well that B Company was a fairly aggressive company, because that's the way I had trained them, and they had confidence in their own ability. I knew that we'd been put on a side that had a fair amount of problems. So we knew we were in for a hard slog and that time was precious. I told them that we must get on, that we were not interested in capturing hundreds of dagos – someone else could do that. What I wanted to do was go through position after position after position and keep battering away at them. Finally, I said to them, 'These people have nicked our islands – we're going to make them wish they had never heard of the Falkland Islands.'

Later we moved to the forming-up point at the neck of the isthmus leading down to Goose Green. A Company had to swing round to the east in order to take out Burntside House before the whole battalion could move straight down. If we hadn't done that, we would have been hitting one another with crossfire. So we moved into position and just lay down in our assault formations. The blokes lit cigarettes and we listened to the night noises of HMS *Arrow*, which was firing away, but unfortunately a mechanical problem nullified her very impressive fire support, which later we were to rue.

A Company started to make their attack, and although there were shells coming over, they caused few problems. Slowly my lads started to get attuned, but there was a tension around because we knew from our own patrols that facing us, about 400 or 500 yards away, there was an enemy company defensive position with a machine gun.

In support for the attack we had three light guns based at Camilla Creek House, which were firing ahead of us. We only had very limited helicopter lift to come forward with the small amount of ammunition that we had. The support boys carried forward two mortars with ammunition. A normal battalion would have six or eight, but we had only two. However, we did have six detachments of Milans, and we also had six heavy machine guns. We had, of course, expected HMS *Arrow* to be the main thrust of our artillery attack.

It was such an awful night in terms of the weather that one of our problems was actually being able to see what we were coming into. Although it was dark, raining and even snowing at times, the Toms got accustomed to it. At least they'd had some experience of night fighting during the previous November while carrying out exercises in Kenya.

The one thing I'd learnt in the Middle East was to keep the momentum going – if you stopped on a position, you got hammered. So all through the night we kept crashing on. Their artillery, which was generally well orchestrated, had a job to find us. When we did stop, because we got disorganised or came across a position we didn't know about, the enemy rearranged their artillery to fire back on us. What saved us in these situations was that the ground was very soft and a lot of shells ploughed in or blew up the peat. If it had been a very hard surface, I think the casualties on both sides would have been far worse.

The company killed its first Argentinian about three minutes after the start. This thing actually arose from a trench, in a helmet and poncho; there was no face, just a helmet and poncho. We challenged him twice and nothing happened. The third time, his hands moved and two of my machine-gunners and two riflemen opened up and, rather naturally, this bloke fell over. So that was a release of tension; we knew our weapons worked. As they say in the vernacular, 'Targets scream when hit.' Like the first punch from a boxer or the first run for a batsman, we'd played it and hit home.

That night, in the aggressive trench-to-trench action, we had them all over the place, and we didn't sustain any casualties in my company. We had to fight at really close quarters for four or five hours, which showed our soldiers' durability and stamina; certainly their aggressive, hard training paid off. I think we had, without blowing one's own trumpet, the most problems to overcome, but we kept moving in a classic formation of two platoons up and one platoon back. A Company was on our left and we couldn't link in with them, so it wasn't a classic two-company move, which we achieved later at Wireless Ridge. Many of the actions were led by young NCOs, senior soldiers and young soldiers. I think the little black woollen hat I wore throughout the campaign helped the Toms to identify me, and I'm sure they thought, if that stupid bugger's still running around with that hat on, it can't be that bad.

Come the dawn, we were out of the driving seat. We'd come up against the main defence position, which was the ridge of Darwin Hill in the east, and we were still about 800 metres short of Boca House, which we'd expected to take in one run that night. We'd lost two hours of darkness due to D Company having a punch-up behind us, and we'd also hit another position that had taken forty-five minutes to clear. These things happen in battle. The only thing to do was to move forward, so I ordered the two leading platoons, 4 and 6, to move ahead with Company HQ into the gully, into the bottom and up the other side towards a sort of gorse line, which gave some cover from the enemy's fairly dominant position at Boca House.

As the light increased, so did the accuracy of their fire. I had two options – either withdraw completely, or get forward. I certainly wasn't going to withdraw, so I ordered my two forward platoons ahead with my own HQ. I left my reserve, 5 Platoon, on the crest line to protect the whole of the high ground in case we had to beat a hasty retreat; it was that platoon that took a battering. We also got fairly well larded with artillery and mortars. I said to 5 Platoon over the net, 'Right, once we get down into the gully, you withdraw on to the hill line and just hold the ridge-line position.'

It was during this action we lost young Stephen Illingsworth. He had rescued Private Hall, who had been shot, and then, because we were short of ammunition, had gone back for Hall's kit, and while doing this was killed. It was a classic young soldier's act – extremely brave, totally unselfish, and one can only give the highest praise for him.

A little later there was a pause in the action as each side tried to sum up its own situation. During this period, the Toms were able to see the devastation we'd created through the night, because we were not standing in the positions we'd taken out. We could see the effects of artillery fire, mortars, grenades and our own handiwork. In this lull, a mortar bomb came through the air, spinning rather badly, hit the crest line and very ser-iously wounded my second-in-command, Captain John Young.

We were under increasing pressure, because we'd been in action for four hours during the night without resupply. About 400 or 500 yards in front of us, across a totally open field, was a very strong enemy position. They were in the driving seat and could put down artillery, air attack or mortar fire whenever they wanted. Although we were putting down fire on to their positions and hitting their bunkers, we weren't actually killing the blokes inside. So I said, 'Cool the fire.' I kept one machine gun going, because at the back of my mind was the thought that they could counter-attack. We were in a fairly tenuous position, because Toms were trying to hide behind gorse bushes which, needless to say, hardly provided adequate cover.

The situation changed when Corporal Margerison managed to clear a bunker and Corporal Robinson's lot flattened another. Robinson had a lucky escape when a bullet just missed his balls. All I could hear him say was, 'If you've hit me in the balls, the wife'll kill me!' But once he'd ascertained that he'd still got a pair, he was all right.

I then took command of directing our guns and mortars on to the positions that were giving us problems. To my simple brain, what's hurting you at the moment has got to be eradicated. You worry about positions at Goose Green once you get to Goose Green. It was during this period that I heard that H was killed. When the news came over the net, I said to Corporal Russell, my signalman, 'That doesn't go any further. We've got enough problems without letting that out.' I was close to H – we thought along the same sort of lines. His death certainly stiffened my resolve. I mean, I was always determined that we were going to win, but his death just added a bit more oomph.

Shortly after the news of H's death, I heard that the Argentinians had landed another two hundred people to our south. We were in for trouble. I thought of John Frost's 'a bridge too far' at Arnhem in 1944, and I said to myself, 'We've gone an island too far.' We needed to strike again. Boca House was our major objective, but with the weapons that we had, we couldn't get effective fire on to it, so I called up the Milan team. A Milan is an anti-tank weapon that fires a guided missile with a very substantial warhead over a range of 2,000 metres.

I thought, if we can bust them with the Milans, we can probably get round their flank, get down to Darwin, knock that off, and then worry about Goose Green. The Milan was an unorthodox choice, but it was the only powerful weapon we had. Much to our relief, the first round fired was a perfect bull's-eye. It went straight through the bunker window and blew it out completely, and the second one did the same. Four more rounds and that was Boca House cleared out. Everyone stood and cheered!

A Company achieved a breakthrough in their own right and cleared Darwin Hill. Chris Keeble had taken over command by then and sent D Company off to start attacking Goose Green. We then started to come under fairly intense fire from Goose Green and the airfield. Their anti-aircraft guns had very good optics, so they could see us at about a mile-and-a-half's distance. Chris Keeble had been calling for an air strike all day, but weather conditions were bad. However, at last light the Harriers came and I would say their effect was critical. They flew in on a low pass and dropped cluster bombs, inflicting a lot of casualties. It was a surgical strike – very precise – and I think this undermined their will to keep fighting.

Prior to the aerial attack, we had continued towards Goose Green with D and C Companies. A Company remained on Darwin Hill. We'd heard that there were 112 civilians being held in Goose Green, so our idea of going in and flattening the area was out of the question. I said to Chris Keeble that I would swing down the isthmus itself and come in from the south. I'd been looking at the map and seen there were a couple of streams and I realised that if we could get round and come in from the south, they would feel they were encircled. So psychologically the whole thing really shifted to our advantage; we'd broken the crust, they had no escape.

However, their anti-aircraft guns were still extremely intense. I remember telling the two leading platoon commanders that I wanted to get to where we could see the tracers in the sky.

I'm sure one or two of them thought, JC's deaf or daft – or both. I told them that we were going to go underneath the trajectory and, although there was a lot of fire, we had a fairly reasonable passage and got through, only to realise later that we had been walking through a minefield!

We had to try and neutralise their anti-aircraft guns; some were forward and some were on the promontory of Goose Green. They had their guns amongst the buildings and were going to be difficult to shift. When we arrived within 300 or 400 yards to the south of Goose Green, we engaged them with machine guns, and they returned very fierce fire. We then heard that six helicopters had landed to my south with reinforcements, but we managed to get off a few rounds of mortar ammunition, one of which landed right on top of them and dispersed them.

There was still the thought in the back of my mind that there were 100 or 200 blokes who had been landed fresh, and could catch us with a possible counter-attack. So, after the Harrier attack, I gathered everyone together and told them to go and scrounge all the ammunition they could find. They went off and plundered everything and carried back about 7,000 or 8,000 Argentinian rounds, which fortunately were the same calibre as ours.

I told the lads to go firm, go get into fours, dig in, and then we'd have to wait and see. I don't think anyone knew quite how far round we were, so we withdrew that night and dug in to a tight defensive position around a hill. It was a very long, cold night – it snowed and froze very hard, but the Toms were very good indeed, considering they'd been on their feet fighting for twenty-four hours. They'd had a bit of a baptism and they'd come through very well.

The news had filtered through during the day that we'd lost H. I gave them a sort of Winston Churchill pull up. I said, 'Look, we've done bloody well today. Okay, we've lost some lads; we've lost the CO. Now we've really got to show our mettle. It's not over yet – we haven't got the place. We're about 1,000 metres from D Company; we're on our own and an enemy has landed to our south and there's a considerable force at Goose Green, so we could be in a fairly sticky position.'

While we lay there, two guys in a hole received virtually a direct hit, but fortunately it had gone into the peat. It hadn't wounded them, but it had blasted them, and they were shaken. I shouted to them to come back to the Company HQ and have a cup of tea. It was just what they needed; to get back into the main body and have a cup of tea and a cigarette. You could see the relief on their faces.

We were really set to go in for the last push, but that wasn't necessary, because the following morning the surrender negotiations had started. 2 Para had captured two senior Argentinian NCOs. Chris Keeble explained his terms of surrender and sent them off to talk to their garrison commander. Eventually they accepted Chris's terms.

After the surrender, we were told to stay firm and dig in where we were on the high ground. Later I went into Goose Green and was pleased to meet some of the very relieved civilians, who had been released. The casualty-clearing process then started. We swept the battlefield, trying to get all the Argentinian casualties in and their bodies tidied up. Their officers appeared to have little interest and an extremely vague knowledge of how many men they had. We just lined the enemy bodies up against a hedge; there was nothing else we could do. Our padre, David Cooper, had the task of attempting to organise some kind of burial for them, with little help from the Argentinians.

We then flew to Ajax Bay for what we'd assumed was a memorial service for H and the others. When we arrived, there was a hole dug ready to receive eighteen burial bags and a lot of people gathered round, saying their last farewells. We'd understood that the bodies of those killed would be repatriated – yet here we were, burying them. We didn't know what the hell was going on, and a lot of people were, naturally, very upset. The company commanders acted as bearers for H and for the adjutant David Wood, Chris Dent and Jim Barry. The Toms under Regimental Sergeant Major Simpson, who had flown down with us, were the bearers for the other Toms.

The first time I had a moment of quietness, I sat down and wrote to the parents of Stephen Illingsworth and told them of his great gallantry. I also wrote to Sarah Jones about H. I hoped these letters would bring them some comfort. I felt responsible for Illingsworth. I don't mean that in a trite sort of way – I was his boss and basically he'd been killed working for me. I also wrote to Cathy Dent, whose husband Chris had been killed in A Company's action on Darwin Hill. I then asked the NCOs and officers to put down on paper the names of those they thought deserved some kind of award.

Things were good within our little group, but I was very keen that now we had finished at Goose Green, the company got some rest.

Having called a nearby farm from a local telephone to ascertain if it was clear of Argentinians, we moved on to Fitzroy. The six days we were there were interesting, because there was a slight feeling of 'You've done your bit, 2 Para – you can stand back now', which was very dangerous. My message to my Toms was quite simple: 'You can stand down when you get to Ascension Island on the way back, because that's when it's finished. Drop your guard now and you will get one straight on the chin.' So we set about improving our positions and making ourselves comfortable.

Naturally they were tired. After all, we'd been in a fairly major fracas for thirty-six hours and we'd lost eighteen men and had thirty-eight wounded. In *The Anatomy of Courage*,

Lord Moran talks about the 'bank of courage'. Our reserve had been pretty drained; it needed to be replenished – banked up. The next seven days were going to be a useful recuperation phase. After twenty-four hours we began preparing for other tasks. This kept the element of tension up sufficiently and didn't allow the Toms to think too much about their experiences.

It was a great responsibility and also a great privilege to lead such high-calibre blokes. If you have the privilege of commanding such men, then the battle is half won before you start. So I think it behoves you to try and think things out before, because there's no doubt that they are looking to you. I say this humbly, without meaning to sound pompous, but I think that within the battalion, I was the barometer. People knew that I'd had a lot of experience and therefore they were looking at me to see if there was any shake. If there was, then things could have been serious.

We had a very good team led by H, and I think the Toms knew that such a team thought conscientiously about problems and wouldn't commit them to something that they had no control over. People have said, 'Well, why the hell did you go to Goose Green?' And the answer to that is that the Toms were keen to get at the enemy and attack them. It's a great privilege to have people of that nature ready to follow you.

*Sergeant John Meredith, 2 Para*

I moved down with D Company from Sussex Mountain to our objective, Camilla Creek House. The artillery had fired on the area around the house and there had been no response from the Argies. So 10 and 11 Platoons went in and searched the house and found it empty. As it was the only house around, every company decided that they wanted to get their men in, which caused a bit of chaos. The next day, the World Service told its listeners exactly where we were, which obviously upset Colonel Jones and really pissed us off. We were then briefed by our company commander, Major Phil Neame, as to what the plan of attack was on Goose Green.

As we began to prepare ourselves for that, from out of nowhere a blue-and-white Land Rover carrying four Argentinians came on the horizon. A patrol of C Company opened fire, wounded two of them and brought the rest in. These were the first Argies we'd seen. They were interrogated by Captain Bell of the Marines who spoke Spanish and he got some information from them. We'd been given a piece of paper on the ship with Spanish phrases suitable for Benidorm on it – like 'hands up' – but it was all double-Dutch to me. We worked it out that if we pointed a rifle at them or stabbed them with a bayonet, they'd stick their hands up anyway.

We moved off that night, but a lot of people weren't happy with the artillery support we were going to get. We could only use two of the battalion's mortars because we didn't have enough ammunition to keep the six of them going. We'd taken a whole artillery battery down there with us, but they'd taken them away and given us three guns from another battery as support. So we had three guns and two mortars instead of a full mortar platoon and a battery of guns.

As we moved off down across the creek, A Company was to go over to Burntside House and B Company was to swing forward to the right, and we were in reserve at the rear. There was a navigational error on the way down, so we ended up somewhere in front of Colonel Jones, which didn't please him. Major Neame realised the mistake and told everybody to come back up to Burntside House. They opened up on it and luckily, they didn't hit any of the three civilians in there. Then B Company went and did their attack on the right and had trouble from fire coming from their left-hand side as they were advancing. Colonel Jones realised that A Company had to reorganise, so he pushed us through and we cleared a position in the centre. We took out about a dozen trenches in front of us and then went firm.

Unfortunately, in this move 10 Platoon ended up with two killed and 11 Platoon, who should have been on our left, crossed over behind us and went in on the right as well, and had one killed and one injured. One of my sections became split up from us and I had to go back and try and find them, but I couldn't. As I was moving back in, coming up a fence line to my right I could see four helmets moving. I asked the second-in-command if we had anybody forward on my right, and he said, 'No.' We put a mini-flare up and these four Argentinians stood up – so we wallied them. We went firm around the trenches that we'd cleared.

B Company had sorted out their problems, so the CO decided to revert to the original plan, which meant that A and B would go forward to carry on the attack, and we had to sit it out. By then it had become daylight. A Company then got caught up at Darwin, and B Company was starting to get caught up at Boca House, so Major Neame decided to move forward. Behind us we could see Argentinians coming out of trenches and moving along the beach, which was a bit worrying, so we just opened up on them with the GPMGs, and wiped out quite a few. Again, owing to sniper and artillery fire, Major Neame moved up forward behind the ridge that B Company was on, which sheltered us from the shelling. While we were waiting there, we had another lad named Mechan killed.

We sat there and the OC passed the word to brew up. It was then we were told that the Colonel was injured. Major Crosland and Major Neame had a confab, because B Company had one of their platoons in a very exposed position. They brought the

Milan up and attacked Boca House. Before we started our next move to the beach, the Argentinians began to surrender. There were white flats, so we started to go in, but were stopped. I think Major Keeble, who'd taken over, had decided that B Company needed a supply of ammunition before we could move.

After waiting a bit, we went forward through a shallow valley going towards the Argentinian position that appeared to have surrendered. Ahead of us was a minefield with anti-tank mines below the surface; they had orange cord tied between each mine to act as trip-wires. I told the lads to watch the cord while we were moving through – then suddenly there was a great bloody bang and the next minute we were lying on the ground with our ears ringing. As I got myself together and looked around, there was one of my lads, Spencer, with this cord on his foot, saying, 'It wasn't me! It wasn't me!' Somebody came running over and said, 'Get him out.' I said, 'Leave him in the bloody minefield – he tripped it.' He was all right, just bowled over. I wasn't very happy with him at all, and so we left him there.

There was another little Irish lad attached to us, who'd also been knocked over and was groaning a bit. One of the other blokes said, 'There's nothing wrong with you,' and he got a boot for his pains! We then moved up towards the Argentinians who had surrendered. We gave first aid to their injured, some of whom were badly hurt. We got them out of the trenches and laid them there, but they were obviously going to die. We then dealt with our own casualties and left a section to look after the prisoners.

Major Neame then pushed us straight on towards the school-house at Goose Green and 11 Platoon opened fire on the little house first. The trouble was, they used 66s (anti-tank rockets) and phosphorus grenades that caused a fire – which didn't give them very much cover. Then our C Company came down, ready to go in. My platoon were tasked to go up the track and give covering fire on the schoolhouse and also cover behind it to get anybody that tried to withdraw. The plan was to bottle them in there.

One of the rear sections saw some white flags waving near the airfield and he reported this to our platoon commander, Mr Barry, who said to me, 'I'll go forward and take the surrender. You look after these two sections.' So I moved to where I could control both sections and see what was going on. I told the radio operator so that he could get into contact with the company commander about what was happening.

Mr Barry went over the rise with his men and I watched them move towards two Argentinians who had come forward with their hands in the air. The others were sitting behind them on the floor with their hands up. Because I had to watch my own section, I had to keep my eyes in both directions, as I was a bit concerned about Mr Barry going forward. I saw him talking to two Argentinians, who seemed to be worried about the firing still going on at the schoolhouse. Then, for some reason, Mr Barry put his rifle against a fence.

Suddenly a burst of fire, probably from someone who wasn't aware that surrender was taking place, came whistling over the top. The Argentinians who'd been sitting there reacted immediately by picking up their weapons and firing. Mr Barry was killed instantly. Knight, the radio operator, killed two with his SMG, but Corporal Smith, who was trying to give covering fire with a 66, and Corporal Sullivan were also killed. Shevill was wounded in the shoulder and the hip. There was now an awful lot of firing going on.

As the senior man there, I was doing the chasing about. I saw some of my lads hit the deck, because of the volume of fire that was coming our way, but I got them up and firing. I was covering a lot of ground, but that's my job – that's what

I'm paid for. I got across another section and picked up a machine gun and knocked off three Argies with a couple of bursts each. Then, as I moved up again, I took out two more. We moved forward and took their position, and dealt with Shevill, who was badly hurt. He crawled back into cover, and so did Roach, who shouted that he thought he'd been hit. I shouted back that he would know if he'd been hit! But he'd only had the arse shot out of his trousers. Roach, with the help of Wilson, then gave first aid to Shevill while still under heavy fire. Unfortunately we couldn't get him out for five hours.

There were so many sensations at that time that I had to think fast and hard, because everything was changing from second to second. There were rounds going everywhere. I didn't have time to be frightened. When Mr Barry was killed, there was a lot of anger. The thing was to kill them as fast as we could – so for each one I knocked down, I thought, well, there's another. It was just whack, whack – and the more I knocked down, the easier it became . . . the easier the feeling was. I was paying them back. The feeling was anger – a mixture of both anger and sadness – sadness that three good blokes should die that way.

Then, as we reorganised, we were told that there would be a Harrier strike coming in – three friendly aircraft from the north. But the next minute we got strafed by enemy aircraft coming in from the south! We had to get Shevill back, as he had taken off across a fence as soon as the strafing came to a close, with his trousers down around his knees and a saline drip hanging out of his backside. We obviously wanted to go forward and collect our dead, but we weren't allowed to, so we dug in and stayed there all night.

They then attacked us with a Pucara that dropped napalm. It just missed the sergeant major's party with the prisoners and wounded. It also missed a big ammunition dump – so we were lucky. However, this napalm attack did the CSM some good, as he had his first crap since the *Norland*. We shot down the Pucara and captured the pilot. (He was one of the ones they sent in for the surrender, which they did the next day.)

We moved into Goose Green the next morning and dug in. I kept the lads working – most of them were all right, but one or two were a bit shaken. I had one who was very shaken, and it took us about three days to get him really back round. He was usually a cheerful lad, but he'd lost a couple of NCOs who'd looked after him, and he'd taken it badly. So I kept him working. After Goose Green I felt that I had to look after those who were alive rather than worry about people that had been killed. I wanted to get those that were alive performing properly, because we were out on a limb at Goose Green. But I was very pleased with the way the lads had behaved. I had mixed feelings about the battle, but it felt good to have won.

Then there was the shock of seeing all those hundreds of Argentinians at the surrender – I couldn't believe it. We'd attacked with a battalion, which was about 400 to 500 men, and they'd had 1,200. In the end, we sent one platoon of twenty-four men in to guard them. I felt we'd won a strategic battle – if we'd bypassed Goose Green we'd have left 1,200 men there with a usable airfield, and later that could have been a big thorn in our side. They could have caused a lot of damage from there.

*Sergeant Dave Abols, 2 Para*

We went towards Darwin for a dawn attack on Goose Green. As we advanced, we stopped by a little inlet and a recce party went forward. It seemed all clear. Ahead of us there was a fence across our path: 2 Platoon got over it, but as my platoon got halfway across, the Argies opened up. Half of my blokes ran back to a bank, and the rest of us ran forward. So I had lost control of my section. Luckily we found cover in a gorse bush area. Very soon, 2 Platoon took out about three trenches that were in the area. They didn't have time to get orders – they just ran forward for a place of cover, and as they were running, they noticed the trenches, so they took them out straight away – it was just instinct – what they were trained for. When we got to the gorse it was burning from the phosphorus grenades – burning the cover that we needed. Everything was on fire, and it seemed everyone else had lost control, because there were men split up all over the place.

I pushed on through and joined up with two other section commanders, so we stuck together, us three. We had one or two Toms with us, so we just went on using common sense, trying to find out what was going on and where the shooting was coming from. We went up the side of the little gully, took cover, and as we did so, we could see rounds landing in front of us. There was a sniper after us.

We doubled forward to a bank. In front we saw two blokes – Private Elliot and Private Worrall. They were the front part of 2 Platoon, which had gone through. We shouted to them to get back – as they did so, Worrall was hit in the stomach, so Stevie Prior and I went out to give him first aid. As soon as we got out there, this sniper was after us. It was only about forty to fifty metres back to the bank, but as we dragged Worrall, I could hear the rounds whizzing past my ear. Both of us were saying, 'He's after you – no – shit! He's after me,' because he was so accurate. It took us about twenty minutes to get him back. There wasn't only the sniper, because when we left the bank it was about four feet high – and now it was about two. They were firing anti-tank weapons at us and at the bank, because they knew we were getting covering fire from there and that we'd have to get over it.

We got him to about five metres from the bank. We said we'd count to three, drag him and drop him over. We got to three, went to jump, but his webbing got caught on the roots. So I said, 'Right, I'll go over, organise someone to give us cover fire, and we'll get him off the root.' I did that and went back to tell Steve, but I'd forgotten to ask for some sort of signal, so I had to crawl back again and tell them that when I threw the smoke, that was their signal to open fire. Throughout all this, the sniper was still after us, and Steve and Worrall were out there in the open, very exposed. I got back to them and told Steve that we were going to have to move as soon as I threw the smoke, but Worrall's webbing was still stuck, so by the time we got it off, the smoke had run out and so had the covering fire. But we were still out there, so we said, 'Bollocks. Count to three and we'll go.'

We got hold of him, got to three, then bang. The sniper got Steve right in the back of the head. He fell on top of Worrall. One look at him, and I knew he was dead, so I jumped back across the bank and told Corporal Hardman and Lance Corporal Gilbert to come up and give me a hand. We got both of them over so fast that I can't even remember how we did it. We gave Worrall some morphine, even though he had a stomach wound, just to stop the pain, and got him back down the bottom of the hill. We just needed a rest then, and a few ciggies and that.

We then started to organise ourselves. I was with Farrar-Hockley, the 2IC, and about four others, so we made our way to the top of the hill, where ahead we could see ten or eleven trenches. We said, 'No chance,' not unless we did a company frontal assault could we take them on. We came back down, reorganised ourselves and went back up again, but each time we went up this hill, we were losing blokes. I lost Corporal Hardman, shot in the head – we think that was the sniper again. Captain Dent was shot and fell back on his radio. Then another time I lost my number two on the gun. Farrar-Hockley was nearest the gun, so I said, 'You'll have to go number two.' He knew the crunch was on and he wasn't going to say no.

When we got back, the CO, H. Jones, came over and started having a go at us. His actual words were, 'Come on, A Company, get your skirt off,' and I felt like telling him what we'd been through, because we must have lost at least five blokes. At one stage there was just me and Corporal Toole up there with two 66s, trying to fire them at the trenches – that's two blokes out of a whole company.

We tried to show the Colonel, this time with the sergeant major and the CO and everyone that was there. We all went up this slow round hill, yet again. When we got to the top, he went round to the right, moving forward of the gully. We saw the Argentinians open fire on the side that we hadn't seen before. H went down and the next minute everybody automatically opened up at once at all the trenches. There must have been about seventeen of them. Then there was a sudden lull, and we began to shout to the Argies to come out of the trenches. One of our blokes could speak Spanish – he tried that, but they wouldn't come out. They started firing again.

Our sergeant major fired a 66 at what he thought was a command trench, but it went above it, so I fired a 66 at the same trench, hit it on the parapet, and obviously got the bloke who was inside, because straight after that they stopped firing completely. They jumped out of the trenches and started running towards us, surrendering straight away, so it must have been the command trench.

We got forward and tried to give the CO first aid. He was in a bad way. I left him with the sergeant major and others to deal with the casualties, and went to search the prisoners and clear the trenches. The next minute, these two fellas were on the skyline coming forward, obviously going to give themselves up. I shouted to them to raise their hands, but they couldn't understand me. So I said to my gun controller, Jerry, 'I'll go halfway and then I'll get down and wait for them to come forward. If they move their hands, open up.' I was about a quarter of the way towards them when Gerry noticed them raising their hands or weapons, either to shoot or to put their hands in the air. He wasn't sure, so he told the gunner to open up and he cut them down.

We got up to them and we found that one of them was the sniper. He had an American-made sight on a Chinese weapon with little handmade silver rounds. When we got back after sending all the prisoners down, we heard the Colonel was dead. We reorganised ourselves, cleared up, got fresh stuff and that, and then we waited there.


*Major Christopher Keeble, 2 Para*


Lieutenant Colonel H. Jones was the inspiration for making it happen in 2 Para. The way the unit was constructed, its morale, the training with the emphasis on speed and the offence, stemmed from him. I found my relationship with H extremely straightforward and, of course, because of the nature of the man, very demanding – as indeed did the company commanders.

We were on leave prior to departure for the jungle in Belize, Central America, as the crisis blew up. Our sister battalion, 3 Para, had been selected to embark with 3 Commando Brigade, and it was felt that 2 Para should remain to fill the gap created by their departure. H, of course, was very impatient, as we watched the Task Force depart, and more so when our overseas tour to Belize was cancelled. Despite these developments, we did not stop planning for the possibility of war.

It was clear the Falklands could only be recaptured by attack. We therefore made it our business, in the few days we had, to acquire what additional weapons and equipment we needed to increase our potential for offence. We also spent much time studying the topography, the Argentinian armed forces, and even working out how we could launch an airborne assault directly into Stanley, such was our enthusiasm to go. All this effort paid off when we heard we had been tasked to join 3 Commando Brigade at Ascension Island. We were to be the best jungle-trained battalion in the South Atlantic!

As soon as the battalion had been selected, H left for Ascension Island, to link up with the 3 Commando Brigade staff, leaving me in command. He said, 'Chris, train up the battalion and bring it down to me. I'll meet you at Ascension.' We then spent a week training in Aldershot, getting all the equipment we had planned to acquire, embarked the battalion on *Norland* and worked out a training programme for the remaining three weeks afloat. So I spent four weeks commanding 2 Para – a measure of the trust that existed between H and me.

We had a meeting as we departed to plan the training priorities and programmes and devise the seamanship skills required to turn the *Norland* – a commercial ferry – into an amphibious platform. More importantly, there were several weaknesses in 2 Para which I had seen on Salisbury Plain and at a major field exercise in Norfolk in January. These had to be put right.

The first was our ability to deal with casualties. The existing principle was based on patching up the injured and withdrawing them to expert help well behind the battle. We quickly appreciated that movement, other than by helicopter, would be too slow for casualty survival, so we decided to concentrate on battlefield resuscitation, rather than simple first aid. In other words, to prevent the onset of shock and sustain the injured for as long as possible, at or near the site of wounding.

This was put into operation by our young medical officer, Captain Steve Hughes, RAMC, who had researched the medical experiences of various campaigns, particularly those of the Israelis. I discussed with him, before we left, how we would achieve this objective, and what additional medical resources we would need. As a result, he acquired 1,000 drips for intravenous infusion to cope with blood-loss and even bought a dummy forearm, veins and all, on which to practise. The idea was that we would distribute these IVs to each man, along with the more usual morphine and shell dressings. A soldier would then have his own medical repair kit, which either he or a combat medic could administer at the site of wounding. During the journey south, we taught everyone how to set up a drip, either intravenously or through the rectum, should the former not be possible. As a result of these measures, we were able to reduce the loss of life dramatically and sustain the casualties until evacuation could occur.

The whole point of war is to apply violence to break the enemy's will, not simply to destroy his weapons or his cities, but undermine his will to fight for what he believes in. Now, how do you reinforce that will in a body of people who've never been to war? This is where our padre, David Cooper, was so marvellous. He took each section (nine men), the smallest fighting unit in the battalion, and he sat down in front of them and said, 'Look, when we go on this battlefield, it's going to be bloody awful. Now, I don't know about you, but I'll tell you how I'm going to feel.'

He attempted to penetrate that macho façade that soldiers build around themselves in order to reinforce their own inner resistance to fear. By voicing their own fears for them, he got them to talk about how they would actually cope with the trauma of war. Being a padre, and to some extent apart from the military structure, he gave them the opportunity to share their emotions with each other, which developed a 'spiritual' bond within the sections, which is so essential if people are going to work successfully together and, for the 2 Para team, to die for each other. It was a tremendous contribution.

In that week after the Goose Green battle, there was closeness between everybody – they were fused by fire. Very difficult to describe, but there was this tremendous brotherhood. It's a word used frequently by people who fought in the Second World War – the Brotherhood of Arnhem – and it is a brotherhood, too. War is a very emotional business – more than people realise, and much more than I'd ever anticipated and appreciated. I was enormously attracted to the Parachute Regiment because of this wonderful feeling of comradeship. We all have to go through a traumatic selection process, which weeds out a great number of people. We are united in our hardship, by what we have done. It is a very good way of preparing for the actual trauma of war. Soldiers do not fight for Queen and Country – or even for Maggie – they fight for each other. But they need to know that their comrades would do the same. Selection produces that mutual trust.

I remember parachuting on to the Arnhem drop zone with our sister battalion, 10 Para, on their annual pilgrimage to the battlefield and the war cemetery. After the jump, we visited the Oosterbeek crossroads, the scene of fierce fighting on the outskirts of Arnhem, and we listened to one of the very few survivors of the battalion describing the battle around the junction.

Someone in the audience asked the speaker, 'What made you go on fighting when the battalion had been largely destroyed, the cause lost and defeat inevitable?' He paused, looked across to the suburban junction, and with tears brimming up in his eyes, he said quietly and simply, 'They were my friends.' That's how it was for 2 Para. We had spent our peacetime training fusing the individuals into a team together. The fire of war merely tempered that process. We would never have given up. We would have fought to the last man rather than compromise the trust that existed between us.

When H died, the situation was really very simple. A Company's battle around Darwin in which H lost his life trying to sort it out, sounded a shambles and the ground favoured the defence there. There was little point in reinforcing failure. B Company with Johnny Crosland, on the other hand, was in a reasonable position, despite being part-caught on a forward slope down, and so I told him to assume command until I could get forward with Major Hector Gullan, the ubiquitous brigade liaison officer, who had a direct line to Brigadier Thompson. I also took with me my orderly room clerk, Corporal Kelly, who had been at my side throughout, to man the battalion radio link.

As we left, the RSM, Mr Simpson, called me back, much to my irritation. 'What is it?' I asked sharply. He looked me in the eye and said, 'You are going to do fucking well, sir!' I felt a million dollars! A wonderful touch. He did terribly well in the battle, dealing with the procedure of accounting for the casualties – normally the adjutant's job. Very sadly, David Woodhead had also been killed on Darwin Hill with his CO.

The outcome of the battle was really achieved by the skill of Phil Neame's and Johnny Crosland's companies, D and B, reinforced by the Recce Platoon commanded by Roger Jenner. Subsequently, the devastating violence created by the Harriers, who attacked the outskirts of the settlement at last light, clinched it. It was at that moment, it seemed to me, that the will of the defence began to break. We, on the other hand, were very short of ammunition and so overnight I prepared two plans.

I remember sitting in a gorse bush behind Darwin Hill that

night and saying to A Company commander Dair Farrar-Hockley and others that the way to crack the problem was to walk down the hill the next day and tell the bloody Argies the game was up and defeat inevitable. Dair looked at me wearily as if I had lost my marbles! If that failed, well, we would reinforce and launch a massive assault with aircraft, artillery and infantry, and destroy the settlement. There was really no other option, since not only had we little ammunition, we were all exhausted, having been on the go for some forty hours without sleep. In addition, and perhaps the most significant fact of all – there were 112 civilians locked up in the Community Hall in Goose Green. This fact was discovered overnight and re-emphasised the need to use more subtle means than the bayonet. After all, we had not journeyed 8,000 miles merely to destroy the very people we had come to save.

And so, standing in a small tin shed on the airfield next day with Tony Rice, the battery commander, and our two bewildered journalists, Robert Fox and David Norris, we confronted the Argies with Plan A. It was clear that the three Argentinian commanders we negotiated with (Navy, Army and Air Force) had had enough. It became apparent later that one of the principal causes of this collapse of will was the breakdown of trust between the officers and conscripted soldiers.

The surrender was arranged on a sports field outside Goose Green, close to the hidden position of D Company, who had closed up on the settlement. It was a straightforward affair, requiring the defenders to lay down their arms, which I allowed them to do with a degree of honour, to avoid the humiliation of defeat. About 150 assembled in a hollow square and, after singing their national anthem, the commander, an airman, saluted me and handed over his pistol. We were very concerned that we could not see any Argentine army personnel in the mass of defeated airmen. Some minutes later, everything became clear as we watched about 1,000 soldiers marching up in files to surrender in the same way. It was an incredible sight. We held our breath hoping they wouldn't change their minds!

Victory came from H's leadership and the way he inspired the team, and is a vivid example of Lord Slim's view that, 'Leadership is of the spirit, compounded of personality and vision; its practice is an art.'

# 2

# THE FALKLANDS
# 1982

## Mount Longdon

*Company Sergeant Major John Weeks, 3 Para*

3 Para waited five days before we got our orders for the attack on Mount Longdon. We were told that there were seventy men on the hill and that ours would be a company silent night attack. I was surprised, because the lesson we'd learnt from Goose Green was that no way should we ever do a silent attack. I thought we should stomp everything, but we didn't have artillery on call because it was being used in the other battles. I got the company together and told them that some of them would not come off this hill. I'd been their company sergeant major for two years – I'd like to think all of them were pretty close to me, and I knew them well – but I knew some of them were going to die. I knew because I had a feeling that there was more on that bloody hill than seventy guys.

I told them, 'It's going to be hand-to-hand fighting from trench to trench, and it will be very, very slow and, believe you me, you can't visualise, lads, what it's going to be like, because it's going to be so slow and you're going to have things happen that you've never had before when we've been practising. You're going to have live things coming at you and exploding around you and it's going to confuse you – but you will do well. Now, if you have any thoughts, or if any of you believe in Christ, here's the time to sit down and have a little talk to Him. It's not stupid, because I'm certainly going away now to have a little prayer.'

I think a load of them probably did pray. I'm not a religious person, but having spoken to the guys afterwards, they all said that at some stage during that night they'd said a prayer. After that battle I sincerely believe that there's Someone who listens to us – but if your number's up, your number's up.

Then I went to speak to personal friends like Doc Murdoch. It was new to him, so I said, 'Well, it's the same for me, Doc, because I've never done anything like this, but all we can do is give of our best.' You don't know how anyone is going to react in battle. You couldn't line up many people you've known for years and say, 'Well, he's going to be all right in battle,' because guys you wouldn't dream of are those that come up and shine, and the guys you thought would be brave are not very brave at all.

The battalion did a sort of follow-my-leader up to the start line, where we split up to our fighting order. I was with B Company commander, Major Argue, and we were deployed to the rear of 4 and 5 Platoons; 6 Platoon was taking the opposite way up. We crossed the start line on time. It was a very eerie, very quiet, cold night. We were going quite well towards the hill and were 500 metres short of the rock formation when Corporal Milne trod on a mine. That was the end of our silent night attack. It then became like Guy Fawkes Night – I've never seen so many illuminations. I think most of the Argies must have been asleep – but what came at us was bad enough, so if they'd all been awake, they'd have wiped our two platoons off the face of the mountain. For the next eleven hours it was unbelievable non-stop action.

Initially there was confusion. We branched off right and ran into the cover. Myself, Sergeant Pettinger and Captain McCracken, the gunnery officer, all got down into this rock division. The platoon commanders, on the radio, were telling us what was going on up front. You didn't need the brain of an archbishop to realise that 4 Platoon were involved in some considerable fighting, but there were no decisions being made from Company HQ at the time, because we were in limbo.

I called to Major Argue, who told me to push forward and clear the way. Sergeant Pettinger and I then went forward, rock by rock, and cleared the position to make sure there was nobody there. Once we'd cleared it, we shouted back to Major Argue, 'Okay, sir, it's clear.' I then started to clear another side with Captain McCracken, but we were stopped and held up by snipers. We couldn't move because we couldn't see them and we didn't have the night scope with us, but later John Pettinger's sniper came up and – his rifle had a night sight – took them both out.

We then eventually got up into the rock grooves where they had been. The first thing I heard was John Ross shouting up front, and I realised that we were close to the enemy now. As we went forward, we cleared a bunker that someone had obviously gone through before us. There was a body lying with a blanket over it. I stopped the Company HQ moving towards it and said, 'Stay there. You don't find a body on a battlefield with a blanket over it. Something's wrong.' I said to the Engineer corporal, 'Stand at the bottom with my SMG, and when I pull this blanket, if his hands move, shoot him.' As I pulled the blanket, his hand moved to release a phosphorus grenade. My lad just let loose the magazine.

We had to push forward and from then onwards I was on the net a lot. We'd taken casualties by this time, and Sergeant Des Fuller was looking pretty grim about what was going on. So he was dispatched forward to find exactly what had happened to 4 Platoon. He came back a half-hour later and said that 4 Platoon had been virtually wiped out, there were bodies all over the place, the casualties needed to be evacuated and the lads were out of ammunition. They were now using the enemy weapons and ammo. He said that Sergeant McKay had gone forward with a few guys to try and take out gun positions, but the rest of the platoon were either injured or without leaders. Fuller was then given the order that he would take over 4 Platoon.

I went forward with Privates Lewis and Clarkson-Kearsley to see what the situation was. When I got down there, an officer was lying injured and alongside him was Corporal Kelly. Further forward of them there were a number of dead, and to the left, Sergeant McKay was in action, although I couldn't see him. I could hear Corporal McLaughlin shouting and a number of other people doing their best to try and fight forward to take out these gun positions. I heard over the net that 6 Platoon had taken some heavy casualties. I then went back to HQ and told them that I needed guys to evacuate casualties. Something had to be done – they were lying there in the battle zone, and they had to be got away from there and have treatment.

I didn't have enough guys and because there were so many casualties, it meant a number of trips – which took a couple of hours. These four or five guys and I were going backwards and forwards under fire, taking guys out. I remember carrying one young lad out. I'll never forget him. He was alive when I carried him out, but he died in my arms – it was terrible. It was his eighteenth birthday.

I had only one medic, so on the net to Major Patton, I said that I needed more, and I needed stretcher-bearers who could carry out my casualties to the RAP. He was trying to reassure me that they were coming, but they were a long time getting there. So I was still going backwards and forwards with the casualties. I didn't move the dead – there was nothing I could do for them. The priority was getting these casualties back. I got hold of Corporal Kelly, who was badly hurt, but he said, 'It's okay, John, I'll walk,' and he did. He was holding on to us, walking; it was unbelievable.

The first man I carried out was Lieutenant Bickerdike, who was heavy. I was running with him on my back, and he was screaming with pain. We got him out, but the problem was going back for the rest, because all the time we were getting sniped at. We couldn't just run in and run out, because it took so much time. By this stage I'd got Corporal Proberts, my medic, who did some fantastic jobs. The lads started to cry for ammunition, i.e., grenades and 66-mms, so I had to go forwards and grab the ammunition from the casualties and the dead, and then get back and give it to the guys who needed it. But I wasn't the only one doing this.

I then got back and briefed Major Argue about 4 Platoon's situation. There were only a few guys left with Sergeant Fuller out of the twenty-odd. He'd taken command and just as I got back he'd also come back to brief Major Argue. He'd seen Sergeant McKay killed, and all the other men that had gone in with him were either injured or dead, so it meant we had to go down again to get the casualties out. While I was doing this, Sergeant Ross and Mr Cox had lost contact with each other, so 5 Platoon had got split. Mr Cox was running in one place and Sergeant Ross in another. It was chaos.

Something needed to be done to regroup and establish what we wanted to do. I got back from looking for the second-in-command to find a platoon commander crying. He'd seen death for the first time and it had shaken him. I gave him a good smack in the mouth, because he was hysterical. I said, 'Pick your weapon up and get back and sort your platoon out. They need you.' I'll give him his due, he went back and sorted himself out, and did bloody well. It was sheer inexperience, because he'd never seen anything like it.

I then went back to see the casualties, and although Corporal Proberts was still doing a fantastic job, I was still having no joy on the net trying to get somebody to help. I needed people to get the injured down to the RAP, because they were losing blood. Corporal Kelly, who knew that if he lost much more blood he would die, also told them in fairly tough terms that he wanted somebody up there to get him out. The second-in-command had his problems, because he'd been ordered to bring ammunition up on the stretchers, and the stretchers had got some distance away. So some of my injured guys were there seven to eleven hours, which is a long time. Eventually we got stretcher-bearers up and the guy who came up and down that hill the most times was Cook Sergeant Marshall. He was up and down that hill all bloody night long. He was excellent and got a Mention in Despatches.

Other guys throughout the night were bayonet fighting, taking out the enemy, trench by trench. I saw Gray and another lad take ground: they threw a grenade into the trench and then as soon as it had gone off, they'd go in with bayonets. I jumped in one trench which they had cleared and there was a bloke lying in the bottom. I got the shock of my life when he moved. I nearly shot my toe off with my SMG trying to unload it! The enemy had to be taken out and the only way they could be taken out was by actual bayonet fighting. Dominic Gray and Ben Geoff and another little guy were into it all night long, because they had to be – there was no other way of taking the ground.

We then got A Company coming up and the first person I saw was Sergeant Major Docherty, who was the sergeant major of B Company before I took over. I said to him, 'Sammy, they've done bloody well tonight, but we can't do any more – we're just out of numbers.' Then I saw Major Collet come up and go forward to where he could see what the problem was. It was an anti-aircraft gun and obviously A Company would have to take that out – but that was their problem.

Before A Company arrived, some of our company had tried a left-flanking move and four had been killed when they opened up on us. Captain McCracken came forward and fired a 66 straight into where the enemy were – which stopped them straight away. He was really switched on, that guy – he was everywhere – he had a great big walrus moustache. We then went in and pulled the casualties out. But this time I'd got another medic, Lance Corporal Lovett, who was helping. Sadly he was killed by shellfire.

The Argentinian artillery now realised we'd taken their positions so they were stomping us and we were starting to take casualties from this. We moved all platoons to the bottom of Mount Longdon. We stayed there about another twenty-four hours getting stomped. A Company moved forward and they called in Captain McCracken and asked him if he could bring in artillery fire. He said that he could bring it in within twenty-five metres. He brought it in brilliantly and without that we would have been bollocksed, because we'd never have taken that ground. It was a natural feature for defence. There was everything you could want for a defence and the only thing they didn't have was the bottle – they didn't have the guts to go with it. By the time they had moved off, or surrendered, my lads had given everything, and I mean everything – and some had given their lives.

The next thing we had to do was get the bodies. The following morning, when it was light, in-between the artillery and the mortar coming down, we had to go and sort out the bodies and do the documentation. Although it sounds stupid, in battle you still have to account for everything and everybody and you have to fill in the bloody paperwork. I went round to the lads who were left and I asked if any of them would come and help me remove the bodies. I didn't particularly want to do it. I found it terribly hard to ask the guys, and they found it terribly hard to say 'no' outright. They tried to make an excuse that they were too busy doing other things, rather than say they didn't want to go down to their friends and bring their bodies up. Lewis and Clarkson-Kearsley were the only ones who said they'd come. Sammy Docherty also came, because it needed four to carry a body on a poncho and get them all down to a central place.

Then Corporal Proberts and myself had the task of doing the documentation, taking off wedding rings and any personal effects and leaving one dog tag on. I then filled in the form to say where they had got the wounds. There was still artillery fire going on all the time we were doing this. Sammy Docherty and I were in tears taking Ian McKay's body – we knew him so well. I've seen dead bodies, loads of dead bodies; bodies don't actually bother me, but when they're people you know, and you've got to get them into a body bag, which is a flat polythene thing, it's terrible. Sergeant Brian Faulkner and his crew came up to remove the body bags, then I went down to the RAP to the padre with the personal effects of the dead.

One of those who died that black night was Corporal McLaughlin. He'd been a tower of strength, though. Everywhere I looked, there he was, directing blokes, encouraging blokes forward to take these positions out, screaming and shouting, 'We're taking this one, I am now going right.' Telling the guys what to do, then moving back to brief the boss on what was going on. And again, when I went forward some hours later in a similar sort of area, there he was, screaming at blokes, 'We're taking them out – follow me!' He then came back after I got the casualties out and said, 'Is there anything else?'

He was one of those guys that, if there was anything going on, he wanted to be amongst it. He was an extremely brave man. He was with Ian McKay when he took out bunkers and came out of that unscathed. People like him and Dominic Gray were the lifestay; they were all over the place, assisting everybody. Gray got two rounds in his head and still carried on fighting until he actually collapsed through lack of blood. Yet he didn't want to be carried back out – he wanted to stay till the bitter end. He was doing things beyond his job as a Private soldier.

When there was a lull in the battle, we had to check equipment. We'd carried 84s (anti-tank rockets) all the way across the Falklands to find that every one we fired, misfired. The lads had carried a weapon weighing 35 pounds plus four shells, weighing six pounds each, only to find the bloody thing didn't work. That made them really angry.

We then moved towards Stanley itself to take the racecourse, but on the way down, the surrender went up. Then it was a race between 2 and 3 Para to get into Stanley. The helmets came off for the first time and the red berets went on.

The next two weeks in Stanley gave the lads time to think, and there were a lot of sad boys in my company. They had time to reflect on what had happened. They'd lost friends. One minute their mate had been standing there, and the next he'd been hit by a shell and was a mass of flesh all over the place. That scars the mind. It took a while to reassure them that they'd not died for nothing, but like us all, they understood that we couldn't allow the Argentinians to take over the Falklands. Thank Christ we had Maggie, because she proved that you can't hold this country to ransom.


*Major Philip Neame, 2 Para*


We began our move to Wireless Ridge with Lieutenant Colonel David Chaundler as our new CO. The move there involved a long night march in the snow. Just before, I'd had a dose of the cook's special brew, as had most of the company. Every time we stopped I had to step out of line and drop my trousers in the freezing cold for a quick one, much to the amusement of everyone else.

We went up into position just north of Longdon and waited for the order to assault Wireless Ridge. Our CO had promised that next time we weren't going anywhere without our full ration of artillery, so we began to feel a little more confident. But there was still a lingering feeling that we had already been through the mangle – my company had picked up eight dead, over half the battalion's total, at Goose Green – and we would rather not go through the whole thing again, but if we had to, we had to.

Come the night, things weren't helped by the fact that the plan had changed at least three times. But then we had the reassurance that we'd never known an airborne exercise go off as planned. So when we went ashore at Sussex Mountain and again that night before Wireless Ridge, the Toms took the very phlegmatic approach that it was like any other exercise they had ever been on – one big fuck-up!

I didn't beat around the bush on this, reckoning it was better to admit things weren't going as planned, but at least keeping them in the picture. That made them feel involved in what was happening, not just pawns, and they were more ready to accept last-minute changes as a result. This helped morale, which I think was the difference between us and the Argentinians. They weren't used to all this fucking around, and when it happened, as it always does in war, it got to them. In the case of our Toms, it was almost a source of strength.

The main thing about Wireless Ridge was that we were the only company in the whole of the battle that had to assault in the face of organised opposition. We actually carried out three separate company attacks in that one night. The initial attack, however, went in with little opposition. We had really leathered it up with artillery before we actually got on to the position. We had also had light tanks from the Blues and Royals, and machine guns supporting us, so by the time we started moving through it, whatever enemy had been there – anything between a platoon and a company – had already thinned out, and all we found was isolated resistance, which was quickly dispatched. So we got on to the position quite pleased with ourselves.

The thing about the Argentinians really was that you'd attack positions, and you'd find a large proportion of them completely unready. With all this battle going on around them, they would be lying in the bottom of the trenches, or even asleep in their sleeping bags with their hoods up – a sleep of fear, really. It's what I call the ostrich factor: they had buried their heads, thinking, it's not happening, it won't happen to me. I'm not here . . .

At Goose Green we never met co-ordinated resistance, but here for the first time we did. We were still clearing the first position when we began to get extremely heavy artillery down on us. I had been told to reorganise on the position, but there was no way I was going to do that, so we pushed straight through and reorganised about 300 yards further on. The enemy's own artillery completed the job of clearing the position for us!

After A and B Companies had taken their objectives, we set off for our next target – the first part of the main ridge line. Again with artillery support and the Blues and Royals providing spot-on response, we met very little opposition. We should have gone straight into an attack on our third and final objective, which was known to be very strongly held. I told our FOO (Forward Observation Officer) to fire on the final target, but for one reason or another he called for the wrong target number and the next five rounds landed straight on us – which completely broke our momentum. It wounded one section commander and killed another. This lad had already been injured and casevaced; he'd recovered, returned to us and now, of all things, he'd been killed by our own artillery. It seemed a complete waste. These things happen in war – far worse had happened in the past and far worse will probably happen in the future – but it made me really mad.

We tried again, but the rounds were now landing rather closer to B Company than the enemy. I was getting ready to assault and then had to call a halt while the artillery went through this long system of adjusting the fire on to the target. We were actually overlooking the enemy position at this time and thank God we had the tanks in support, because they were able, from the flank, to keep firing at the enemy positions and keep them occupied. The enemy remained totally unaware that we were sitting on a bald, open slope just a few hundred yards to their left and above them.

The artillery finally got some rounds on target. At last, I thought. We were literally about to assault when once again the artillery had to stop firing because some rounds had again been landing on B Company. It clearly wasn't B Company's night! I could not advance without fire support and my feelings were, especially having already had thirty-odd rounds of our own artillery on my position, that B Company could live with one gun sending the odd round their way while we got on with the war and out of a very nasty situation. But there was no way I could persuade anyone to change their minds. So we then had to go through the farcical rigmarole of firing each gun in turn to try and find out which one needed realigning. There we were, literally within spitting distance of the enemy, while this sort of peacetime safety procedure went on – and I got a bollocking for not assaulting earlier! I began to think that it really wasn't my night either, and began to get extremely short-tempered with a number of people.

Eventually we had four out of six guns lined up. I said, 'Sod it, I've had enough. We won't bother with the other two – we'll just go in with what we've got.' I gave the order to attack. The trouble was, we'd completely lost our momentum. The Toms had almost grown roots waiting in the cold, and by this time we were very sceptical of our artillery support. I yelled, 'Advance!' and stood up myself – and nothing happened. I thought, shit, and yelled, 'Advance!' again, and the cry was taken up and slowly everyone began to move forward unopposed.

We got to within about 100 yards of the enemy position when one of the Toms put up an illuminating round earlier than he should have done, which attracted the enemy, who realised that the assault was coming not from the front, but from their flank. So, of course, everything that they'd got was turned on us. There we were, in the middle of a very exposed, totally bald little valley with no cover at all, suddenly confronted with this withering hail of small-arms fire, accompanied all the time by incoming enemy artillery! Everyone hit the deck. Direct fire at night is always rather more frightening than in daylight.

I thought, fucking hell, what do I do next? I was almost at a loss, knowing that it was my job to get the assault going, but not at all keen on moving myself. I learned a great truth from that moment – if in doubt, start shouting. I'm not normally a great shouter, but I started shouting for all I was worth! Then I heard other people start to shout. I got up and ran a few yards and I could see other people moving and suddenly it all got into its stride again. The blokes started working as they had been trained to do: fire and manoeuvre, moving in pairs, and so on. It suddenly began to happen once more. I lost my signaller in the middle of it all. I thought he had been shot, but as he is as black as the ace of spades, there was little chance of finding him that night, so I moved off without him.

Fortunately I had my own personal radio, so I was able to talk to the platoon commanders, but there was no way that I could talk back to Battalion HQ. I had also by that stage lost touch with our artillery observation officer. So the only fire I had in support were the tanks which were on the company net. I was able to keep talking to them and they did a great job in chasing the enemy off the ridge in front of us. As we hit the enemy they began to cut and run.

If I had gone by the School of Infantry handbook we'd have cleared each position systematically step by step, at a relatively slow and controlled pace, one position at a time. But I remember this distinct feeling that all we had to do was to keep moving very fast and keep the enemy on the run ahead of us. If we went slowly, they'd leave one set of positions and reorganise in a further set of positions and we'd have to fight all the way along. So I started to keep the pace moving as briskly as I could, but the platoons on either side of me were trying to conduct things as they'd been trained, in a slightly more measured and controlled way. At one stage, Sergeant Meredith or Sergeant O'Rawe was yelling at some of his guys, because the company commander was ahead of them.

We kept on the move so quickly that the enemy didn't have the chance to go firm anywhere until we got to this area called the Telegraph Wires. This was the limit of our exploitation, as the SAS were operating further east of that. The ridge line carried on ahead of us, so it was an absurd place to stop – with no obvious feature – but we stopped there as ordered. I guess the Argentinians who were running along ahead of us must have thought we had run out of steam, because from that direction we got this counter-attack.

Jon Page, whose platoon I had left up that end, managed to get hold of our artillery by flicking his radio on to their net, as we were still without our FOO. That broke up their attack. I made my way back to Meredith and Page. In the last 30 or 40 yards I had to get across the top of the hillside itself. I became vaguely aware of a lot of shit coming my way. This was confirmed by Meredith, who told me to 'fuck off' as I was attracting all the shit his way! His platoon was having a very, very rough time indeed. They couldn't move without attracting extremely accurate small-arms fire.

There was sporadic artillery fire going on the whole time, which one began to live with, but this was really most uncomfortable, and the whole platoon was virtually pinned down and couldn't move. A lot of this fire was coming from Tumbledown, as 5 Brigade's attack had started late and the Argentinian positions there dominated Wireless Ridge. But I think a lot was coming from snipers on the slope above Moody Brook that we hadn't cleared. There was a lot of shit flying around, and it was very hairy for what ground I wanted 10 and 11 Platoons to cover. I'd sent my runner, Hanley, back to try and locate the rest of my Company HQ, but he'd not found them as they were further back, still dealing with casualties. So he'd got the two platoon commanders together and started tying up details with them on his own initiative.

Then, as daylight broke, we got another counter-attack – this time from the Moody Brook side on to Sean Webster's platoon. I wondered what we had got into, and thought this was most unlike the Argentinians. For a while they were quite persistent. They got close enough to throw grenades, but didn't drive home their attack – a 'Latin' gesture – and we won.

I then met up with Corporal Osborne, my signaller, whom I'd lost at the start of the attack. I thought he'd been hit, but he'd actually fallen into an Argentinian shit-hole. As I could now get on the battalion net again, I called up a fire mission on to the Moody Brook area, which quickly discouraged any other counter-attack. Those three hours between starting our final attack and daylight were, for me, the most harrowing period of the whole war, especially with the cock-ups from the artillery breaking our momentum and losing contact with the CO, and then the counter-attacks. But about half an hour after daylight, we saw the Argentinians pulling off Tumbledown. It was an amazing sight. They virtually marched off in single file.

I had been trying to get fire missions down on the retreating, closely packed formation of troops, but was told that there was no artillery available. I was going quite spare, because I was supposed to have two batteries at my priority call. Here was a golden opportunity being missed. I assumed the enemy were withdrawing to regroup on Sapper Hill and the last thing I wanted was another major battle.

Eventually we got the artillery and started blasting away with everything else we had as well. But as soon as we opened up, we got very accurate artillery fire back at our own position. I guessed that they were adjusting on to our muzzle flashes, so I told the company to stop firing with their small arms. I decided that the only thing was to keep fighting this battle with artillery; otherwise we were going to have a lot of shit knocked out of ourselves.

The CO then came up and couldn't understand this, and I tried to explain what my reservations were, but he told me to keep firing with everything I had. Very gingerly, I got only two machine-guns to open up to avoid exposing our own position. The machine guns opened up and nothing came back at us, so I felt an absolute idiot! What had happened, of course, was that during my conversation with the CO, the Argentinians had thrown in the towel. We were now able to do anything we liked, so the whole thing turned into a turkey shoot. We were firing away with machine guns and it was just a slaughter. I think for different reasons, David Chaundler told us to stop firing. The change was so abrupt, within the space of a few minutes, from well-organised opposition to surrender. We were still on the hilltop when the news of the ceasefire came over.

Everyone stood up and took their helmets off and put their red berets on for the first time in months, just to let everyone know that it was the Parachute Regiment who had won the war. And in much the same way as at the end of an exercise, everyone who had spare ammunition fired it off – smoke grenades, the lot. What really won the day was the quality of the blokes we had, probably the best-trained soldiers in the world. We had come through the cauldron and had lost some very brave blokes indeed. Now this fantastic little force one had built up and worked with had done its bit. We marched into Stanley knowing that we were never going to do anything like it again. That was difficult to come to terms with.

What really scored for us was team effort. I think I was lucky – I had some excellent subordinates and it didn't need too much from me to produce results. It was all very effortless and rewarding, very rarely lonely or frightening. As much as I led them, they carried me, and though not all of us got back – and I'm sad for their families – I never really mourned them, because for me they're still there, part of the team.

*Lieutenant Colonel David Chaundler, 2 Para*

We had fought all night amid driving snow flurries and comparatively heavy Argentinian Artillery fire, which they used effectively to shell each one of our objectives soon after their capture when, standing on the final objective captured by Phil Neame's D Company, we saw a remarkable sight. Off to the east we could see Port Stanley under a pall of smoke, but below us the Moody Brook valley seemed suddenly full of Argentinians as their army broke and, looking like black ants, were pouring out of Moody Brook and off Tumbledown and Sapper Hill across the valley and walking back to Port Stanley – an utterly defeated army. We were, of course, firing at them with everything we had. The machine-gun platoon was up, as were the Scorpions and Scimitars of the Blues and Royals, and the battery commander was in seventh heaven, having asked for – and got – a regimental fire mission. It is difficult to describe the elation we felt when, all of a sudden, I realised we were in danger of crossing that moral threshold where what we were doing was no longer acceptable. I ordered a ceasefire.

It was now evident we must get into Port Stanley before the Argentinians had time to reorganise. John Crosland's B Company moved down through Moody Brook on to the high ground on the other side of the valley, followed by Dair Farrar-Hockley's A Company on to the Port Stanley road. And so, at one o'clock, some six hours before the official ceasefire – with D Company, the troop of the Blues and Royals and C Company of 3 Para, who had come off Mount Longdon, following up – we entered Port Stanley, the first British troops since the Argentinian invasion eleven weeks before. As we walked down that road and the realisation began to dawn that it was all over, without orders, steel helmets came off and out of pockets came crumpled red berets as yet another generation came of age, proud to wear the beret that has symbolised the airborne soldier from North Africa, through Sicily, Normandy, Arnhem, the Rhine Crossing and the many campaigns since 1945. Like them, we had come through.

## Post Falklands

*Pathfinder Platoon*

In 1984, 5 Airborne Brigade was in the process of developing its Leading Parachute Battalion Group (LPBG), to drop a parachute battalion from nine Hercules with six heavy drop-configured aircraft for vehicles and stores onto drop zones (DZs) in under five minutes, by day or night. To do this, there was a requirement for the DZs to be clearly marked, in order to ensure that the crews had an easily identified reference point to allow them to drop accurately and consistently.

Pathfinders had always been used for this task from as early as 1943. However, the demise of 16th Parachute Brigade in 1977 and the disbandment of the Pathfinder Company (No 1 (Guards) Independent Company, The Parachute Regiment) meant that the expertise was lost. From then on the parachute battalions were required to develop and maintain that skill themselves, which proved difficult.

The requirement for a brigade-level capability led to the re-establishment of a pathfinder unit and the formation of the Pathfinder Platoon in 1985. From the beginning, much emphasis was placed upon High Altitude Low Opening (HALO) parachuting as an insertion method. In addition to the pathfinding role, the platoon acted as the Brigade's own medium-range reconnaissance force, bridging the gap between the tactical recce of the battalions' Patrols Platoons and strategic-level recce carried out by Special Forces.

The Pathfinders currently operate within 16 Air Assault Brigade, which succeeded 5 Airborne Brigade in 1999. The Pathfinder Selection Cadre is open to soldiers of all cap badges, although there remains a very strong Parachute Regiment contingent. The selection cadre currently lasts six weeks and includes a rigorous process to test aptitude, endurance, soldiering and fieldcraft skills. Soldiers who successfully pass the cadre undergo a period of further in-depth weapons training; high-altitude parachute training in America; and survival, escape, resistance and evasion (SERE) training before deployment to the Pathfinders.

# 3

# KOSOVO
# 1999

## Operation Agricola

In May 1999, 1 Para was directed to prepare for possible operations in Kosovo following the NATO air strikes directed at
Serbia to prevent the 'ethnic cleansing' of Kosovar Albanians
by Serbs.

On 6 June, the 1 Para Battle Group reinforced by 125 men
from 3 Para was forward deployed to the former Yugoslav
Republic of Macedonia under 5 Airborne Brigade to spearhead
a forced entry by the NATO KFOR Peacekeeping Force. The
aim was to clear any pockets of hardline resistance that might
impede the negotiated Serb Army withdrawal.

At H-Hour on 12 June, 1 Para Battle Group secured the
Kacanik Defile with an air-mobile helicopter insertion on
the Serbian border with Macedonia, and later participated
in the KFOR ground advance to the capital Pristina. After the
initial deployment, the battalion was engaged in peacekeeping
tasks in Pristina, protecting Serb civilians from Albanian
reprisals, overseeing and negotiating with the Kosovo Liberation
Army and recording evidence of Serb war crimes. With emotions
running high because of inter-communal violence, it proved a
Northern Ireland-type experience conducted in circumstances
similar to Aden in 1967.

On 30 July, 1 Para handed over the civil administration of
Pristina to the 1st Royal Irish Battle Group and returned to the
UK, having earned a DSO, QCB and a Mention in Despatches.

*Lieutenant Dan Jarvis, 3 Para*

We left Aldershot on 6 June 1999, a historic day for the regiment, and went not really knowing what we would encounter. Our battalion, 1 Para, didn't go to the Falklands, so whilst we'd been to Northern Ireland and we had seen other people go off to the Balkans, this was the first opportunity for a generation for the battalion to show what we could do.

Having deployed to Macedonia, within a few days we found ourselves moving up the Kacanik Defile by Chinook helicopter into Kosovo and Pristina. One of the things that confronted my platoon was an area we had to patrol that included a mass grave. I remember very clearly seeing an arm protruding out the side of this grave. I looked at it and there was a watch on the arm, the watch was still ticking. There was very significant evidence of the atrocities that had been committed in Kosovo. Very quickly as a battalion we organised ourselves and conducted a whole series of patrols to try and secure the area and reassure the local population.

It was a very demanding operation, there was a lot of movement – we moved around the city to secure different areas, it was a rapidly developing situation. We had to be prepared to fight if that was required, but quite soon we also had to shift to a different posture where we would seek to keep and protect the peace. It was a demanding operational tour, which demonstrated the flexibility of our paratroopers to adapt to rapidly changing circumstances. At one point we discovered a Serbian torture chamber in the basement of a house that had clearly been used to enact the most terrible treatment on people. The infrastructure and detritus of torture remained; it was a very, very grim place. There was evidence of the carnage and killing wherever we went and it was our job to bring some peace, stability and order and that's what we tried to do.

We were welcomed as liberating heroes by the indigenous people who came out on to the streets. It was an amazing reception and atmosphere when we first arrived. But then we rapidly got into the routine of soldiering and we soldiered incredibly hard. I remember my platoon went three nights without sleep, because we were establishing a patrol base. We were getting into routine patrols, getting to know our local area and conducting a number of operations. On one occasion, my machine-gun platoon was tasked to support a hostage-rescue operation being carried out by Support Company and we tore off into the night to a location, put a cordon around an area and worked our way through a whole series of houses to try and rescue an individual we believed had been taken hostage. There was this constant change of posture between peace enforcement and a higher level of soldiering. It was a very demanding time.

There was the odd contact. Tragically, two British soldiers were killed by unexploded munitions; there was a constant threat of mines and booby traps. There was the occasional contact with the residual Serbian forces, but there was no sustained contact with the enemy. Nothing like the intensity we were subsequently to experience in Iraq and Afghanistan.

*Corporal, 1 Para*

It was one of these things; we didn't know what we were going to do, because we didn't know the nature of the battle and more importantly how it was going to go. We went to Macedonia first and then we started to get more details about how we were going to enter into Kosovo. We would not be going into there, guns blazing. The first thing I remember is going along roads looking at the countryside and thinking, what a wonderful place. Then you'd look at all the destruction of the houses and stuff and you realised the Serbs were there making lives unlivable. They were just wrecking things and abandoning things. The infrastructure was getting shot to pieces.

Once we got into Pristina, there was a lot of revenge killings going on there. I remember going on patrol and as soon as we were out of the way, they would go and assassinate somebody. We were put into areas where there were old people (Serbians) that wanted to live the rest of their lives in their family homes. I remember there was an old couple, both of them got shot – it was a youngster who wasn't even ten years old. An adult had given the kid a gun and set them up – that's what we were dealing with. They knew that we wouldn't shoot kids. But an adult with a gun – that's a different thing altogether.

The biggest thing was dealing with the aftermath of what was going on. People had been killed and just left and we ended up having to deal with their bodies. But if you took all the soldiers away and simply looked at the area, it was straight off a chocolate box.


*Sergeant Andy Newell, 1 Para*


I did two months in Kosovo in 1999 with 1 Para as acting Colour Sergeant for Support Company. I had roughly 190 blokes and all the support weapons to look after during the deployment, on the regiment's first real operation since the Falklands.

The battalion gathered in Macedonia and began planning whilst the NATO Kosovo Force (KFOR) held negotiations with the Serbians. At one point, we were all stood to and placed into chalks (groups) by helicopters ready to deploy to the airport, as we had heard the Russians were driving from Bosnia to the airport at Pristina in armoured personnel carriers to take control of it. The rumour was that there were Russian MiGs in there that the Russians had lent them and they didn't want us to see them. The helicopters rotors were turning and we were getting very excited about seeing some action against the Russians, but negotiations headed by General Mike Jackson prevented the possible catastrophe of Brits versus Russians at Pristina airport.

Once a peace deal had been agreed between NATO and the Serbs, we had the green light to advance into Kosovo. The Pathfinders were forward placed on the high ground, the armour (tanks) drove straight up the Kacanik Defile and we went through by helicopter and entered Kosovo. We were dropped off at Kacanik, which was completely deserted except for the odd body lying around the place. We then found a couple of mass graves, which turned out to contain ninety-eight civilian bodies; and we'd only just arrived! It was our first day inside Kosovo, and we thought, bloody hell!

I think that was the first time I realised that people can be evil, totally and utterly evil.

We had to sit there and watch some of the Serbs drive away to Serbia with smirks on their faces, waving at us, knowing they'd get away with genocide. That really gripped us, because our hands were tied by the peace agreement when we really wanted to waste them all. They deserved nothing better than that in our eyes. Before they left, they went around trying to mop up and hide what they'd done by burning bodies, and stuff like that.

Eventually we got choppered in to a memorial park on top of the hill, where we were enthusiastically greeted as heroes by the locals. We started putting patrols out in the immediate vicinity, and this Serb policeman came out of a bar, pissed as a fart and started rattling off rounds at the guys, who said,

'Stop. NATO. Or we fire!' But he fired again, and so one of the lads who had only been in the battalion about three months shot him twice in the chest. Bang – and down he went. Our lad was a hero, then the next day he had a Negligent Discharge of his weapon (firing his weapon by accident), and he went from hero to zero in twenty-four hours.

We moved out from the park and set up our main logistics base (A2 Echelon) in the grounds of the university with the gymnasium being the focal point. Battalion HQ moved to another location and the individual rifle companies moved out into the town and surrounding areas around Pristina to set up patrol bases from which to work.

Support Company ended up with five or six different patrol bases where the guys worked from – and most of my time was spent driving around with Norwegian containers full of food and feeding them.

Before we got a decent place to stay, we'd literally take over a café or building, declaring this is now Company Headquarters, then break into another house, saying this is now a platoon house. We would clean the places with bleach and stuff like that, so we didn't get hideous diseases. I remember speaking to one of our interpreters, an Albanian, about these ghost towns that were formerly held by the Serbs. He told me about one of his mates who was killed by the Serbs and left lying in the street and was eaten by dogs. The remaining Albanians were hiding in their basements, they daren't come out. They just sat there and watched their mate being scoffed by dogs. It was horrible. It was utterly shocking, and when I came back from there, my girlfriend at the time said I'd changed. You don't see that many dead bodies and NOT change. It was all right seeing one or two, but seeing this waste of life *en masse* definitely changed me.

Support Company HQ ended up living in the local TV

studios, which had some Serbs staying in one of the buildings. One night they left suddenly and went to the A2 Echelon location asking for safe passage to Belgrade. After the Serbs had left Kosovo, their old and disabled were left behind. Most of them had been given weapons and uniforms, no matter what age they were, to act as a rearguard force. So you had little grannies turning up at our locations with AK-47s and uniforms, saying, 'I don't want this kit anymore.' All the confiscated weapons and uniforms were taken to the university gym where A2 Echelon was located and put on display. I think we took about 2,000 weapons in the two months we were there, including a German WW2 Luger, Tommy guns, MG42s and modern-day weaponry.

The Albanians went around slowly killing the stay-behind Serbs one by one, so we ended up like some funeral removal service, picking up what was left of the bodies, bagging them and taking them down to the local morgue. The morgue had no electricity and no lighting, so you used to go in there with your body bag and with your head-torch on and stack them on top of each other. You'd go in there and the stench – you'd have to swim through it, it was that thick. You trod on what you thought was broken glass from the lights, but it was maggot casings in the body fluids on the floor. I used to come out of there and for a couple of days afterwards people would say, 'Just go away – ugh – you stink of death.' It was minging – absolutely minging.

We even found a couple who looked like they'd been walking their dog, they'd been abused and mutilated and killed – but they shot the dog as well– and that's what really pissed me off. I found some local kids trying to stone to death a puppy that was about six weeks old. We told them to 'Fuck off,' and we took him in, fed him up, had the veterinary corps guys de-flea and inoculate him. He was a really nice dog, whom I named

Shithead, because I found him trying to eat my beret one day and called him a little shithead and the name stuck. Shithead followed me around everywhere and was handed over to the Royal Irish when they took over from us.

None of the Intelligence people had picked up on the fact that the 4th July was celebrated in Kosovo. I think like the US, it was their Independence Day. That evening as it was getting dark, the streets started to fill up with people and all we heard was lots of gunfire and saw tracer arcing across the sky, and we're talking not just AK tracer, but DShk (Soviet heavy machine gun) tracer. We all thought, fuck, what's happening!!! We rushed out ready to shoot everybody and all the Albanians were cheering and celebrating! Cars and lorries were going past us with people hanging off them. We nervously watched the celebrations continue throughout the night until they all dispersed.

We managed to get some of the guys away once for a day's R&R (rest and recuperation) at a big lake. They pulled up at the lake and there was a bridge across it, and as they were swimming in the lake they found this bloated body hung from the bridge, half in and half out of the water. Their day's R&R finished at that point and they were gutted, absolutely gutted because of a big, bloated body.

One day I was in the gym attending the daily meeting with the RQMS to sort out the logistics of running the battalion, and there was this almighty explosion that rattled the whole gym and we thought the windows were going to fall out.

We rushed outside and saw a huge mushroom cloud in the distance and thought, oh SHIT! What the fuck's that? It turned out that the EOD had found an ammo dump, or something like that. They couldn't gain access to it, so they'd put charges on the roof to blow it up. It turned out to be rather full of explosives, which caused the largest and loudest blast I've ever heard!

Another day, four of us got together with some civilian parachute rigs that guys had packed in their follow-on kit and conned a helicopter pilot into taking us up a couple of thousand feet above the football stadium so we could jump out. What an experience that was. Why did we do it? Because we could.

We handed over to the Royal Irish Regiment after two months in country without suffering any casualties. I think the general feeling amongst the battalion, on returning to the UK, was of a job well done under sometimes very grim circumstances.

## Formation of 16 Air Assault Brigade

Following the Strategic Defence Review of 1999, 16 Air Assault Brigade was formed on 1 September, amalgamating elements of 5 Airborne Brigade and 24 Airmobile Brigade, to combine the versatility of airborne forces and the formidable power of the attack helicopter. The name came from combining the 1st and 6th Airborne Divisions of Second World War fame that had been used by 16 Para Brigade post war and the Striking Eagle Badge was taken from the Special Training Centre in Scotland, where Special Forces and Airborne troops had trained.

16th Airborne Assault Brigade is the largest brigade in the British Army. Its core role is to maintain the Air Assault Task Force, a Battle Group held at high readiness to deploy worldwide for a full spectrum of missions, from non-combatant evacuation ops to front line fighting.

# 4

# SIERRA LEONE
# 2000

*Prior to the Operations Palliser and Barras, Captain Andy Harrison was an observer with the UN Assistance Mission.*

*Captain Andy Harrison, 2 Para*

The future looked bleak. I had been at the Ministry of Defence for over a year. I was facing another twelve months behind the same desk and the subsequent two years at Staff College. After that I would probably be in a staff job for two more years. I said to my boss, 'That's six years away from real soldiering. Can I have a break; will you release me for an operational tour prior to Staff College?' He agreed.

I sought out a friend in the Ministry of Defence's Commitments Directory and asked him where the most interesting place in the world was. He said, 'In Sierra Leone, they've just had the ceasefire and we think there are some UN observers jobs available, so throw your name in the hat for those.' One came up. So I completed a short three-day training course and in February 2000 flew to Freetown as an unarmed observer in the burgeoning United Nations Assistance Mission to Sierra Leone.

The Lomé Peace Accord had been signed just before we arrived, and in this UN brokered deal with the rebel Revolutionary United Front (RUF), they had agreed to a process of demilitarisation, demobilisation and reintegration. The UN observers would oversee this process and the peacekeepers were there for some form of protection. In Freetown I met up with my Royal Marine boss, a gruff Falklands conflict veteran and recipient of the Military Cross, Colonel Peter Babbington.

We couldn't move out of Freetown initially because the UN mission was still expanding town-by-town into the areas that had been dominated by the rebels in the civil war. Colonel Peter had to decide which of the 12 British observers was assigned into each town. I was posted to Kailahun, a godforsaken town deep in the country adjacent to the Liberian border. Kailahun was the heartland of the RUF and the place where its leader, Foday Sankoh, had started the barbaric revolution a decade before. I hoped Colonel Peter sent me there as a reflection of my soldiering ability, rather than simply a nod to the traditional Royal Marine Parachute Regiment rivalry!

It took a few weeks for the UN to negotiate access into this rebel area. When we eventually gained authority, I flew into the town in a battered old Russian HIP helicopter. We landed in a small jungle clearing on the outskirts of the town. I was appalled at what I saw. The town was horrible; I've never, before or afterwards, seen anything like it. The place stank. It was a fetid hell-hole of an ex-town which, like some recently discovered Aztec city, had been mostly reclaimed by the jungle. It was full of wounded RUF fighters clustered into mud hut hospitals that the Red Cross had never been able to access. There were dozens of mortally wounded rebels who had never received any medical care; the stench of their gangrenous, infected wounds was appalling. Everything was filthy and infested with rotting, putrid decaying jungle matter.

With the rebels, we negotiated the terms of our deployment. I was the deputy commander of the new patrol base working under the command of Dwi Ujianto, an Indonesian colonel who spoke hardly any English. We lived in the jungle initially, in tents on the outskirts of a derelict building. An Indian

Gurkha peacekeeping company was located in a clearing close to us and we gradually started building up relationships with the rebel leaders. Slowly we gained their trust and started negotiating a plan for disarmament and demobilisation. We got on well with them. They were never armed and escorted us from village to village. It was a fascinating couple of months as we got to know them and explore a part of West Africa that was returning to primitive existence after being shut away from any outside contact for decades.

By early March we had moved out of the jungle tents and were living in a dilapidated concrete house in the centre of the slowly regenerating town. At this stage we had established strong relationships with the RUF, were engaged in a series of meetings with their leadership and in some cases had formed friendships. We played volleyball against them every day and, when they weren't drunk or drugged up, could have detailed conversations about the genesis of the barbaric civil war. The rebels were a happy-go-lucky bunch, mostly only teenagers, poorly educated and misogynistic, but conscious that the peace accord gave them an opportunity to avoid a brutal death and perhaps improve their primordial lives. We had started to raise the complex issue of disarmament and I was optimistic that our team could make a real difference.

Early on the morning of 1 May I received a message from the young RUF colonel in charge of Kailahun that he would like a meeting in his house to discuss how we were going to commence the process of disarmament. This appeared to be another in the series of meetings that had been taking place to discuss the modalities of the Lome Peace Accord.

What I didn't realise was that during the night before all hell had broken loose in the town of Makeni, close to Freetown. Without leadership authority, some of the Makeni rebels had unilaterally started the process of disarmament and were handing their weapons in to UN peacekeepers. The RUF central command was incandescent at this unauthorised disarmament and rallied their loyal troops. A bitter standoff ensued which rapidly led to a series of arguments, which in turn escalated into a full blown fire fight. Within a few short hours the harmony between the UN and the RUF had deteriorated into war and, isolated in Kailahun, we were unaware of the violent conflagration erupting across the country. It was therefore in blissful ignorance that about ten of us travelled to what we thought would be a perfectly normal meeting.

We were gathered in the derelict ground floor garage of the RUF colonel's house. The meeting started with an address by the grandiosely titled 'adjutant general' of the RUF. In the middle of his extended monologue praising our efforts towards peace he said, 'But there have been some problems and as a result we are going to detain you for your own safety.' This was obviously his signal, because as he said it, a crowd of about 100 rebels smashed into the building. They had AKs and a range of weapons but my overriding memory is the vivid image of a huge woman in a canary yellow dress standing screaming at us with an RPG on her shoulder. If that had gone off everyone would have got a slice.

We were rapidly overpowered and our arms were trussed up behind our backs before being dragged into the back of our Land Cruiser and driven off into the jungle. That was the start of a long and interesting experience. After an hour of slow and painful driving we arrived in a clearing and were made to sit on some rough wooden benches. Nothing happened for a number of hours until, later that day, we were joined by two Indian peacekeeping officers and a few of their soldiers. All were bound like us. After a few minutes one of the Indian officers accused a rebel guard of stealing his sergeant's watch. It was obvious the guard had done this as we'd all had personal belongings stolen but this was neither the time nor the place to make such a confronting accusation. The guards saw the watch on this RUF rebel's arm and – on the order of their boss – attacked him viciously with big bamboo sticks. As he curled on the floor his clothes and skin started to be flayed from his body. One of the Indian officers and I were shouting at them to stop. Suddenly the assault stopped. The RUF boss came up to us and said, 'Okay, we'll stop beating him'. In silence they dragged him in front of us and shot him through the back of the head.

In that moment everything changed. For the first time in my career, my one overriding thought was just to stay alive. The situation was dire and there wasn't going to be any pleasant outcome; all the rules had changed. They pulled the boy's bloody body into the boot of our car and drove it off.

As I recoiled from the barbarity of what had just happened I was separated from the others and marched at gunpoint a few hundred metres to a concrete blockhouse on the edge of the village. I was unceremoniously shoved into a small improvised cell, a concrete room about twelve foot by six foot with a metal door, metal shutters, and iron bars over the window. The fierce tropical heat beat down on the tin roof and the temperature in the enclosed cell soared. I'd last had a drink at breakfast and as the sun began to set, my thumping headache gave a clue to my growing dehydration.

The first night seemed to last forever. The tumultuous events of the day, the dehydration, the rock-hard concrete floor and the constraining belt holding my arms behind my back all conspired to prevent any sleep. But as the first shafts of dawn filtered into the cell my morale rose. The cacophony of nocturnal jungle sounds and the reasonable temperature were slowly replaced by distant village noises and the beating heat of the African sun.

I tried to talk to the guards outside the building with little success, trying to establish what had happened, why the situation had degenerated and why we were being held. One by one I could hear the other rooms in the blockhouse being filled with observers and Indian peacekeepers, but it was a disorientating mix of movement and noise and most of the rebels were talking in incomprehensible pidgin English.

There were small victories. After asking for hours we were eventually brought a bucket of water by some local boys. My cell door was opened and the filthy plastic tub was placed by my body. As the guards stood over me menacingly, I knelt up awkwardly and plunged my head into the water to drink, half expecting a hand to hold my face under the water. Eventually someone released the belt constricting my arms behind my back and feeling slowly returned to my hands. Perhaps best of all, my solitary confinement came to an end when Andre was launched incongruously into my cell on the second day.

Hours turned into days and each day seemed slightly worse than the last. Even though we weren't being fed, our cell and the blockhouse became more and more unsanitary. At night the incessant mosquitoes were joined by rats, scurrying around and interrupting our fitful bouts of sleep. There was constant sobbing from one of the observers on the other side of the house. It was a grim place to be and I was constantly thinking about how to escape. From the very start the RUF had been very clear that if any individual tried to escape they'd kill those that were left. In hushed conversations between the cells we had talked and agreed among ourselves no one would attempt an escape unless we knew one of us had been killed, and then it was a free for all. We had not reached that stage – yet.

On the third night we were lying on the concrete floor when a distant sound of vehicles became louder and louder. Eventually the light from the vehicles flickered into view and the voices of furious rebels resonated around the house. All eleven of us were dragged to the front of the building in the blinding light of the two vehicles' headlights. The rebels were giving Andre and I a particularly hard time, ostensibly because we were the only white guys. A knot of fear grew in my stomach as I realised that their anger was growing, not abating, and Andre and I continued to be the incessant target for their vicious beatings.

It gradually became clear what was happening. They told us that we were going to be executed because two RUF soldiers had been killed by the UN in a fire fight elsewhere in the region that night. This particularly psychotic RUF officer knew the two dead rebels and was determined to avenge their deaths.

Eventually the beating subsided and we were tied up again. Then my worst fears were realised. Andre and I were picked up and dragged across the track to another abandoned house. It was obvious what was happening and I hoped and prayed that someone was watching and an impromptu rescue would be launched from the dark tree lines. But nothing happened. The seething mass of rebels, clearly high on bloodlust, kicked, rifle-butted and punched us into the house. There we were told to kneel down. I was convinced the end had come. With bowed heads Andre and I caught each other's eye. Almost simultaneously we both said we would not kneel. There was a sense of resignation in our voices as we waited for a trigger to be pulled.

But for whatever reason, a miracle ensued and the rebels degenerated into chaos. They somehow got into a fight among themselves about what to do with us. Eventually they must have decided that a serious beating would suffice and we suffered a torrent of rifles butts and boots. Curled up in the foetal position as the blows rained down, I remember seeing rebels stamping on Andre's head and swinging their rifles by the barrels as they launched attack after attack. After what seemed like an eternity we were picked up and dragged back across the track to our cell.

On about the fifth day a couple of kids brought some mangoes to the guards and they gave them to us. That was the first time we'd eaten since capture. I was spending all my time just trying to talk to the guards. Many of them had shortwave radios and gradually a picture emerged of the chaos the country was in. Each hour we could hear snippets of the crisis developing as they tuned it to the World Service to hear the news. It was clear that British forces were coming into Sierra Leone and the situation across the country was rapidly degenerating. So we knew what was going on in Freetown, but we didn't have a clue what was happening around us in Kailahun. We were right on the Liberian border, totally out of reach from my mates in 1 Para who were by now streaming into the country.

Throughout all of this I learned to hate the BBC's correspondent in West Africa, Barnaby Phillips. The rebels knew I was a paratrooper and they understood that it was the Parachute Regiment spearheading the stabilisation of Sierra Leone. On the hour, every hour, Phillips would deliver his assured and confident report, describing the influence the Battle Group was having and the impending violence. And immediately after each radio report finished the guards would walk into my cell, say, 'So you're the great Para,' and then launch into me. That cell was far from the most pleasant experience of my career. The radio beatings were supplemented by the nightly assaults when they were high on drugs or blind drunk. Strangely the fact that we knew the violence was coming was almost worse than the actual beatings.

On the eleventh day the women of Kailahun bravely decided they were going to hold a rally to protest against the RUF holding us hostage. Unbelievably, this seemed to work and eventually, after one of the biggest tropical storms I'd ever experienced, we were moved from our jungle cells back into our house in the town, but still as prisoners. We were put onto the top floor with four rebel guards posted around the outside.

By this time I knew that 1 Para wasn't going to simply sit in Freetown and do nothing. Dwi, our team commander seemed to have lost the ability to do or say anything. I didn't realise until much later that a few years earlier he had been captured and held hostage in Bosnia. He was one of the observers chained to the bridges to stop NATO planes from bombing them. No wonder he was ill.

In the top floor of our concrete house I corralled the team together and said, 'Look, I know we've got this deal about escape, but the bottom line is my battalion is in Freetown and they will take the fight to the RUF. Then in retaliation I will be killed. So I'm getting out and I think we should all go.' We debated this for a couple of hours, and in the end Andre and the Indian and Pakistani officer agreed to come with me.

I knew one of the young guards particularly well and I thought he'd be the most acquiescent as we planned our escape. We tracked his routine for a couple of hours and when he was located at the most isolated sentry point, out of sight of the other three, I climbed down to him. I told the lad about the four members of my team who were ill with malaria and that I had to get to the Indian peacekeepers compound to obtain medical resources. He was only a kid and was clearly confused about how to react. Terrified on the inside and waiting for him to either fire or shout a warning, I then walked, as calmly as I could, until I was behind the corner of an adjacent mosque. The other three followed.

Although my right knee was damaged from one of the beatings, as soon as we were out of sight of the house we limp-sprinted off into the dark jungle as fast as we could manage. Within five minutes we had slowed to a trot and linked onto a track that led in the direction of the peacekeepers' camp. A nagging sense of guilt pervaded my every step. I began to imagine what might happen to the seven colleagues we had left behind and didn't feel proud of my actions.

As the first light of the day started to permeate through the dense jungle, we glimpsed a figure on the track approaching us. We took cover in the thick undergrowth and squinted through the foliage. I recognised him as a friend from my previous time in the town. He was carrying an enormous bunch of green and yellow bananas. We talked for a bit and he said that we didn't look too good, before giving me about twenty of his bananas. After he left we gorged on the welcome food and set off again.

As we started approaching the high ground surrounding the peacekeepers' camp my guilt reached a crescendo and I said to Andre; 'I'm going to go and see the RUF colonel and get the medical supplies. You three go to the camp and I'll see you in an hour'. Cutting back into town, I carefully made my way to the old decrepit terraced house where the RUF colonel lived. I knocked on the door. It was eventually answered by a girl who looked about 14 years old. Although she looked nonplussed to find a filthy and bedraggled British army officer carrying the remnants of a bunch of bananas, she scurried off to wake the young rebel colonel. I greeted him and gave him the remaining bananas. Once again he was obviously confused but I told him that I had to collect some medical supplies at the camp as my colleagues in the house were in a terrible state. He nodded sleepily and I thanked him, spun around and set off. He never questioned how or why I was at his house and I didn't want to give him the opportunity.

I continued my trek to the peacekeepers' camp. From previous conversations with guards I knew that rebels surrounded it but the absence of any shooting gave me some confidence that

Andre and the others had made it safely. I thought it best not to approach on the track and carefully crawled through the jungle until the outline of an Indian sentry position was visible. In a hushed voice I kept repeating 'UN, United Nations' until I had the guard's attention. With my heart pounding I carefully stood up. He ushered me forward and I crossed the open ground to his post.

Once in the camp I quickly found Andre and we went to see the Indian major in charge of the beleaguered company. I told him that we needed two of his vehicles to try and get the other observers from the house. He sensed our urgency and lent us the vehicles. Having just reached safety, it was a nerve-racking feeling to be driving back out of the Indian location. With adrenalin pumping we travelled through the morning light back towards our house. It was good to be doing something active rather than simply being the passive victim of the rebels' whims.

We drove up to the house that we'd left only a few short hours earlier. I challenged the guards with as much confidence as I could possibly muster, 'Your colonel has ordered us to get these men to medical facilities.' We seemed to have the moral authority for such an order and there was no dissent. I hobbled up the external staircase and told the remaining members of the observer team to get into the vehicles as fast as possible. Amazingly, a few of them didn't want to go and I spent a desperate five minutes persuading them it would be better to risk the journey back to the peacekeepers' camp than be left to the violent recriminations of the rebels. 'Look,' I said 'we've got a route out here, just get in the cars and we can finally get to safety.' Eventually we persuaded them all to move to the vehicles and drove off, leaving a rather bewildered looking gaggle of now-redundant guards.

As Andre drove back through town I was in the front seat next to him trying to operate the Indian vehicle's short-wave radio. I was flicking through all the UN frequencies I could remember, repeatedly transmitting: 'Hello any station, this is Oscar India 2 (my UN call sign). Is there any Uniform Kilo (the code for UK) call-sign out there?' There was no reply and I soon ditched any pretence of code and switched to clear speech. 'This is Captain Andy Harrison, is there anyone who speaks English out there.'

All of a sudden, 'Yeah.' Then a pause, 'Andy, is that you?' It was Joe Poraj-Wilzynski, a Parachute Regiment colonel based on the other side of the country in Freetown. It was the first communication I'd had for 12 days with anyone from outside Kailahun and my spirits soared. He then said, 'Where are you?' 'I'm in Kailahun, I'm making my way back to the Indian base, they're surrounded but it hasn't kicked off,' 'Understood, I've got all available means here if you need it, just give me the shout. Do you understand, ALL available means.'

I immediately knew what he meant; the Parachute Regiment were stood by if I needed help. A huge wave of relief swept over me; I now knew I wasn't alone. Help was at hand if I needed it.

We re-entered the Indian compound without incident. The eleven of us were now under the protection of over a hundred armed Indian Gurkha soldiers and nothing would ever lever us out. The rebels were clearly angry. They sent a delegation to attempt to negotiate our return but there was no way we would leave the security of the enclave to return to their control. The atmosphere deteriorated and a series of skirmishes around the outskirts of the jungle base elevated the state of tension to stratospheric levels. We had now armed ourselves from the Indian's makeshift armoury and dug ourselves shallow trenches in the area we were allocated.

Hours turned into days, and days into weeks. We had a sizeable store of rice and a well for water. Gradually we improved the defence of the jungle enclave, digging bunkers and communication trenches. It was a Rambo-like existence; sneaking to the perimeter at night to create traps of spike-filled pits and hanging tin cans with stones to act as early warning of any rebel approach. Working like ants, we chopped down hundreds of trees with the Gurkhas' kukris and used the wood to provide overhead protection in the bunkers and to strengthen the perimeter. Slowly the vulnerable jungle clearing took on the appearance of a defendable military strong-hold.

With the occasional contact with the UN headquarters through the Indian soldiers it became clear that British troops were involved in operations around Freetown. It was also clear that the rebels had butchered dozens of peacekeepers across the country and were holding hundreds of UN hostages. We well knew how the rebels treated their prisoners.

After the two months, supplies in our camp began to run out. We were continually anticipating a UN attack to relieve us but the UN couldn't authorise any action that might place their other hostages at risk. Instead the UN negotiated a deal whereby the rebels would drive a UN food truck to our enclave. In the deal they'd struck, we would then unload the food and the rebels could keep the truck.

In a ration pack labelled for me, the UN had concealed a satellite phone, batteries, maps, money, malaria tablets, and a host of supplies. They then took it to my British UN mates in their house in Freetown and said, 'Now fill this box with stuff that Andy would want on top of the supplies we've put in.' As they started to put in additional medical kit, the mischievous sense of humour of the British soldier mixed with Freetown's 'Star' beer and a plan was hatched.

The first we knew of the deal was when the rebels brought the truck to an area of high ground visible through the jungle canopy about 800 metres away from our camp. We watched them with curiosity as they then started throwing the food off the truck and wantonly destroying it. Clearly high on drugs or booze, they were jumping up and down on the food, firing their weapons in the air. The rebels were playing psychological games, enjoying destroying the desperately needed supplies in front of us. The team watched on in silence.

Late that night we sent a covert Gurkha patrol out to see if they could recover any of the food. It was a risky move and the first time anyone had left the enclave since our trip to the house. They managed to recover a few battered boxes full of rations and decaying food. The next morning the Indian soldiers were going through the contents and one of them came up to me with a box marked 'Oscar India 2', my UN call-sign. My heart was racing with anticipation as I ripped it open.

The first thing that I saw was a video cassette. It was a 'Join the British Army' recruiting video. Underneath was a yellow plastic blow-up sword with a message on it saying, 'In case you need to fight your way out.' Next was a cardboard helicopter, 'So you can fly out.' All of these plus condoms and hangover tablets and a tin of Barbie spaghetti! Around me the observers were scratching their heads and looking on with incredulity. I was shaking my head with wry amusement, fully understanding that I was at the receiving end of a dose of fantastically inappropriate military humour.

The jokes came to end in the lower half of the box and at the bottom was a satellite phone and an anonymous note giving me instructions and a phone number to contact. I grabbed the phone, set it up and, with trembling fingers, rang the number.

No one answered. It rang and rang. At last, after about two minutes, a male voice answered. I asked him who he was and met the same question in response. Whoever I was speaking to probably didn't have as much to lose as I did; 'It's Andy Harrison,' I heard an intake of breath and then, 'Just wait a sec, wait a sec, boss, boss, it's him!' There was some commotion, and another voice came to the phone and calmly asked, 'Right, what's your dog's name?' Well, I knew that and so did he. I now had comms with the ops room in Freetown.

After a lot of planning and negotiating I was briefed that two UK helicopters would pick us up at dawn. As the first massive Chinook flared to land in a cacophony of wind and noise, I expected the rebels to kick off. They didn't. The helicopter landed and I sprinted up the rear ramp. As my observer colleagues raced on, I went through the ID cards of the guys who were supposed to be boarding the helicopter. As soon as we were content all the observers were on board, the Chinook took off and circled overhead, the huge mini-guns providing top cover for the second helicopter picking up the wounded Indian soldiers and the ammunition we didn't want to get into the hands of the rebels. We flew off and a huge sergeant grabbed me by the collar and, with an enormous smile, shouted above the din of the rotors, 'You owe me a fucking slab of beer, I've been in this shitty country for three months because of you.' Brilliant! The helicopter tilted and we accelerated away, skimming a snaking brown river and racing towards safety. Bright smiles covered every observer's face, we were safe!

We landed in the small town of Daru where I met the Indian Force Commander. The Indian artillery around us was pounding the rebel positions as the Indian Gurkha company fought its way back to the UN lines. With all the UN hostages now released, the gloves were clearly off.

In Freetown that night I met my mates and after a medical we went out to celebrate. I'd lost a couple of stone in weight and my emaciated frame collapsed after my second pint. At the High Commissioner's residence I had a long, glorious shower and then, on crisp, clean bed-linen, fell fast asleep.

## Operation Palliser

In May 2000, 1 Para minus A Company, but reinforced with D Company 2 Para, intervened as the Revolutionary United Front (RUF) advanced on Freetown. Their actions prevented the collapse of UNAMSIL, evacuated EU nationals and stopped the rebel advance and pushed the RUF back from Freetown's outskirts. A follow-on training and security mission relieved 1 Para. In September 2000, elements of 1 Para deployed again as part of a mission to rescue captured British soldiers from the West Side Boys (Operation Barras).

*Lieutenant Mark Jackson, Pathfinder Platoon*

It was the summer of 2000, and I had just handed over to Gareth Hicks as second in command of the Pathfinders; with the sunny Friday afternoon feeding a growing sense of freedom of an imminent carefree stretch of leave, I'd popped in to grab some kit from 1 Para's barracks in Aldershot. I bumped into the CO, Paul Gibson, outside battalion headquarters, and he asked if I wanted to join a briefing. An hour or so later, all thoughts of leave banished, I rang Gareth: 'Get all the blokes back, now, it's Africa. And I know I've just handed over, but I'm coming!'

Following a sketchy brief to the platoon back at our base in Suffolk the next morning, catalysing our own deployment preparations, Gareth and I plugged back in to 1 Para's briefings for a few hours on the Saturday, and, after a combined admin explosion on the grass outside the Officers' Mess (hidden from everyone's sight, and therefore apoplexy), we rejoined the Platoon at the air mounting base in Oxfordshire. Brigade Commander Peter Wall shook Gareth and my hands through an open window, and wished us luck. There was a confirmatory ministerial meeting at Chequers at 4 p.m. that afternoon, and the first patrols arrived in the tropical heat of Freetown as part of 1 Para battle group the following morning.

Op Palliser was in many ways a watershed deployment for the modern-day Pathfinder Platoon, a coming of age. Formed in 1985, though only formally established in the British Army Order of Battle in 1993, the Platoon had for the intervening years operated largely on a black economy; the legacy of those years was a bureaucracy-bending and entrepreneurial spirit, a stubborn willingness to achieve much, with little, and a confidence – both individual and collective – in operating with great self-sufficiency and minimal support.

The deployment to Kosovo the previous summer had been the first for the Pathfinders as a formed unit, and had been a good run-out for us all, our equipment and procedures, in an (albeit low spectrum) operational environment; there lingered still a doubt in some quarters that we were as good as we committed ourselves to be, that our entrepreneurial spirit wasn't actually a thin veil for the cowboys' spurs. The Platoon's role, performance and mission success on Op Palliser shook off the last of these doubts, and properly launched the Pathfinders as a battle-proven organisation.

The Platoon had been tasked to push forward of the battle-group into a village called Lungi Lol, to provide early warning of an attack on Freetown Airport. Exposed and with limited support, we set about creating a defensive perimeter, building relationships with the villagers and local Nigerian troops and building a picture of nearby rebel activity. Increasing numbers of displaced Sierra Leoneans sought shelter in the village by night. I then flew back to the airport to take over command of the Platoon headquarters, leaving Gareth with the patrols in the village.

This was a classic, deep recce role, but with an emphasis on an overt posture to reassure the locals and deter the RUF against a northern approach on Freetown's international airport at Lungi. When we landed at Lungi Lol, we had very little in the way of belongings. Indeed we had sort of anticipated landing and going straight into a scrap, such was the paucity of accurate intelligence. Port Loko to our east was on fire and being heavily contested by the RUF, but resolutely defended by a Nigerian detachment and the SAS.

The village of Lungi Lol had become inundated with refugees, some of whom had been previously captured by the RUF; their missing limbs the proof of their ordeal. They were all desperately fleeing the terror that approached them from the east. They passed us information and relayed stories of mutilated corpses strung up in those RUF-controlled areas of Port Loko. Our little village, Lungi Lol, was the next area of interest for the RUF. It sat astride the most significant two roads/tracks that approached Lungi airport and northern Freetown. Colonel Paul Gibson knew its significance, as did the RUF.

We joined a small Nigerian detachment, very lightly armed (they had two magazines apiece and a pocket full of bullets), and despite them knowing very little about what was unfolding around them, they were very jovial and they looked immaculate!

Given our overt posture, we were very vulnerable to a well-thought-out attack by the RUF. But the twenty-four of us busied our defences, clearing fields of fire through the bush and laying obstacles to channel any attackers towards our strengths. The defences continued to be enhanced, using fields of punji sticks and homemade claymores. In the half-light one morning, ten days after our arrival at Lungi Lol, Lance Corporals Andy Heywood and Bryan Budd and a Private were manning a GPMG in a forward sentry position, when they started to pick out vague figures emerging through the misty dawn. 'Maximise' (stand-to) was called over the net.

As we occupied our positions, the forward sentry position was now faced with a dilemma: some of those approaching us were wearing UN berets (we had been forewarned of this RUF tactic being employed at Port Loko further to our east). This dilemma passed when the leading four figures engaged our forward sentry position from a distance of about 20 yards. This threat was swiftly removed, which caused the remaining thirty or so RUF to try and flank us. This was hard going for them, as our innovative obstacle plan worked and helped channel the attackers towards our strengths.

After what seemed like an eternity, but was in fact about three hours, the attackers withdrew to consider their options, leaving fourteen dead. Subsequent intercepted RUF communications suggested they would try again the next night in much larger numbers, which triggered the deployment of the 1 Para QRF (including a section of 81mm mortars) to strengthen the position at Lungi Lol. The RUF's re-attack never came and the threat to Freetown's northern approaches and its international airport was removed.

Op Palliser was a watershed moment for the Pathfinders. It was our first operational deployment in our 'deep recce' role. The difficulty of the operating environment, especially the secondary jungle and bushland, and the ability of the guys to retain the highest standards of soldiering over a two-week period in close contact to the RUF, was a testament to the ethos, selection and training of the Platoon. The Platoon required highly motivated, self-disciplined, professional soldiers with a determination and pursuit of excellence. Every Finderman distinguished himself during Op Palliser, none more so than the Platoon's sergeant, Steve Heaney, who would subsequently be awarded a Military Cross for his outstanding soldiering and courage in the face of the enemy.

*Corporal Andy Cutting, 1 Para*

We had an MMG section attached to my platoon in B Company, and every day the OC would get them to site their trench in a different place. They used to get the local kids to help them dig and fill sandbags and reward them with sweets from the ration packs.

One sunny afternoon, two burly Paratroopers (hard guys and built like barn doors) were sitting in the MMG trench watching their arcs, which was the track junction ahead, with a GPMG on a tripod (SF model) with about 1,000 rounds of 4 bit. When a four-year-old local lad came up and said, 'Snack, snack,' the lads told him to fuck off, as they had given him some sweets earlier; but he kept on saying 'snack, snack' and again they told him to do one. The little lad then pointed in the trench and said, 'Snack, snack!'

The guys looked round and there was a snake in the trench with them. That must have been the fastest I have ever seen two hairy-arse Paratroopers leave a trench, weapons and ammunition flying everywhere. The four-year-old jumped into the trench and picked up the snake, flicked the back of its head, killing it instantly, and took it home for his tea.

## Operation Barras

*Corporal, 1 Para*

In Sierra Leone, the West Side Boys were an armed militia and that was their thing. They were a bunch of thugs and they terrorised people. If you were to look at everything they did beforehand, they always seemed to be in the news. I remember from when I joined the army back in 1987, the number of times that we nearly went to Sierra Leone before Palliser. It was on the radar because of the conflict that was going on there.

When we landed in Sierra Leone, we got straight from our aircraft onto transport and went up to our training camp. This camp was in the middle of the jungle. It was out the way. We spent several days going through various rehearsals for what we were going to do – our option. Right up to before we got deployed, the friendly forces on the ground, they were recceing or trying to recce various places for us. Meanwhile the negotiating team was still trying to arrange the hostages' release without us being used. Obviously that didn't go to plan and the evening before, we'd had a briefing from our OC and one of the negotiating team, who were trying to put things in perspective for us. Since the Falklands, this was the first time the Parachute Regiment was going to be doing anything in anger. He said he'd never met such a deserving bunch of bastards in all his life! Let's get this done.

There were two assaults. One to get the Royal Irish hostages out, while we had our bit on the other side of the river where the equipment was and the Land Rovers – that's why we went back in there, to get the vehicles – we wanted our equipment back.

Although we had rehearsed everything over and over, we didn't know for sure what we were going into, and what we were going to be landing on. We found out the hard way, because as the tailgate went down, water started coming in. I was two back. My machine gunner was in front of me, but as he went out, because of the weight he was carrying, he disappeared in the water. I went after him and just grabbed him, pulling this fella up. Though it turned out to be a better landing place than the one we were originally going to land on.

We were in the jungle, hot, wet and sweating, trying to get away from the landing site as quickly as possible to the tree line on the edge of the village. We were the point section of the point and we soon got to the outside of the village, but due to where we landed we had approached it from the west instead of the south. I identified the building that we were going to be taking first. All I remember was the platoon commander saying, 'That's your building there, you okay with that?'

That was it. We basically crossed this track, sprinted through the jungle through the right-hand side of the track. The West Side Boys had the vehicles camouflaged with jungle, palm leaves – they were just basic pickups. I remember turning to my 2IC, Tom, and saying, 'I'm going to go round and as soon as I'm ready and in position, fire a 66 into the side of the building and then we're going through the front door. At the same time, I want somebody to hose this vehicle down. I don't want them coming out.'

The 66 went in, bang – I heard the gunfire going into the vehicle, so me and Eddie started to bomb burst in towards this vehicle. As we were charging towards it, somebody popped up. All I heard was gunfire: it was Eddie shooting at this fella who legged it, but didn't get far as he had an armour-piercing round in him.

We then found the building was empty; they had all legged it. We had a Hind Helicopter gunship as well as a Lynx, which was providing air support over our village and the village where the hostages were. They got the biggest shock of their lives, because our company rolled through that place in seconds. We just hammered straight on through. It was fast and it was furious. With one hundred-plus paratroopers determined to do one thing and do it very well.

We did our bit quite quickly and secured the houses and the village. I saw that one person and that was it. The rest left in a rush, as we found signs of life – fires, etc. – leaving this one bloke to guard it. Basically, they ran away, they gave up.

Once we got to our level of exploitation, then we secured the area for the vehicles we'd recovered, to be extracted. As soon as we were on that helicopter, we flew straight to a ship. From when we started on that morning in the training camp, we were now on a ship within a few hours waiting to go home. I remember speaking to one of the lads; he was ex-1 Para. He was part of the recce team and he thought the game was up for us. He thought it was all going to go wrong, because he could hear the helicopters, three big Chinooks, the Lynx and the Hind starting up in the early morning!

I got a joint Commander's commendation for my efforts that day. I don't know why. I just turned up, did my job and went home again, like most people do when they go to work. On reflection, it was nice to be recognised for doing your job. But everybody did their job that day.

In my section they were young lads straight out of Depot. I remember meeting them and they were still standing to attention when I walked by. It was trying to get a different mentality into the young lads straight away. And we did. In the period of time from when we left Dover to arriving into Sierra Leone, we started to change their mind-set.

In Catterick they were doing it in a training area with a Section Commander telling them exactly what to do and where to go. Then they evolved as Paratroopers by coming to a Company where a Section Commander would still be telling them what to do, but not by standing over them but expecting them to one hundred per cent get it right. I had a job to do and it wasn't babysitting the younger soldiers; it was training them to get them to do what they needed to do. Their learning curve was really steep. We had a strong group of senior NCOs and Section Commanders within the company: a mix of experienced and inexperienced Private soldiers.

That was it. It was good.

*Sergeant Andy Newell, 1 Para*

In May 2000, I was out in Jamaica with A Company running their jungle training package. I basically lived in the jungle for a month, with fifteen of my Patrols Platoon guys, and it was brilliant. The rest of the battalion deployed on Op Palliser to Sierra Leone and we tried like hell to get over there, but the powers-that-be said no. By the time we'd got back to the UK and had a couple of weeks leave, the rest of the battalion was back. So they'd been off to war, come back and they gave us a right slagging.

Then a short time later, some soldiers from the Royal Irish Regiment were caught and held hostage by the West Side Boys in Sierra Leone. The UK decided to send troops out to secure their release in case negotiations broke down. A Company group was the most experienced at jungle operations at that time. Then I heard that the CO had said, 'Well, they're the only ones who haven't got any medals yet, so they can go.' We deployed to Sierra Leone on Op Barras where we went through the planning phase, zeroing weapons, kit preparation and rehearsals.

The West Side Boys were located in two camps; the main camp was called Gberi Bana, which held the hostages, and the other was called Magbeni. Running in-between the two camps was the Rokel Creek. The hostages consisted of some Royal Irish Regiment soldiers and SL armed forces and civilians who were with them. Recce troops tried to get down the river to observe the camps, but there were too many obstructions in the river and it wasn't deep enough to support boats for an attack. So they decided to use Chinooks and fast-rope in during the attack, whilst 1 Para simultaneously assaulted Magbeni. Alongside the Chinooks there were a couple of Lynx helicopters with 50 calibre machine guns mounted, whilst the Chinooks had mini-guns fitted. The windows were removed from the Chinooks so you could fire out the windows whilst flying.

There were ongoing negotiations conducted with the leader of the West Side Boys, Foday Kallay. When the negotiations broke down and the government decided that the hostages were in grave danger, the order was given to rescue them.

The attack went in early the next morning and was a complete success. What we didn't realise was that the previous night they'd had a big drugs party in Gberi Bana, so the majority of them switched over and went across. So when the strike went in the next day, it was a bit stiffer resistance than they had expected. The guys fast-roped directly into the camp containing the hostages and went about their business. The Lynx were firing on the perimeter with the 50 cals, and the Chinooks were using their mini-guns. In a short time they'd secured the hostages, but unfortunately Brad Tinnion got hit by a ricochet, and died. Whilst this attack was going on, the 1 Para guys had been dropped off waist-deep in a swamp, but were dealing with the camp at Magbeni. We had a few injured in an explosion, which was initially thought to be from a drop-short of one of our mortars, or one of their mortars, or a landmine, or what? The whole operation was over in a relatively short space of time.

After everyone was back at the jungle camp, it was decided that within an hour or so, 'We're going to get you out of here just in case there's a counter-attack.' They flew us out to the *Sir Percival*, which was moored offshore. When we landed, the ship's captain gave a big speech on how we were the big heroes of the free world. They lowered us down below the decks using one of the big deck lifts and there was this huge pile of beer sat waiting for us – then they said, 'Just help yourselves, lads.' The rest of the night was a bit of a blur!

# 5

# MACEDONIA
# 2001

## Operation Bessemer

In August 2001, 2 Para and 9 Para Squadron (with logistic support from 13 Air Assault Support Regiment, RLC) provided the UK (Operation Bessemer) contribution to the 3,500-man NATO Operation Essential Harvest mission led by HQ 16 Air Assault Brigade. The mission involved disarming ethnic Albanian groups and destroying their weapons as a part of confidence building measures following the Lake Ohrid Accord.

*Captain Peter Flynn, Adjutant, 2 Para*

Operation Bessemer was a significant milestone for the battalion, after years of residential and roulement tours of duty in Northern Ireland. From our base in 'Arnhem Factory' on the outskirts of Skopje, the capital of the Former Yugoslav Republic of Macedonia, 2 Para Battlegroup launched a series of operations to help deliver the NATO-brokered Ohrid Agreement. This saw the insurgents of the Albanian National Liberation Army (NLA) agreeing to disarm, in return for greater political rights being given to Macedonia's ethnic Albanians by the Macedonian government.

  2 Para conducted a series of operations to establish weapon collection sites in the mountains on Macedonia's north-west border with Kosovo. The Patrols Platoon and Snipers would

typically deploy at D-1, to conduct liaison, recce and over-watch the intended weapon collection site. On D-Day, inner and outer security cordons would be established, using a combination of support helicopter insertion and a road move. Convoys with light and highly mobile Pinzgauers and Weapons Mount Installation Kit (WMIK) Land Rovers were used, with Support Company either providing firepower and protection to the convoys, or attached to the companies providing the outer security cordons in depth.

Once the weapons collection site was established, shipping containers would be flown in, to store and transport the weapons that were to be collected. The NLA would arrive on foot to hand in a variety of small arms and portable weapons of varying quality and occasional antiquity. This drew some fairly wry observations from the Toms, on the suitability of some of these weapons for museum collections. The weapons would be cleared before being carefully registered and handed over, with the NLA displaying a far more relaxed attitude to weapon safety handling drills than a Small Arms School Corps instructor would be altogether happy with.

Every Paratrooper in the battalion was keen to get in on the action, after years of the same old routine in Northern Ireland; every attached arm and platoon had a role to play in the operation, whether it be recce, over-watch, inner security, escort duties, route marking, convoy security, flank protection or quick reaction force tasks. The Assault Pioneer Platoon, keen not to be left out, constructed an impressive, carpeted and door-framed entrance to a field latrine, with bits and pieces of rubbish and timber they'd salvaged. Once through this rather dramatic portal, the user was then almost completely exposed to the entire world behind the door, whilst sitting on a hastily constructed 'throne'!

With weapons collection complete, the shipping containers

would be flown to a handover area, from where Support Company would escort the weapons to an official site for destruction. As each weapon collection operation was achieved, it marked the next progressive step in the reading of the Ohrid agreement in the Macedonia Parliament. It was during a gap between these weapon collection operations that the attack on the World Trade Center in New York took place and the Regiment and the world's future changed in a matter of moments.

For 2 Para in Macedonia, when not on weapon collection operations, the warm September days were filled with routine briefings, planning and administration in Arnhem Factory. At this time, the battalion was involved in a fairly long-running battle with an outbreak of diarrhoea and vomiting. The virus took its toll on almost a third of the battalion at some point over a couple of weeks, with a key contributing factor being the close and unsegregated living quarters. The factory accommodated a majority of 2 Para, on a sea of US-style camp cots, which had eventually made their way up the logistical chain (considerably depleted in number by the REMFs, it was noted).

Being hit by the infamous 'shit sniper' brought out the gallows humour. A cheer went up when the first Gurkha from a seemingly immune C (Gurkha) Company succumbed and had to undertake the 'Bataan death march' walk, camp cot in hand, to the tented quarantine area that the Med Platoon had set up at the back of the factory building. The ever-innovative Pioneer Platoon and irrepressible Cpl Chadwick constructed a 'shit sniper' hazard road sign on a wooden stand, which was placed in the vacant bed space of the most recent victim.

Arnhem Factory also had a television in the communal living area, which showed what was going on in the world by screening BBC News throughout the day, then any big sports matches and more adult-oriented entertainment for a couple of hours during the evening. What was going on in the world was clearly illustrated to us ten days after we had keenly watched England beat Germany 5–1.

It was early afternoon in Macedonia on 11 September 2001, when a plane smashed into the South Tower of the World Trade Center in New York at 9.03 a.m. Eastern Daylight Time. Given that the North Tower had already been hit, it was immediately apparent to both media commentators and viewers that this was more than a freak accident.

I went to find the Commanding Officer, to let him know that there appeared to be a major incident in New York. Major David Buckingham, the US Exchange Officer and OCC (Bruneval Company) was found, and he joined hundreds of us as we watched the coverage unfold. Major Buckingham was in stunned silence and I watched his jaw drop as news came in that the Pentagon had also been hit; it was clearly difficult for him to comprehend.

Everyone knew that this was a 'Question 4 moment' – a useful bookend to the mission analysis process, when the planner is asked 'has the situation changed?' Yes, it had. Everyone from the Commanding Officer to the most junior Tom knew that with an attack on 'Fortress America', the world was going to change.

The potential for military reaction and potential operations was discussed at great length, by a battalion of 'camp chair General Montgomerys'. The appetite of the Paratrooper for challenge, adventure and warfare was on full show. The popular consensus over the following days was that the battalion was well placed. As we were already mobilised and deployed and halfway to the Middle East region, optimists held that we could simply roll on from Macedonia to the next operation, wherever it might be. Even more so as we were co-located in Macedonia with the Brigade Headquarters. Excited talk of potential parachute operations was mixed with a worry that one of our other battalions might get to go ahead of us.

Our operations in Macedonia completed the following month, but the reaction to the events of September 11th turned out to be a little slower than we had at first predicted. However, a matter of weeks after returning from Macedonia, on New Year's Eve 2001, I found myself in a convoy of coaches pushing carefully past revellers spilling out of the pubs in the Cotswold villages between the joint Mounting Centre, South Cerney and RAF Brize Norton. In the early hours of New Year's Day 2002, I would fly forward to Oman with 2 Para's advance party, bound for Kabul, Afghanistan.

2 Para's deployment to Macedonia, swiftly followed by Afghanistan, saw the battalion right at the fulcrum of a pivot in political and military interest and activity, from the Balkans of the 1990s, to Afghanistan and the Middle East. The next chapter in the Regiment's history had begun.


*Lance Corporal Tom Blakey, Pathfinder Platoon*

During Op Bessemer in 2001, the Pathfinders deployed as part of 16 Air Assault Brigade to Macedonia, in order to stabilise the area following tensions that had spilled over from neighbouring Kosovo (where we had deployed as part of Op Agricola in 1999).

Pathfinder patrols deployed in WMIK Land Rovers to remote villages and towns in order to provide some 'ground truth' to the situation. Basically, one village would start shooting at another village and it escalated from there, and whoever you asked would blame the other. Amongst my team was a good mate of mine, Bryan Budd, who was posthumously awarded the Victoria Cross for bravery in Afghanistan in 2006.

It was quite surreal to be located with a Government Army unit one day, who were fighting the rebel forces, then being with the guys they had been shooting at the next day. Not to mention the fact that we were intentionally travelling directly into the hot spots where all the shooting was going on at night. However, the locals were very friendly, and we often had to resist their offers of homemade moonshine, whilst trying not to offend them.

After returning from a couple of weeks on the ground, we went into the Ops Room in camp, to find everyone quiet and crowded around the TV. It was 11 September 2001 and everyone was watching the planes crashing into the Twin Towers. No one knew exactly what had happened at this stage, but we all knew that things were going to be very different from now on, and that we were going to be busy.

*Lieutenant Colonel Chip Chapman, 2 Para*

I was in the middle of a letter to my children when I was called downstairs to witness the breaking news on CNN. Even worse, my family had been standing on top of the World Trade Center only five months earlier, and my wife had spent two months of 2001 working in New York. It will forever be one of those events where you will remember where you were when you first heard the news. As I said to our battalion 'O' group on 12 September, what we were doing in Macedonia would be a mere blip on the radar of history, whilst the events in New York and Washington would fill the radar screen for months or even years to come.

The first dusts of snow covered the high features around Skopje after 9/11 and it was certainly crisper. The 'al fresco' dining that occurred at every meal was coming to a close with a move indoors bringing an increased risk of spreading viruses. Our first outbreak of D and V produced twenty-two cases.

Many more followed. We had more than enough troops to cover such numbers easily, but as is the case in every deployment in history, sickness from hygiene factors trumps those of combat. We had sadly lost Sapper Ian Collins to massive head injuries when his vehicle was stoned by a group of youths by the side of the road.

As the tour was ending, our thoughts turned to Afghanistan. The battalion 'head shed' were invited to an extended lunch with the 2nd REI (Foreign Legion), who hosted an excellent meal, most notable for the singing and protocol of the Legion. The singing is a tradition and we were all given the 'Chants of the Legion' songbook. Inevitably, I asked the French CO, Lt Colonel Philippe Bras, what he thought of the events of 9/11. He believed that there would be a military response in Afghanistan in three phases: 1. Bomb it; 2. Concrete or tarmac it; 3. Hold the victory parade on it – or at least that is what the Legion would do.

# 6

# AFGHANISTAN
# 2002

## Kabul

*Corporal Jim Newell, 2 Para*

After seeing the 11 September 2001 terror attacks in New York happen live on TV, it was pretty obvious that the battalions would be getting very busy in the near future. What wasn't expected was to receive a phone call on Christmas Eve that said that all personnel in 2 Para must return to Colchester on Boxing Day. I happened to be making a rare visit to my in-laws in Aberdeen and only arrived on Christmas Eve, so I had an extremely short Christmas before returning to Colchester and picking up one of the guys on the way down.

We finally deployed to Afghanistan in January, and it was certainly a country that I never thought we would be deploying to in my lifetime. We initially moved into a battalion location which was nicknamed Telecom Towers due to two large, red-and-white radio masts in the rear. Locations were quickly found where the rifle companies could move to and establish patrol bases. C Company went to an old school in the north-west of the city and D Company moved into a police station near the palace in the south-west.

The mandate we were working under restricted us to only patrolling within the city of Kabul; I think it was a one-kilometre limit around the city. We were told that there were no armoured vehicles within the city and we would be providing stability and security for the population.

I was a corporal at the time, but due to others being on courses or promoted, I stood in as Platoon Sergeant. I had done my sergeant's course, so was OK to go out with my own patrol of twelve guys. Being in command of a patrol is the best job you can do in the infantry, especially as a corporal. I was tasked with a job and all the planning, tactics and details were down to me.

We started off patrolling our part of the city and the north-west quarter was our area of responsibility; it had been absolutely decimated over the last twenty-five years by one of the Afghan warlords called Gulbuddin Hekmatyar. He had basically shelled the west of the city and it was about ninety-per-cent destroyed. Because it was so damaged, one of the most difficult parts of patrolling it was working out routes that we could drive down and which part of the city corresponded to the maps.

We soon discovered that the 'no armoured vehicles' claim was utter crap, I was finding them in parks all over our area. We tried to get as close as we could so we could give accurate details of vehicles, weapons and ammo for the patrol reports. Several of the areas had so many vehicles in them that we couldn't work out what they all were. On the next patrol, a top vehicle recognition guy came out with us and even he was surprised at some of the vehicles we found. Everything from BM-21 multiple-launch rocket systems and ZSU-23/4 anti-aircraft guns to T54/55 main battle tanks, as well as BTR-2 armoured personnel carriers, plus nearly everything in-between. These were all listed and reported back up to the battalion Int Cell.

On one particular patrol, we moved out of the city to the extent of our limit outside and headed into the hills, and when we got over the hill we discovered how Hekmatyar had shelled the city. He didn't have many artillery pieces, so they had parked tanks on the back of the hill and then used the main gun as artillery firing into the city; the target was several miles wide so it didn't matter where they hit.

One day, we had reports of bandits moving into the civilian areas at night and robbing the locals, we also had reports about young girls being abducted. The guy responsible was believed to be the second in command to Hekmatyar, a guy called Saif. He had a walled compound down the road from our patrol base, which was heavily guarded and had 12.7mm machine guns and RPGs all over the front of it and a massive metal gate. While on a foot patrol a few days previously, one of my section commanders, Paul 'Scouse' Radcliff, had spotted that at the back of his compound was a break in the wall that was hidden by destroyed buildings. During all our patrols so far, no one had been acting aggressively, including Saif's compound. After a bit of a discussion with the section commanders I decided that on the next patrol, we would try and find a way to get the vehicles to the back of his compound.

We ended up driving past the front gate a couple of times and although we were being watched, the guys on the sanger were waving back to us. Eventually we managed to find our way round the back in the vehicles and could see the break in the wall, so we stopped off and after a quick brief we moved in. The plan was that we would move into the compound fast and as soon as the vehicles had stopped the guys would deploy all around the compound covering all the arcs and the sanger positions, while I would stroll up to find the commander. Everything went as planned, we steamed into the middle of the compound and the guys spread out covering any targets that could be hostile.

The first thing that stood out was that he had a T64 main

battle tank in there, as well as two four-barrelled 23mm anti-aircraft turrets mounted on trucks. Over to one side were two containers, one of which was open and several hundred mortar rounds had spilled all over the ground. It looked like something had detonated and blown them out of the container. Many were damaged and missing fuses.

One particularly flustered Afghan guy came over to me to find out why we were there; he turned out to be second in command to Saif. Once he discovered we hadn't come to detain anyone or confiscate equipment he became very friendly. I told the guys to stay alert but be nosy and get as much information as possible. James 'Cheeks' Brudenell was one of the team commanders and had previously been in the Int Cell; he came up with the excellent idea of getting lots of tourist-type photos of our guys with all the Afghans in the compound. However, in every photo would be some piece of equipment or pile of ammo that was the actual target of the picture. He even got the Afghans to let him get in their tank to take a picture so we could even tell the Int Cell how many rounds of ammo he had for his main gun.

I was asking whether we could buy any pistols or assault rifles, so he was getting them out for us to see so we could count them, too. We ended up staying for a cup of Chai and some sweets before we said our farewells and moved back out. When the patrol report went in the Company 2IC called me up to the Ops room to explain exactly how I managed to get all the information, as my multiple seemed to be finding everything in the city.

One of the funnier stories that happened when we were there was about one of the guys in HQ Company. All we had in Telecom Towers for toilets was a large hole in the ground with a row of toilets placed on top. The hole was probably a metre wide by five metres long and about three metres deep. As this got filled with shit by the several hundred people living there, a new hole was dug and the old one filled in. One night the hole was full, so the engineers moved the toilets to the new location, but didn't fill in the old hole. In the dark, a young Welsh private needed to go, but couldn't find the toilet as it seemed to not be there anymore. While he was wandering around looking, he found the full hole where the toilet used to be by falling in.

Eventually his cries for help were heard and people went to assist, but in true army fashion, most blokes stood around laughing at him and some went and got their camera to take pictures of the guy covered in shit.

*Private Simon (Foz) Foster, 2 Para*

We landed in Kabul in early January 2002. The first thing that struck us was how bloody cold it was and the second was what a shit hole it was, having had the shit kicked out of it during the civil war.

Rudimentary arctic kit given to us by the battalion wasn't really cutting it and most of us had gone out and spent a few quid on kit like Therma Rest roll mats and proper warm kit. Being patrols we were always buying ally kit anyway so it was a good excuse!!

We were housed in a former telecommunications college on the Jalalabad road and went out on patrol in the back of Pinzgauer 4x4 wagons and on foot. The locals seemed friendly enough, but everyone was wary as we had heard all the stories from the Russian occupation and what the locals did to captured Russian soldiers.

A week or so into our tour, we were tasked to TV Hill in the centre of Kabul to mount the first of our ops. In its heyday, a nice restaurant had been built on top of the hill, but it was now rubble thanks to the fighting and an American bomb.

The place was bristling with antennas and we heard rumours the Iranians had listening devices up there. Consequently every device we came across we would give it the boot, and before long we had a Mexican stand-off with the Afghan police, who didn't seem to like us trashing their gear. We spent a couple of weeks on the hill with not much to report other than a hell of a lot of snow, and soon enough we were back at the college.

After a few days, we were told to get ready for another op, this time on the other side of the city. The location was an old Russian bread-making factory with two 100-feet-high grain silos ideal for observation of that side of the city. The Taliban hadn't given up the ghost (as we were later to experience in Helmand) and reporting their possible movements became our main aim. Deploying a few days later, we had to take all our food and water for the foreseeable, so carrying it up 100-foot-flights of stairs was a right bastard given that Kabul is at 8,000 feet altitude.

Once in situ we started our routine, two blokes on and two off, pissing into bottles and shitting into a bag, which is standard practice in this type of op. It was bloody freezing until the sun came up and we chased every ray as it crossed the floor of the silo. After a couple of days, we noticed some odd behaviour from the so-called Afghan police, stopping people and robbing them. One of D Company's platoons was informed and went into the area that night with over-watch from ourselves. Before we knew it they were surrounded by armed men claiming to be police, clearly not happy we were taking their earning potential away.

This was just one of many close calls the battalion had, but everyone was super restrained as most of us had been to

Northern Ireland years previously and didn't just open fire at fuck all, unlike our American counterparts.

A few nights in and we all stood to early doors as a 4x4 full of armed blokes tried to enter the grounds of the bread factory; it was clear that they were not there with good intentions. All of us in the patrol knew something was not right and this was made evident the next day when we were watched closely by the so-called police for most of the day. All of this information was constantly being fed back to Battalion HQ to gain a bigger picture of the general situation on the ground.

Then at 0130 the next day it happened: as me and Jim were on watch there came a burst of gunfire aimed directly at the OP. Through the thermal imaging we could see armed men taking up fire positions some 400 metres away at the base of a small hill. My first thought was 'cheeky bastards!' They must be bloody mad shooting at a Para Reg patrol. We got the rest of the blokes up and all clambered on to the roof just as another burst headed our way. This being for all of us the first time of being shot at for real, it was all a bit bizarre initially, then our instincts and training took over and we all got in a position to return fire.

We were all still in Northern Ireland mode, so a bit hesitant to return fire. In the end, I put the Minimi light machine gun on top of the rail and thought, fuck this, and opened with a burst of 5.56 mm from the belt-fed weapon, which 2 Para had only just taken delivery of. The gunfire echoed around the deadly still night, even D Company some way away said they could hear it.

Sully, our patrol sniper, let rip with the L96 sniper rifle and Steve stood by with the GPMG should we need it. Fire continued back and forth for what seemed like ages, but was probably just seconds. Jim, our patrol commander, was busy sending a contact report back to HQ, who would then alert the QRF in case we needed back up asap.

Before long a car appeared to our right moving towards the firing point; we all thought these clowns were now getting reinforcements and so the car became our next target. It was also serving as a good source of cover for the first bunch of the enemy who had decided to have a go.

I was having a lot of stoppages, so decided to take the entire link out of the bag and sling it over my arm, which did the trick nicely. As the fire died down, all that could be heard was the screams of women coming from the direction of fire and dead bodies being dragged away. Pretty soon we were told the QRF was on its way and we were to be bugged out asap; we started to pack all of our shit away and took fire positions awaiting our pick-up.

I was shaking like a shitting dog due to the adrenaline rush of my first contact and buzzing knowing we had all reacted like Paratroopers are supposed to do, and judging by the sounds we could hear coming from the enemy, we had got a few of the bastards as well. The QRF appeared and secured the compound, as we jumped into the back of wagons and sped away to D Company's location.

Nobody slept; all we did was what generations of soldiers had done before us, we relived every second of the contact over and over again.

*Captain Justin Tancrel, 2 Para*

C Company had just been re-formed after the manning gap had been covered by a company of Gurkhas for a number of years. I arrived at the Company just as they were sent to Kabul. We didn't have any platoon commanders and so the sergeants all had to step up. I led some of the patrols at night because of this. Our OC was Major Dave Buckingham, a US Army

82nd Paratrooper on exchange. We were sent to the east of the capital and turned a school into a sound Forward Operating Base (FOB) from where we would launch our operations day and night. The entire place was utterly deserted when we arrived, eerily so. At night, it was surreal watching the flashes of shell fire light up the snow-capped mountains and hearing the sounds reverberate through the valleys where the Taliban were still fighting. They hadn't gone away at all, as we were to find out.

After only a few days of us being there, and the police structures being set up again, news spread that it was safe and literally tens of thousands returned to reclaim their homes. It was wonderful. On my twenty-seventh birthday on 4 Feb 2002, I was leading a supply convoy back to Battalion HQ when the Taliban attacked a police station 100 metres ahead of us. It was carnage, as horses reared up and the packed crowds panicked – we couldn't see in front of us, never mind fire back. Eventually we got to the police station, but they had done a shoot and scoot, whilst flying their flag – it was a statement.

Later as we patrolled much further out from the city and outside our area of operations, we came to remote villages and found fighting age men with 'make up' on. My very old interpreter, Ghullam, became extremely nervous and said we must go – they were Taliban, who were equally nervous and surprised to see us. We didn't venture out that far again.

On one memorable occasion after dark, our Patrols Platoon were contacted whilst manning an OP on the roof of the Soviet-built bread factory. They asked to be extracted as they were compromised and didn't want to be cut off. Led by me, the Quick Reaction Force (QRF) was crashed out and we identified the firing points including the 'getaway car'. This turned out to be a taxi that was fleeing the shoot-out, with a pregnant woman on board. There was blood everywhere inside and drag marks into a nearby compound. We made our way to the doorway and basically conducted a house clearance, but quickly found a family that had been shot up very badly, including one dead nineteen-year-old with a perfect sniper-round head wound.

As we began treating the family, they explained they had been caught up in a firefight and evidently the Patrols Platoon has assumed this was an accomplice car. Then in one of the outhouses, a soldier found the pregnant woman hiding with bullet wounds to the thigh and neck. As we began treating her, she fought us like hell! What was going on? The family was becoming hysterical, too. Then a little head appeared between the woman's legs, a sight I'll never forget.

I shouted to Sergeant Hone, our Company medic, to leave the seriously wounded and deliver this baby quickly (I was medically trained for basic wounds, but not for this!). The family and the mother didn't want us near her private parts, but we explained, through my crying teenage interpreter, what we were doing.

Basically, Sgt Hone saved her life and the baby's life together. We patched up the family and extracted them at first light just as the RMP arrived to conduct their investigations. Western media later visited the family and by then the warlords had persuaded them to change their story so that they said there had been no rogue gunmen firing at the Patrols Platoon in the bread factory. It was very frustrating for us to read some of the published articles or what we would now call 'fake news'.

On another occasion, I led a platoon ambush against forces that were coming down from the mountains every night to pillage from the locals, who had now asked us to defend them (many years later, we realised these 'rogue bandits' were probably unpaid/disgruntled Northern Alliance soldiers fed up with not having enjoyed their war-spoils after liberating Kabul). Instead my ambush recce group was ambushed itself whilst patrolling down a river bed by the same terrified locals from three different compounds.

Between their point-blank range sporadic fire, I heard women and children crying and the gunmen shouting to each other across compounds. I knew this wasn't the enemy, but frightened civilians firing at us. I stopped my soldiers from firing at all (thank God – and I had a similar experience in Helmand in 2010, when something wasn't right and I stopped my call sign firing at 'hiding Taliban' that turned out to be a petrified farmer and his son).

We met up with the families, who were grateful and relieved to see us. Our OP on the mountain, who watched our patrol enter the river bed, said they saw green (Chinese) tracer criss-cross and assumed that we 'were a goner'! Then they heard my somewhat shaken voice deliver the radio contact report to Company HQ and couldn't believe it. The steep-sided little river bed and the pitch-black darkness had saved our lives that night.

*Lance Corporal James Brudenell, 2 Para*

The day before we deployed in January, the film *Black Hawk Down* was to be shown in the cinema for the first time. That evening the cinema was buzzing with 2 Para and I seem to recall the blokes thinking this was what Afghanistan was going to be like. Needless to say, it wasn't like that at all!

C Company was located in an old school not too far from probably the only remaining tall building in Kabul; a granary factory. One evening, the Company was to establish an ambush and we received our Orders from Capt. Justin Tancrel (Company 2IC). Due to the lack of vehicles, a number of us would be moved forward and be dropped off while the vehicles would go back to collect the remainder.

The op went ahead at night and I was moved on the first lift in a Pinzguaer. In the interim, Capt. Tancrel was to move forward to the proposed site with Cpl Skid Ewen, L/Cpl Tyrone De Silva and an RAMC corporal. Myself and a private remained with the interpreters and Afghan police. Capt. Tancrel and his group moved forward down a dried stream/track in between some compounds and must have gone 80 to 100 metres when they came under contact (out of sight to me). I saw the tracer bouncing into the sky and it went quiet after what seemed like only seconds. Nothing came over my radio and I honestly thought they were dead. As we started to move gingerly forward, expecting to come under fire, a shadow appeared ahead, and looking through my CWS I noticed it was Capt. Tancrel beckoning us towards him. I was relieved to find everyone alive and uninjured.

After a while, the remainder of the Company arrived and it came out that Capt. Tancrel's group had been mistaken by the locals for thieves (they had been robbed the night before) and they were now waiting to catch them again. Apparently, Capt. Tancrel stood up during the contact and shouted 'ISAF', which resulted in the stopping of firing. He was later awarded a Mention in Despatches (MiD) for his actions that night.

One evening in the Company location, I was walking to the Company Ops Room and heard a bang and someone shouting 'medic!', which I started repeating while running towards the sound of the shot. On entering the room, a private from another platoon was holding his left hand in the air and was being treated by a medic. On looking at his hand, the fleshy web between his thumb and first finger had a hole in it. In essence, he had put his hand on top of the rifle, leant down and pulled the trigger. Lucky for him his head was not over his hand at the time or it would have gone through his hand and into his head. There was a hole in the roof where the round exited.

As I said, the tallest building in our Area of Operations was an old granary factory. An Observation Post was established on top of the building by the Patrols/Snipers. One evening, the position came under fire from a car. Our returning fire resulted in one dead and the rest in the car injured. After the contact, a cordon had been put in place and later that morning 7 Platoon had been tasked to take over the cordon. I passed the vehicle and the back seat resembled a scene from *Pulp Fiction*, where the guy is shot in the face. The vehicle was to be towed away, probably for forensics, and Private Fell was tasked to sit in the car and steer it. As he closed the door, all the windows shattered; I don't think he enjoyed his drive either!

*Sergeant Dean Stokes, 2 Para*

I was the Company Ops 2IC and as such as I planned all the patrols and gathered the intelligence reports from the ground. When D Company deployed into the south of Kabul (first Company in) we were based in the ISAF compound opposite the US Embassy. One night, not long after deployment from Oman, a young officer came into our compound and asked who was in charge? I was in the company ops room (very basic at that time) and I said, 'That would be me, sir, how can I help you.'

He said he wanted us to send a patrol out onto the street now, as the US Embassy gates had just been petrol bombed. The gates were only 400 metres away, so I told him that I would not be sending anyone out. He was quite shocked with this, as I was a sergeant and he was a captain trying to flex his muscle, but exposing his lack of operational experience.

He then demanded to speak to the CO. I asked him if he would like me to wake the CO and said that if I did, he would not be happy with him and in any case, he would support my decision. He then left with his feathers ruffled. At first light, it became apparent that this was a blatant 'come on' by the Taliban, with several AP mines scattered on the road and paths in front of the embassy!

Shortly after arriving into Kabul, I mapped out the city with squares like we had done in Omagh in Northern Ireland with the Kilo squares. I numbered all the squares on the map from top left to right: Kabul 1, 2, 3, etc. This offered Op sec with Loc stats and quick reference, i.e. K34, 3, 6 (K34 and 3 along 6 up for an accurate grid), and this was taken on by ISAF. After doing this, Major Lawrence and the Battalion Ops officer coloured the routes and gave spot numbers for junctions and, like the squares, they are still in place today.

I planned the patrol matrix and Sgt Dave Caskey came to me and asked if he could stay out for four days. I told him that was no problem, as long as he followed the schedule. This was cleared by the OC, Major Christie, so Dave went out with his men on patrol. On return, he made reference to the patrol briefing map, which I was pleased to have covering the whole 15 feet x 10 feet wall. He pointed to some positions and said, 'We should go here, here and here.' I asked him why and he said, 'It's a fucking minefield, that's why!' They had found themselves in it as there were no markings, but thank God, they patrolled out safely.

We all bought Ray-Bans from the German camp, as we didn't have sun glasses. On leaving, we handed over to the Royal Anglians. We told them that if they wanted Ray-Bans, there was a part number and you got them issued at the German camp. As we were all wearing them, it was easy to believe and they did – hook, line and sinker . . . the OC even played along.

Two memories: we were offered AK-47s for $5 and the Afghan bread was good, but you occasionally found a fingernail in it!

*Lance Corporal Simon Connor, 2 Para*

I was part of the Anti-Tank platoon of 2 Para, situated at the old communications site on the Jalalabad road; also in the same base was the main 2 Para HQ. The base itself was about 200 metres x 100 metres, with two parallel, white derelict buildings at the front, and an MT yard at the rear. The usual sangers were situated on all corners, with a front gate and also a position in the roof of the front building to give us a bit of elevation should we need to spot any incoming fire. A small shelter had been made to protect us from the elements, but nothing more, as it was made of thin wood and looked like it had been made by Stevie Wonder! There was no furniture in the camp so the blokes improvised, making shelving from the cardboard boxes that the twenty-four-hour rations came in, and sticking photos of girlfriends and loved ones on the walls of their bed spaces, which consisted of a doss bag and a roll mat, which we put on any flat cardboard we could find.

We sourced gas-bottle cookers from the locals, the kind that you would plug into your BBQ at home. They also had a detachable cooking ring, which allowed us to cook food in our rooms as well as heating the rooms, as there was no heating in the block. The blokes also fashioned tin cans into cooking implements. A favourite meal was chips cooked in oil got from the locals. We used the improvised pots to fry them in our rooms and it made a welcome break from ration-pack corned beef hash, which for some reason was the only menu we got for four weeks; I still can't eat it now!

On one occasion, I was about to go on guard in about an hour, so I decided to get my head down for forty minutes before I started. All was well as Kev Sheriff started to make some chips, but the 'chip pan' burst into flames, which prompted Kev and anyone else in the room to evacuate, leaving yours truly sleeping happily while the room filled with smoke. After an unknown period of time, I was woken by Corporal Bond from the mortar platoon as he was about to give me mouth to mouth. He had been unable to wake me, as I was succumbing to smoke inhalation. Now being half asleep and seeing Bondy up so close would have been a shock for anyone, but looking like he was about to stick his lips on me as well was way too much, and we gripped each other and exchanged expletives until he told me the situation!

Close call, you might think, but the evil chip pan (which was still alight) had not finished with this young Paratrooper. Corporal 'Mac' Mcleary, a mega bloke in our platoon, had been out finding a fire extinguisher, and stormed past me and proceeded to point the extinguisher at the flaming chip pan. As I looked hazily at the large words WATER on the side of the extinguisher, everything went into slow motion as I shouted, 'NOOOOOOOOOOOOOO!', which could probably be heard across Kabul. The chip pan erupted into a spectacular fireball, which lit up the MT yard and the whole corridor and blew the window out! After zigzagging dizzily down the corridor, I was whisked away to the APOD to spend a couple of nights in a comfortable bed talking to nice nurses and being told with heavy sarcasm that I was 2 Para's first casualty of the deployment.

Kabul itself was an explosion of smells, some good, most not! In the summer, everything was dusty and it was very warm. In the winter, it snowed and you were ankle-deep in shit of every kind, human and animal. I was always amazed how the locals lived there. The place had had the crap shelled out of it and most of it was rubble, or so we thought, but when night fell and the oil lamps came on throughout the city, the rubble started to come alive as little beads of light confirmed the location of a family home or a workshop.

The morning alarm was what got most of the camp up in

the morning. It wasn't actually an alarm, it was when the 'puffing Billy' water boilers got lit in the morning. Some unfortunate soul would be picked to light the boilers, so that the blokes would have warm water to shave and wash; only problem was that very few people knew how to light them properly. Lighting the dripping fuel was an art form to the uneducated and what followed was normally a dull BOOM (the morning alarm) followed by a Tom staggering around, looking like he had come down a very sooty chimney!

# 7

# IRAQ
# 2003–2005

## Operation Telic

In February 2003, 16 Air Assault Brigade with 3 and 1 Para deployed together as part of Operation Telic (jokingly said to stand for 'Tell Everyone Leave Is Cancelled' – one of the largest deployments of British troops since the Second World War, and considerably larger than the Task Force sent to retake the Falklands.

This was the first time the Brigade had deployed complete on an operation since its inception in September 1999. Within days of the invasion of Iraq, 1 and 3 Para with the air-mobile 1 Royal Irish battle group had occupied and secured the Rumaylah oilfields to the south, and started to move north, with the US Marine Corps to their west, to secure the Main Supply Route (MSR) that runs north to Basra on Route 6. Meanwhile 7 Para RHA had fired its first regimental fire missions since Suez in 1956.

By late March, 3 Para had entered Basra with units from the 1st Armoured Division, encountering no significant opposition. The rest of the 16 Air Assault Brigade had moved north, crossing the Euphrates River and occupying Al Qurna, the biblical Garden of Eden, at the junction with the River Tigris.

War-fighting moved to a stabilisation phase, whereby 1 Para was pushed north with brigade elements to occupy and administer the Maysan Province and city of Al Amarah. One company was detached to Baghdad to secure the British Embassy, prior to its reopening.

The Brigade lost eleven soldiers during Operation Telic. Six of whom, from 156 Provost Company, were killed by a hostile mob in the village of Majar Al Kabir.

The Brigade was back in the UK by July, having demonstrated its capability as a potent quick reaction force, able to work alongside armoured troops.

*Lieutenant Dan Jarvis, 3 Para*

I spent a bit of time in and out of Northern Ireland, but the next major deployment for 3 Para was Operation Telic. The battalion had been involved in providing civil contingency support to cover fire stations at various locations across southern England, which wasn't ideal preparation. The CO was determined to make sure that we weren't left in Essex whilst our regimental brothers went off to the Middle East. That wasn't the case and from the end of January through February 2003, 3 Para deployed out to the desert in Kuwait. I was the adjutant.

Although we'd had Kosovo a few years before, this was the first major battalion deployment since the Falklands. We had to do a lot of things very quickly: we had to deploy the whole battalion and all of our kit and equipment out into the desert over a relatively short period of time and then get ourselves ready for what we might face next. We were told by the Brigade Commander, Brigadier 'Jacko' Page, that it wasn't a question of whether Saddam Hussein would use chemical weapons against us; it was a question of when. We deployed from a freezing cold February Essex into the scorching desert, having to do a lot of training to prepare ourselves for a likely chemical attack, which very much focused people's minds.

We got people ready, we did our training, and we waited for confirmatory orders that we would be tracking north up into Iraq and that's eventually what happened.

We were following up behind the US Marines, so any Iraqi army opposition had already been neutralised. We followed up behind through the scattered ruin of the Iraqi forces. There was the odd skirmish, but nothing significant. We went briefly into Basra to provide some support there, but then we were given an AO around the North Rumaila oil fields to secure that critical infrastructure. There were various attempts to fire them; part of our responsibility was to secure that asset.

I can put my hand on my heart and say that my soldiers did everything that was asked of them and (mostly) kept a smile on their face while they were doing it. And we can be proud of the fact that we still have young people serving in the regiment who aspire to fulfil the highest possible standards of soldiering.

People find different ways of coping with it. Lots of us have to put it away in a box and get on with the job and think about it when we get back. Anyone who has been there and has done something like that, it does give you a certain perspective of what's really important and what really matters and what is difficult and what's not difficult. The training gets you so far but then you've actually got to do it, though it's made easier by the fact that you've got people you know and trust and respect and they watch your back and you watch theirs. That system works today in the way it's worked throughout the history of the regiment.

I quite often get Sergeants' Mess or Officers' Mess visits into Parliament and it's always great to see people. But I'd walk into 3 Para now and not know many people at all. There'll always be new people coming forward, that's a good thing – that's how it needs to be. I miss that contact and comradery of soldiering because there's nothing quite like it – politics is a very different discipline. There's a bond that comes from soldiering that you don't get in politics, sadly.


*Lance Corporal Tom Blakey, Pathfinder Platoon*

For the Pathfinders, it was a great opportunity to deploy in our traditional role, that of long-range mobility recce patrols. 16 Air Assault Brigade had been deployed to Kuwait in order to prepare for the invasion of Iraq. We were at the tip of the spear of the invasion, leading the way in the dark through the burning oil fields of the Kuwait/Iraq border. Once across the border, we broke down into patrols of four Weapons Mount Installation Kit (WMIK) Land Rovers with twelve men to a group. Each patrol worked independently, pushing hundreds of kilometres ahead of the conventional ground forces. We spent the night driving for long hours across the desert, using NVGs (Night Vision Goggles) to drive in the complete darkness.

During the daytime, we established Lying up Points (LUPs) in what sparse cover we could find, 'brewing up' and planning the movements for the following night. Most of the local population we encountered were happy to see us, and relieved to be freed of Saddam's regime. I remember one guy who had walked for miles from the nearest village from our LUP, just to bring us 'chai' (local sweet tea). Nice bloke.

Another time we established an LUP near the River Euphrates, and pushed forward on foot to observe and report on the river traffic and what we could see on the other side of the river. Several boats came very close to our location, gliding by in blissful ignorance as we observed them with a lot of firepower to hand.

*Sergeant Andy Cutting, 1 Para*

I was in the Patrols Platoon and one evening we were tasked to carry out an anti-tank ambush recce. We were in four stripped-out 110 Land Rovers. I was the 2IC and Shaun was commanding the patrol. We had practised all our SOPs over the last few weeks in Kuwait and we had them down to a T. We set off one clear night in the vehicles and the plan was to drive through a series of RVs and then at the FRV we were going to leave a few guys with the wagons and the rest of us would carry out the task on foot. There was a high threat of mines and Improvised Explosive Devices (IEDs) on our route, so we walked the vehicles through VPs (vulnerable points).

Shaun was walking the lead vehicle when on his radio he said, 'Stop, stop!' We all stopped and the atmosphere could have been cut with a knife. All the weapons safety catches were flicked to fire and we waited for the firefight to erupt. I got on the radio and asked what the problem was. Shaun replied saying he was standing about three feet away from an anti-tank mine. Fuck me, we have driven into a minefield.

I patrolled forward to get eyes on Shaun, when my radio crackled, 'It's OK, it's a fucking dustbin lid!' The whole patrol burst into fits of laughter and the safety catches went back to on.

*Sergeant Jim Newell, 2 Para*

I deployed to Iraq in 2005 and we were there over Christmas and returned to UK in 2006 after a normal six-month tour. We were one of the major units doing all the soldiering on the ground. We arrived in Iraq, but we didn't go to any of the well-known areas like Basra or Al Amarah. We were at Al Muthana,

Falklands Campaign, 1982: 3 Para carry out emergency medical treatment and shelter casualties while under fire on Mount Longdon.

Having fought two fierce battles at Goose Green and Wireless Ridge, tired but jubilant men of 2 Para celebrate the surrender of Argentinian Forces at Port Stanley.

Operation Agricola, Kosovo, 1999: Paras on board a Pinzgauer on the way from Kacanik to Pristina.

The deserted town of Kacanik is secured by 1 Para. The graffiti calls for a 'Free Serbia'.

Operation Palliser, Sierra Leone, 2000: A soldier from 1 Para takes a defensive position while securing a village, much to the delight of a local boy.

Operation Palliser: 1 Para carrying out a patrol through a village.

Operation Bessemer, Macedonia, 2001: Boarding a Puma helicopter prior to insertion from Petrovac base.

Paras secure the village of Matejce as they help set up the first NATO weapons collection site to gather arms from the ethnic Albanian National Liberation Army.

Operation Fingal, Afghanistan, 2002: Soldiers from 2 Para and Afghan policemen greet each other prior to their joint patrol on the streets of Kabul.

2 Para observe from a position in the new ISAF military base in western Kabul.

Operation Telic, Iraq, 2003: A Para on the ground sends a sitrep on his radio with a damaged Iraqi tank in the background.

Paras on patrol walking past a statue of Saddam Hussein.

Operation Herrick IV, Afghanistan 2006: A sniper from 3 Para on a quad bike for increased mobility in Helmand Province.

3 Para Mortar Platoon return from an operation having just landed at Bastion.

Operation Herrick VIII, 2008: Members of the Afghan Security Forces wait for a helicopter extraction after a joint operation with 3 Para.

Soldiers from 3 Para take up all-round defensive positions after insertion by Chinook helicopter during the strike operation Southern Beast to search for the Taliban, weapons and drugs.

which is right out west in the desert. It was supposedly the sleepy hollow of Iraq and there was not much happening.

The orders brief was to maintain general stability and support the Iraqi police. There were a lot of civilian contractors training the Iraqi police in the police academy down the road. We used to have to escort the civilian contractors; the rest was framework patrolling around the city. There was a long-distance patrol every now and again, as there was quite a big town about five or ten miles north, and another five or ten miles south. About twenty miles south of us was an American air base, which we used to go down to quite often, ferrying the blokes there from Al Muthana. The unit before us had only had one serious contact during their whole tour. There seemed to be an unwritten agreement between the locals and the troops, if you don't do anything, then we won't come and patrol your estate. So, it was pretty quiet for them.

The group we were facing was led by Muqtada al-Sadr. They lived mainly in a large area to the south of the Provincial Joint Operations Centre (PJOC), as well as the two towns north and south of Al Muthana. I was told that there were three main blokes in charge of the terrorist group; one was a complete lunatic and the other two were more sensible. A few weeks after we got there, the two sensible ones had been called up to Baghdad for a meeting with Al Sadr and left the lunatic in charge! This is when we started getting all the smaller contacts. These were usually quite minor, although on some of them we were lucky not to take casualties thanks to the guys' good drills.

There was one building in the city, the PJOC outstation, away from the main camp, that was used as a patrol base. It was manned by one multiple at a time to provide security and to work with the Iraqi police. We had to go and stay in the PJOC for ten days at a time. We were working in multiples and as a sergeant I was the commander with my twelve blokes.

It's the best job in the infantry if you can get it. If you're a sergeant in a conventional platoon, you're not really in charge, but as a multiple commander you have a lot more freedom.

It kicked off the first night I got there and didn't stop for a week. It would be relatively quiet during the day, but by the time you'd finished scoff at around 1900 hours, 'BOOM,' another RPG would go off, and this would continue all night. The enemy wasn't very professional and the attacks were easily resisted. They fired an RPG during one of the attacks and it stuck in the side of the sangar (temporary fortified position). When it was pulled out by the EOD, it still had the safety pin in the end of it, otherwise it would have detonated.

We could only be hit directly from one side, there was just a small car park and one road between us and the terrorist estate – we couldn't see the other side, because that was part of the building we didn't own. There were three buildings together and the little compound in the middle was the one we had. You couldn't cover everywhere, so you used to get RPGs banging in the side trying to hit the sangar. They also fired a 107mm rocket straight down the street at us, but luckily it hit a fence post and it broke up.

My second in command was an excellent bloke who was qualified as a sergeant, so he could man the ops desk when we were there, so I said, 'You're not getting all the fun. You can stag on downstairs, while I am going up to the roof.' It was a psychological thing, we had some spare sniper rifles in the camp and because I am a qualified sniper, I used to take one to the PJOC for the psychological effect, because the Iraqis hadn't seen them and the police would leak information to the locals. So every time I went up to the PJOC, I'd take a sniper rifle with me and sit there cleaning it on the desk, and all the Iraqi coppers would be amazed and keep coming in and staring. Hopefully the psychological thing helped a bit.

One night it kicked off and we believed we had a sniper firing back at us. You can tell how far away someone's shooting by the crack and the thump of the round. When it passes you, you hear the crack and then because the sound goes slower than the bullet, you get the thump later. You can tell the distance because roughly every second between the crack and the thump is about 300 metres. Most of the contacts we were getting were from 50 to 100 metres, because the buildings were that close and some houses straight down the street looked on to the base.

This night it started off with this guy firing single shots – not automatic – I knew the Iraqis didn't do single shots. They do as many rounds as they can in as short a time as possible. He was firing single shots and the last four or five he did rapid fire, then he'd have a little break as he was reloading; then he'd do it again. We worked out that he was probably about 500 metres away and had a Russian Dragunov sniper rifle, because AK 47s have thirty-round magazines, but he'd fire twenty rounds and change mag. He was trying to get the snipers on top of the roof, because he wouldn't have been able to see the sangar from 500 metres away, but he got nowhere near hitting anyone.

All these contacts culminated with the CO of 2 Para having a meeting with the Chief of Police to try to sort out the problem. Ironically, while the CO was talking to the Chief of Police, the terrorists carried out a drive-by shooting on the police station. I'd already taken my team out, because we were escorting the civvy contractors who were training the Iraqi police, and we left six blokes down at the police academy as a security team for them. The rest of us had returned to the main camp. We were about to go out and pick them up when the drive-by shooting on the Chief of Police's compound happened, and the order was that no one was to go anywhere.

I finally got the authority to move out and pick up my guys, but when I was half a mile down the road, I got a radio call to return to base, so I reported back to the ops room where I was met by my CO. The other call sign had gone to the PJOC already. He told me, 'We're sending a patrol out here to this estate – we haven't been there before because it was out of bounds.' So, I got some extra blokes to fill out my patrol and then the CO asked us what we needed and said, 'The team commander's gone up with his multiple and you're going up there, too. I want you to provide mobile support for him.' Then he said, 'Before you go, expect a contact in the next thirty minutes.' I was surprised, but replied, 'Cheers for that, sir.' He knew that it was going to kick off by sending us back in there. But we didn't anticipate it would be quite so big.

We didn't have permission to go in and out of the area, because it had been out of bounds, but now the terrorists were taking the piss. We were going to go back in to their estate and point out to them that it's only left alone because we say so. It was a case of: 'We patrol the place. If you're sensible enough to shut the fuck up and wait till we leave Iraq, then we'll get on great.'

So, we went back in there; I was doing the mobile cover for the patrol with two snatch wagons. The other multiple commander had already deployed to the PJOC; his call sign was going on foot, and I was giving cover in the wagons. We ended up getting about a mile and a half into this quite large estate, which had a massive main street, like a dual carriageway, with lots of adjoining little streets running off it. We would move forward in vehicles to set up cover and then the ground patrol would catch up and we would bound forward again.

We were sitting at this roundabout, when a little bloke came up to us accompanied by a really enormous guy, who must have been about six foot six tall and built like a brick shit house, but seemed a bit simple. He was blatantly this little guy's bodyguard. The little guy starts chatting away, asking what we were doing there, saying that this was their estate and we were not allowed in there. I pointed out several times that as the coalition forces providing security I could go anywhere I wanted. A large crowd formed around us while I was chatting away with him and he started getting aggressive and saying we needed to leave or we were going to get hurt. I said, 'As long as no one fires at us, no one's going to get hurt.'

As I was talking, I was sneakily trying to get my camera out and take a photo of him for our intelligence people. The top cover guy was trying to do the same as well, but the little guy saw what we were trying to do. As soon as he noticed us, the shit hit the fan. He screamed, 'That's it, you're going to die now!' Literally about twenty seconds after he said that, the Iraqi cops, all twelve of them, got in their pick-up trucks and buggered off, leaving us with the crowd getting very aggressive.

Our interpreter got in the wagon and wouldn't come out, he was shouting, 'They're going to kill us!' I thought the police had been hit on their way out, because as they went around the corner, we heard an RPG detonate from the same area and I thought, fuck, they've just taken the Iraqi police out. But it wasn't them. We were told later from the Int Cell that the guy fucked it up and basically fired from inside his living room and blew out the front of his house, and I believe he also killed his grandmother, who was sat behind him.

I was then told by the platoon commander that we had been ordered to move back to the PJOC. We started moving back and one of the other call signs that had been shot at was now bouncing from contact to contact through the side streets and up the main drag that we needed to get to. All three ground teams and both mobiles were being engaged now. Every fucking street, on the rooftops, up the alleyways, they were just firing at us. We had a few RPGs fired at us and one of them went straight through the middle of the Platoon Commander's team, who were on foot at the time. It flew straight through the middle of his team and blew up harmlessly behind them.

The multiple commander of the foot patrol had only been in the Army a short time and looked like a stunned mullet. I drove up next to him, leaned out of the door and said, 'You might want to start moving, sir, the PJOC is that way.' As we started to move back and try to regroup, it seemed to turn into *Black Hawk Down*, but without the helicopters. You couldn't pick out individual bursts of fire as there was so much of it going on all around.

As we drove around, I was trying to support the ground commander's team by following him up and locating and moving the supporting teams, because the teams were split up. The area was a maze of streets for about a mile before we could get back to the PJOC. Basically, I was bouncing the teams forwards in the wagon one by one then moving back for the next team. On one of the stops at a main roundabout trying to pick up one of the teams, we halted for a bit while the blokes loaded onto the snatch wagon, I remember looking over to the team commander to shout for him to move in as well, but as I looked at him, the wall six inches above his head started falling apart from a large burst of fire, which only just missed him. We then parked the wagons up and dismounted again, but the interpreter stayed in the vehicle and wouldn't come out for neither love nor money. We had to give him a set of body armour and helmet before he would move.

It sounded like all the mosques in the estate were calling everyone to prayer over their loudspeakers, but the interpreter was saying, 'No, they're not calling them to prayer, they're saying, go and get your guns and come and kill the British.' The entire area knew what was going on and were heading our way. We kept stopping and dismounting to try and stop the reinforcements coming into the area. They had a small bus that was driving down the bottom of the estate, picking people up with their weapons and dropping them off in the street next to us. We saw it happen two or three times, the empty bus going past, and then back again full.

Suddenly there were about thirty blokes with AKs jumping out and moving down the road towards us, but luckily no one got a scratch. To be honest, most of the Iraqis when they aim at you, they're shooting above your head or around you. They had no butts on their AK 47s. They thought that it was cool to fire without them. But if they'd had a butt on and aimed from the shoulder, we'd have had serious problems.

We'd parked on the side of the road to give cover as the ground teams moved back and I had picked up one of the teams, so there were eight guys crammed in the back of the wagon. Suddenly a guy popped out from around a corner and lobbed a grenade at us; one of the top cover guys killed him with a burst from his Minimi and his grenade missed the wagons, but rolled for quite a distance, exploding about three metres behind me. I saw the cloud of smoke from the explosion and I thought, fucking hell, it must have been an RPG. 'Okay, move the wagons NOW.'

The front wagon went to move off at speed, but my driver stalled the vehicle! For a moment, my heart dropped out of my arse, I felt we were going to get an RPG through the back door, and the eight guys in the vehicle were going to die. The driver was panicking and I got the piss taken out of me afterwards for the fact that I showed no emotions, no flapping, as I said, 'Just start the fucking engine.' It took him about five attempts, and I was saying calmly, 'Just keep going, start the engine. No worries,' but I was shitting myself that an RPG was going to come through the back door. Eventually he got it started and we left in a hurry. It was the longest five minutes of my life!

Later we had parked at the side of the street, where there were some cars parked further up. We thought we'd pull up in front of the cars, and use them to provide some sort of cover for us. Just as well that we did, because another guy came out and threw another grenade, which went under a taxi and blew it up. This set fire to the row of cars and all the smoke started filling the street so they couldn't see us. This helped us in a way, because instead of us smoking the road off with phosphorous grenades, the burning cars did it for us. We were working our way back down the street using fire and manoeuvre for about a mile, the ground teams first, then my call sign bringing up the rear and providing cover.

When we were nearly back to the PJOC, one of the teams reported it had been split up and two of the guys were missing. I got my guys into the snatch wagons and headed back into the contact area to find them. We were fired on a few times before we heard that they had been found and everyone was accounted for, so we moved back. Everyone was pretty knackered from doing fire and manoeuvre for a mile and a half in full kit while in contact. The other vehicle commander and myself were out on foot, the guys on top cover were covering our rear and sides, all the way back to PJOC.

When we got back there, the captain who was manning the PJOC had got some guys on the roof, but the highest rank there was a lance corporal. So, he said, 'Can you go up on the roof and do a bit of command and control.' I went up on to the roof to see what was going on, they said they'd already been shot at a few times and they had extra ammo, but it was still in its boxes. So I got all the ammo out and dished it out to them, all the GPMG link and grenades we had, everything we could need. I then went around and ensured all the guys were covering the danger areas and we had as much protection as possible. After about twenty minutes there was still fire coming from the estate, so I tried the radio and I managed to get hold of the Airborne Reaction Force (ARF) in a helicopter above us, but I couldn't talk to the heli pilots, or the ops room, I could only speak to the guys in the back on our personal radios.

The last thing I'd heard as I was going up to the roof was that everyone was pulling out, including the call sign from the PJOC, and were going back to the main camp. We were still in contact, when I heard someone saying, 'GO, GO, GO!' Then all these vehicle engines fired up and drove out. I thought, fuck, they're not leaving us up here, are they? I leaned over the edge of the building to have a look and they hadn't abandoned us, there was still a platoon in there. What had happened was the CO had said, 'You're not leaving, you're staying there, just send the ground call sign back.' So, my two vehicles and the ground call sign had all buggered off and left me on the roof, all my other kit was in the wagon and I was left with nothing except my shirt and trousers and an assault vest and body armour. I ended up spending the whole night up there with the snipers and the rest of the guys, freezing my tits off. I was trying to beg, borrow or steal a shemagh or some warm kit, because it's freezing cold in the desert at night in January.

It was an interesting night, though, with a bit of on-the-hoof battlefield planning with the platoon commander. It wasn't the best place to defend, to say the least. There were too many rat runs and it was attached to another building, which we didn't control, so they could literally have filled that building up and that would have left an inch-thick metal door and frame between them and us. We had two GPMGs sat in the ops room facing down the corridor, just in case anyone came through that door.

The only way you could get down off the roof was by going

through this other building. We had to have ropes hanging off the sides, so if we couldn't get through, we could grenade the stairway, block the doors and try and climb off the roof. As it got dark, we saw a mile-long convoy of vehicles full of people with guns on their backs coming down from the town to the north and up from the one to the south to hit this place. We had at least 800 people with RPGs, guns, etc. parading up and down the street in front of the PJOC. Every now and again, they would let loose a burst of fire at us to make sure we knew they were still there. We had to reinforce the gate by parking a vehicle behind it and stack the front sanger with grenades to try and stop them, in case they tried to storm the building through the front gate.

It was certainly nerve-racking and lasted all night. At one point, I came down to grab a hot brew to give to the lads on the roof, and as I was climbing up the ladder with their brew, someone started firing at us. I launched myself backwards off the ladder and got covered in boiling hot tea. I did apologise to them for spilling their brew, though, 'Sorry about that guys, I've just spilt your cuppa.'

The CO had been there all night in the ops room controlling what was happening and pulling in all the support he could – he knew it was going to kick off before we left. We ended up that night with more support than I'd ever had in my life. We had the Australians who had six, big, eight-wheeled armoured personnel carriers known as LAVs, with 20mm cannon on top, parked on the roundabout about a mile away, in case we needed them to support us if we had to get out of there quickly. I'm sure we also had American Apaches in support from the base to our south and we had a couple of F16s on standby, which was quite nice to know, because we were stuck out there in contact all night. The Ops Officer was on the radio and saying to us, 'You've got this or that asset in support of you. If you need anything else, tell us and we'll get it,' which was reassuring.

We heard that the little guy I had met at the beginning, who turned out to be the lunatic commander who had started all this, had been hit and killed in the contact. The whole tour quietened down a lot after he was killed.

I was picked up by the CO's call sign the next day and had a good chat with him about what had happened. We sat outside the TV station, where he had popped in for a meeting. He was an excellent commander. Everyone was aware that he was the CO, but he really knew how to get down to the troops' level and how to talk to the guys and understand their point of view, and get what he needed as well.

We knew it was the biggest contact that had happened in the Brigade for that whole tour. The main camp was only four or five kilometres south of the city and they were all standing on top of the freight containers with binoculars watching tracer fire and ricochets bouncing around and could hear all the gunfire. When we got back they were all amazed – how the fuck did no one get hit? The highest rank on the ground was a lieutenant. He'd only been in the army a short time, but he did a superb job.

But to be honest, the thing that helped me stay so calm was that as platoon sergeant, your ideal situation is that all your corporals, lance corporals and Toms are fantastic and do their job perfectly – and they did. Usually it's: 'Get in cover. Get over there – do this, do that.' But I didn't have to do any of that. I was just there doing my job and the section commanders were all over the blokes. We had two guys – young privates and this was their first tour. These guys were excellent: there were people all over the place – 'gunman half left' – boom! – he's gone. They were awesome, the pair of them.

In that multiple they were mega blokes – the platoon commander did a brilliant job, and when this RPG went through his team, he was stood at the side of the road, eyes like dinner plates. So, I would drive up in the wagon, stop and take the piss out of him to distract him by opening the door and saying, 'Siiiiiiir, you might want to start moving, the fucking base is that way, we haven't got all day. Ignore the hole in the wall – just get going!'

The whole lot on the ground were terrific – I had nothing to worry about. It was quite surreal that I was walking around simply directing where to go and occasionally adjusting the locations of the teams. This left me totally free to deal with the larger problem of extracting us and the foot call sign with as little trouble as possible. To be honest, no matter what you think of the training – it works – and when it comes to it, it switches on like that. You get some people that are crap or do only an adequate job – but you get some that are fantastic.

It was nine months later that I got the news of my Military Cross, two days before it gets announced officially. Me and another lad got called up to see the CO. When the CO called us in and we went in together, the other lad had got an MiD (Mentioned in Despatches) and the CO told me I was getting the MC. One of the points on my citation was my sense of humour, because of how I kept taking the piss out of the platoon commander and section commanders, saying, 'What are you fucking kneeling down there for, you twat? Get in the wagon and move out,' but as far as I'm concerned, I'm not usually very funny.

After we got back, I had a while longer as Platoon Sergeant before I finally left the platoon and because I was so calm in action, they had started calling me 'The Iceman'; so when I left, they gave me this pewter tankard inscribed to: 'Jim, the Iceman, Newell'.

*Corporal Charlie Curnow, 3 Para*

Iraq 2005: We were tasked to do long-distance, counter-insurgency missions on the Syrian, Iranian and Kuwaiti borders to try and disrupt munitions, weapons and insurgents from coming across the border into Iraq. This involved long journeys and spending many days at a time on the ground, completely self-sufficient. We were a company working out of Shaibah Logistics Base. All the other units would patrol in some form of armoured vehicle or snatch wagons. These, however, massively limited the capability to go off-road and cross-country and therefore had to stick to main roads. This in turn meant they were an easy target for roadside IEDs and RPG attacks, and when shrapnel started flying around a snatch vehicle . . . everyone got a piece of the party. Hence being later named as mobile coffins.

Being Paratroopers, we looked at the use of armoured vehicles as nothing more than idleness. Yes, they were a lot more comfy, you could sleep in them sometimes, you could carry more luxury items with you and they offered more protection, but you couldn't get to places that we felt were where insurgents and weapons were being smuggled across the borders. We decided to use soft-skin vehicles, load up as much ammo, food and water as we could, and use any route possible looking for our objectives.

On one particular night, we needed to cross through a large oil field. We had received intelligence that a group of insurgents had embedded themselves with the Iraqi police (who sometimes worked with us) and were planning to kidnap British soldiers. Due to us working in small teams with no support, we figured we were a pretty good option for them. So we arrived at the entrance to the oil field and made our way through. We got approximately five minutes in and we could see a number of headlights screaming towards us with the odd blue light flashing.

We immediately stopped, got out of the vehicles and adopted loose firing positions so as not to show an aggressive stance, in case they were friendly, but also ready in case it got noisy! These vehicles fanned out into an extended line, with heavy machine guns mounted on each vehicle, and then we noticed they were all wearing black balaclavas. This didn't feel right and the old spider senses started to twitch. Being a section commander and having previous experience in Iraq, I started to go casually around my guys one by one and got them secretly and silently to cock their weapons, have grenades ready to go and pick a target in case they started firing at us.

My platoon sergeant at the time was arguing with the so-called Police Commander (PC) to let us go through and also to remove their balaclavas. The PC started talking to what he said was his commander in Baghdad and they were awaiting clearance for us to go, but they would have to keep us there until that happened. We argued we didn't need clearance, but they still wouldn't let us through and with the sensitive political environment at the time, we didn't want to cause a huge fall-out with the Iraqi police and government. At the same time, we were increasingly getting the feeling that we were being set up and I mentioned this on several occasions to my platoon sergeant, who agreed.

By this point, everyone was extremely tense; the situation was clearly delicate and could very quickly get out of hand. Suddenly they said we were allowed to go through, but had to be escorted by them. We got back in the wagons and followed on. I immediately got on the net and said we need to look for any turning or dirt track we can take to get the fuck away from these people, because they could be leading us into God knows what. With that, we spotted a left turn and both of our vehicles screamed into it and went full throttle down a dusty track in pitch black with our lights off so we couldn't be followed.

We saw the 'police' vehicles scream to a halt and start trying to pursue us, but due to the light nature and off-road capability of our vehicles, we were able to lose them. We had no idea where this would lead us, but we had to take the risk. We ended up coming onto a main road near a bridge, where an American call sign was situated with an M1 Abrams tank and a number of Humvees and at least ten American soldiers.

They explained they were out looking for a Brit call sign as they had had a predator/UAV in the air that had spotted a large ambush being laid not far from a British patrol in an oil field. We knew instantly that was us and that the Iraqi Police Commander had been stalling us while the ambush was being set up, and was then going to lead us into it.

If we had been in that ambush, I have no doubt we would have taken massive casualties and fatalities, but we would certainly have taken some of those bastards with us!

# 8

# AFGHANISTAN
# 2006

After the fall of the Taliban, the British deployment of 2002 as part of the NATO International Security Assistance Force (ISAF) was largely Kabul-based and benign peacekeeping (OP Fingal). During the two months they were there, 2 Para recruited and trained the first 600-strong battalion of the Afghan National Guard, which was then to train subsequent battalions and provide the Presidential Guard Force. They also took a Turkish Army company under command and organised the much-publicised football match between ISAF and Kabul United in the stadium previously used by the Taliban for public executions.

By 2003, the Taliban had regrouped and resurged. The NATO expansion of ISAF in the south in 2006 led to British forces deploying to Helmand Province (OP Herrick). 3 Para were the first manoeuvre unit into Helmand Province. Helmand would be the scene of the most intense fighting over the next few years.

## Operation Herrick IV

Operations continued in Afghanistan, and on 1 April 2006, 16 Airborne Assault Brigade deployed with 3 Para for Operation Herrick IV. Instead of the expected role of peace-keeping support in Helmand Province, they found themselves involved in fierce fighting in hotspots around Now Zad, Musa Qala, Sangin and Gereshk, very often in temperatures up to 50°C.

3 Para fought over five hundred contacts with the enemy during the six-month tour, often spending weeks patrolling from the 'Platoon Houses' and sleeping in body armour and helmets, often with only minutes' respite between enemy attacks. At these bases, men were lucky to get two hours' sleep a day and such was the intensity of the fighting that one company was in action for thirty-one days out of thirty-five. Apache helicopters saw action for the first time, with the Joint Helicopter Force evacuating 170 casualties.

Losses were heavy by modern standards and the Brigade lost thirty-three men killed in action, during which hundreds of insurgents were killed and injured. Posthumously, the Victoria Cross and George Cross were awarded to 3 Para's Corporal Bryan Budd and Corporal Mark Wright respectively, and 16 Air Assault Brigade also won two DSOs and nineteen gallantry awards.

3 Para saw combat and also engaged in 'hearts and minds' work with Regional Battle Group (South), operating in terrain which varied from the heat and humidity of the Sangin Valley, to arid desert in Helmand and Kandahar Provinces, the Zabul Mountains and in the streets of Kandahar City.

*Corporal Hugh Keir, 3 Para*

That tour was preceded by some pre-deployment training, which was Northern Ireland-esque with bits of experiences in Iraq thrown in. They weren't sure how the operation was going to go. In hindsight you think, Bloody hell, that was the worst training we could have had for it, it was just ridiculous! But we went to Oman for three weeks prior to Afghanistan, where we did a lot of live firing and working with quad bikes. I think they were Yamaha 500s, good fun when you're training. On the tour we used them to carry water sandbags with a plastic lining on planned ops, although we originally planned to use them for outmanoeuvring the enemy, this did not end up being the case.

The problem with Afghanistan we found is that you carry so much water, it is near impossible. We were going in the helicopters in Bastion or Lash. You get your kit, get to your helicopter landing site (HLS), and next to that would be a pile of water bottles. And we'd have a sandbag to which we'd attach para cord at each end, so the sandbag had a shoulder strap on it, more or less made of string. Each one of us would have to fill a sandbag with water bottles, ready to go into an attack with it slung over our shoulders. You'd have to do it. There was no other way of getting the water in. Again, that lack of resources to ensure resupply. So you'd get onto the choppers, good to go, and you'd land in a hot HLS or not, in a contact or not, and you'd run off the chopper into the battle and you'd dump the sandbag as you'd get off, bang. The Chinook would take off, we'd re-engage in the battle and you'd have a pile of water, which once you'd won the battle and got a foothold on the ground, you'd grab.

There was a bottle manufacturing plant at Camp Bastion. They processed the water, made the bottles and put them all out. Somebody made a mint out of that.

We flew into Kabul in a C130 to the Camp Bastion runway, which at the time was a dirty landing strip in the desert. We were based there for twelve days – at that point, we were the first 3 Para company to go in ahead of the rest of the battle-group, so we were in green canvas tents, not the luxury of the air-con tents we had later on in other tours. It was 50 degrees, sweating our bollocks off, and we went through again a series of briefings as part of our acclimatisation. Most days we'd get a tactical briefing, or a talk by the doc on some subject like nasty animals and bugs you should stay away from.

One of the briefs was about sexually transmitted diseases. We had a couple of female clerks in the group; I was sitting next to one of them. The doctor was saying, 'Don't sleep with each other,' etc., and then added, which I will remember forever: 'Men, remember, stay away from women, they are a reservoir for infectious diseases.' Everybody cracked up. It was one of those moments: she's thinking, there are a hundred paratroopers in this hall – all with eyes on me at this moment.

We were told that we were going to Gereshk and I thought, where the fuck is Gereshk? We soon found out when we got to this little town. We were there for three weeks with other troops, who would conduct reconnaissance missions but no offensive operations. There were Americans there, but we were in very separate areas. On the British side were tents, a little cookhouse and another tent with some computers that were designed for sending texts to our loved ones. On the American side, they had a massive dining facility, air-con tents and in their recreational area, they even had a fucking basketball court.

I went back with my sniper team to Camp Bastion. We went there to work with a rapid reaction force that would respond to big contacts and casualties if needed. In Camp Bastion, we had the JOC (Joint Operation Centre); all the key commanders were there, from Lieutenant Colonel Stuart Tootal commanding 3 Para, the RAF and the Royal Navy, who had naval warships in the Indian Ocean supporting us, I believe.

I remember I was eating in the cookhouse and someone shouted for me, 'Get in the JOC now!' We were briefed that we were going to Now Zad to assist the Afghan police, who were undermanned and under threat of being taken over. We were told that the operation was going to last for approximately eight hours. So I got back down and I grabbed Stu Hale, my sniper number one – when snipers work as a pair you have number one and number two. Number one is the shooter and number two is the commander. So number one is usually less experienced and that's because the harder job is to select the right target, get the right data, assess the environment and give the shooter the data he needs to take the correct shot – deflection, elevation, when was the right time to fire – all the rest of the information he needs. Stu was a great sniper, but actually more experienced than I was. Jared Cleary was also a superb sniper. He became my number one later in the tour. He got the first kill of the Herrick, when he shot a guy off a motorbike.

The Chinook dropped us outside Now Zad. Like a lot of the towns in Afghanistan, if you're looking at it from a distance, it's absolutely stunning. It looks like an ancient village that's never been touched in a thousand years and is surrounded by picturesque mountains and ridges. Then, when you stepped into the town, it was faeces, rubbish and bloody Taliban everywhere. We made our way to a mound, maybe thirty metres across and ten metres high and on top of which was a little shanty hut, probably about twice the size of a telephone box, which was an Afghan National Police (ANP) outpost. In a ring around the shelter were very shallow trenches. The setup was enough to give you a vantage point over the town, but not enough to give you any real cover.

Our eight-hour op turned into five fucking days. We went in there with day sacks, a limited amount of water, no sleeping bags or any other luxuries. There were a few significant contacts and there was other stuff going on with the battle groups elsewhere.

The Taliban would engage from a variety of firing points within the town. You had Stu shooting, I had the spotting scope, a telescope if you like, which went up to x40 magnification – cracking bit of kit. It had a graticule in it, which was the same as what we had in the sniper rifle. The sniper rifle scope was a Schmidt & Bender, but those ones we had at the time were only up to x12 magnification. So as the spotter, as the number two, I'd identify the enemy more often than not because of the better optics. Stu would be looking through his weapon as well. Between us, we'd identify the enemy, I'd give him the data and he'd shoot.

I identified this fighter, he was on a rooftop. As I said, it was a district compound we were protecting in the centre where there were Afghan police. I spotted the fighter, out of the corner of my eye, not the scope, I spotted movement. We're talking about a kilometre away; it was a fair old distance. I watch for movement, so I can confirm it is an enemy fighter. And this rifle comes up, AK-47, comes up over the lip, I think, fair enough: Taliban fighter behind it. He shoots, couple of rounds at the district compound – which he was only a few hundred metres from. Then he popped back down.

I gave Stu a steer on, reference this . . . see this third window along, watch that, etc., . . . gave him the distance, the clicks for elevation and deflection – he had all the data to engage. He wasn't sure where exactly the guy was going to pop up; it was hard to give him a precise steer. Then suddenly the guy pops up, I say to Stu, 'Green' – meaning fire. And he fires. I don't think this fighter was even aware we were looking at him. He wasn't even looking at us. You've got thirty Paratroopers and a bit of ANP on this hill about a kilometre away. He must have thought he was out of the limits, out of range. Our AP round hits the wall maybe half an inch below this guy's chin. The wall fucking explodes, dust, mud everywhere. His head pops back up, he's like 'Fucking hell!' or whatever the Pashto is for 'Fucking hell'.

As Stu is rechambering the round, he disappears out of view, off the roof. So I'm ripping the piss out of him because he's missed, while at the same time trying to identify where he has gone. It's funny, but at the same time it's not, because at that point there's still a contact going on, as we're in the middle of a battle. We were also being engaged by the enemy on a roof, closer to the west. They're trying to engage the DC. It's a cacophony of noise. Snipers are quiet. But the Para rifle sections are loud as fuck in the contact and for good reason . . . shouting orders, target indications and all the rest of it. And it's our first whack. We hadn't experienced it before. It's going bat-shit crazy, while we're trying to focus on killing this fucker.

I am still taking the piss out of Stu while we're trying to spot this guy, because he's not dead, we've not shot him and I'm thinking, fuck, we've lost him. Stu is now scanning elsewhere, I'm still looking, but there's rabbit runs everywhere in this town and he reappears at the bottom of the building in an alleyway, thinking he can't be seen. I can see a gap through a doorway onto the side of the building where he is, so he comes round the corner, puts his back against the wall, rifle in hand, and I can see him taking a breath and thinking he was lucky.

I could see him . . . 'Stu, Stu, I can see him again!' Stu's back on the target, it's the same clicks, the same data, so he fires – fucking misses again! Round goes past the guy's head, must have missed his ear by a whisker and this time, the wall behind him falls in and he's covered in rubble and dust, and he stops, he's looking left to right to see where the round is coming from. He runs off. I say, 'Fucking hell, Stu, luckiest Taliban fighter alive!' And Stu shouts, 'Fucking hell, mate, can't blame me, all I've got is fucking armour-piercing rounds and we haven't got the data for them.' It was hilarious.

No sniper wants to miss. The 3 Paras' sniper platoon has always been highly regarded, within the regiment and outside it. So it made for more ammunition on my part to rip the piss out of Stu. Thing is with Stu is that it was a fantastic shot at that distance, trying to guesstimate what the bullet that we'd not used before was going to do through the air, just one of those things. We were then engaged by a couple of fighters on a roof about 400 metres away, who were out of our line of sight. We got across to the anti-tank platoon commanded by Captain Muzetti, we knew him as Captain Machete. He was quite a gung-ho officer; a soldier's officer, really pally with the guys and with a good sense of humour. He decided to fire a Javelin at the two Taliban who we couldn't get at. He set it up to fire high into the air above where the enemy was. It went up, nose-dived almost vertically and went straight down to the roof and blew the place up. We never heard from those two again. Contact over!

There was then a sort of lull. It all went quiet. This had been our first contact and no one had been injured. Whether it was the combination of the exhilaration, the adrenaline dump, the happiness of having been in contact, everyone at the same time burst out laughing. Apart from Northern Ireland, there had not been a significant contact since the Falklands. I felt that if nothing else happens in my career, I can say I've been in a contact. Little did we know that in six months' tour, there would be more than five hundred contacts.

We then got choppered to Kajaki to help guard the hydro-electric dam. During the day there weren't many engagements as the Taliban were attacking the Afghan National Army (ANA) outpost. They changed that tactic quite quickly – I think they realised that we were supporting them. They started engaging us with a recoilless rifle, which isn't a rifle: it's a long, ten-foot barrel, which fires a missile but it's not a missile, the barrel is rifled. Back on 'Normandy' (one of our three vantage points), there were a couple of trenches, halfway down the hill, which the guys would occupy if the enemy decided to come and attack us. This round came in and the round struck, maybe a couple of yards in front of the guys' shell scrape with a huge fucking bang. Initially we thought the guys were dead, a direct hit, but they had missed. When we found the guys, you could see they were suffering from shell shock, battle shock. One guy was bad, he was a fantastic paratrooper, but he didn't speak for three days. He just locked down, because it had fucked his head.

I came off the hill the next day to see the boss about something, a bit of briefing, and he was there sitting on this step. I sat there next to him, didn't say anything . . . a familiar face you know. This gave him the opportunity to speak if he wanted to, but he didn't even acknowledge me, just looking into space, looking into nothingness. That silent comfort, I'm here. I had to leave him a short time later.

I went to Camp Bastion, after an eight-hour operation . . . five weeks later. I was absolutely stinking, as I hadn't changed my clothes during that time. The only saving grace was in Kajaki, in the reservoir, they had the dam. It was surrounded by minefields so you could go down to the reservoir, which was looked over by our guys, and have a swim. It was surreal, it was amazing. Beautiful! You couldn't even see the villages; it was like being back in Oman. We'd get in with our clothes on, get them clean, then take our clothes off. Then we'd swim naked across the other side of the reservoir where there was a tiny beach and we'd sit there. It was full of minnows which would nibble on you. It was like a massage, with minnows, they would be everywhere. Covered in minnows, they'd be having a little nibble. I was thinking, two hours ago I was on top of that hill being shot at and now I'm having erotica with the minnows!

*Lance Corporal Joe Stevenson, 3 Para*

On 20 August 2006, I was second in command of 2 Section, 1 Platoon, A Company, in Helmand Province. We were located in Sangin. Pretty much every day and night we had been in relentless battles with the Taliban and the next one was going to be no different, we all knew that.

It was still morning and all the commanders had been brought together for a briefing of the day's mission. We were told to take out a section of Royal Engineers, who would be carrying bar mines, which they would place on various walls that the Taliban had been using as cover for themselves while attacking our compound on a regular basis. They would then detonate them, which would ultimately result in the Taliban being more exposed, and would hopefully reduce our chances of them mounting attacks on us from that area.

It sounded pretty straightforward, 1 Section would patrol out and flank up the left giving cover from that side, while 2 Section (my section) would go straight down the middle to the compound walls, which were about to be blown up by the Royal Engineers. In the meantime, 3 Section (Bryan 'Bri' Budd's section) would patrol out and give us protection from the right-hand side.

The previous days, weeks and months had been very mentally and physically demanding and I was feeling pretty fucked as were most people, but we were a strong group of Paratroopers who were probably, at the time, the most combat-experienced in the British Army. My thinking was that it doesn't matter what happens or what we do, or whatever shit situation we find ourselves in, the guys will always have your back and be there giving one hundred per cent.

After our commander's briefing of the mission, we all dispersed to join our sections and pass the briefing on to the guys. I remember walking back to the other guys in the platoon with Bri, and we were chatting about something or other, and I asked him how he thought this op would go. I asked because this was more complex, as most of the ops had been straight, non-stop firefights with the Taliban. He looked at me with his usual unfazed face, nodded and said, 'Alright.' This made me chuckle at the way he said it and that lightened the mood for us. It was also the last time I spoke to him face to face.

When the time came and the platoon was ready, 1 and 3 Section headed off out on the flanks while my section hung back a bit and went out later, as we were the ones escorting the engineers with their bar mines. If I remember rightly, the walls which the Royal Engineers were going to detonate were roughly 500 metres away from our compound and we could see them clearly. Behind the walls were a field of crops at least six feet tall, and various smaller walls and what looked like ruins of old compounds, or just normal buildings that we had blown up on previous missions.

It was pretty nervous patrolling out, as we were so used to being shot at, and all I could see was potential firing positions for the Taliban where we would be easy targets; so my mind was going into overdrive, looking around at various places I could dive into for cover if we did get attacked. Before we got to the area where the mines were supposed to be deployed, I could hear firing coming from the right flank, which was Bri's section. It was nothing new, as it happened every day, so my initial reaction was not of shock, but more calm and collected thinking about what could be happening. I think we were all expecting a contact at some point, whether it was before we put the mines on the walls or after.

Needless to say, putting the bar mines in place was no longer a priority, as one of our sections was under fire: 'no plan survives contact', as they say. We all pushed forward into cover and to regroup. Most of what happened next is a bit of a blur, as when you're in a situation like this, it feels like everything is happening at 100 mph. There was a lot of chatter on the radio, then people running into cover, linking up and passing on information. Our section and 1 Section managed to link up and join each other. Once things had calmed down a little and all of our section was together on the left flank by the river with 1 Section, the platoon commander and sergeant started to brief us on what was going on in the new situation.

I wasn't given many details, because at that point nobody really knew what was going on with 3 Section, although we could still hear rounds being fired, all we were told was that they had been contacted and were in a firefight. Soon after that a message came through that Bri was missing. The new plan was to get the whole platoon back together with Bri, then once we were complete, we would extract back to the compound. The platoon commander and sergeant wasted no time in reorganising everybody, making swift command decisions and giving everybody new roles.

Each eight-man section is made up of two fire teams named Charlie and Delta; four guys in each. I was in charge of Delta fire team in 2 Section and our new role was to provide a safe route for the reinforcements that would be coming from our platoon house, as at this point, it sounded like we were getting fired at from all angles by the Taliban. So much was happening in such a small space of time, it was difficult to keep track of exactly what everybody else was doing, so we concentrated on our own task.

Over a fairly quick period, some reinforcements arrived to help us out. I can't say I knew any of them, as they were mostly attached to us from other units and had now been thrown into the deep end of an intense firefight. I gave a fire control order to some of the guys that were lined out in the dead ground parallel to the track we were near. Everybody was well spaced out and in good cover putting down a blanket of fire towards the enemy. All the time this was going on, I still hadn't heard any update over the radio of 3 Section and whether Bri was back with them.

Apart from Bri's section, the rest of us were in quite close proximity to each other, which made it easier for me to communicate with others and to run back and forth and stay in control of my task, as well as having a quick face-to-face with the platoon sergeant. As usual, it was also a very hot day, which always made everything more difficult and tiring. My ears were ringing so fucking loud from the gunfire and my eyes were stinging from the sweat dripping out from under my helmet. All the time there was so much going on around us, but I gradually noticed some of the guys from our platoon starting to appear out of the crops. Some of them were from Bri's section and they were covered in blood and running, staggering or limping towards us. I moved up to where the platoon sergeant was and could see that he was getting guys together to bring back the rest of 3 Section and Bri.

I looked around and saw one of our guys kneeling on the floor against the wall, holding his leg around the shin area. I asked if he was okay and he said, 'Yeah, I'm all good, mate.' Another one came running out of the trees towards us holding his arm with blood pissing out, but he had his other arm around someone else who was limping. Another was holding his arm with blood all down it and had an FFD (first field dressing) covered in blood wrapped round his face – it looked like he'd ripped eye holes into it so he could see properly, but it was obvious he had bad facial injuries. A few had been shot in their body-armour plate, which was lucky as the plate was no bigger than a large hand and basically covered your heart front and back – those guys were okay, but in a little bit of shock; it was like something out of a modern video game.

While we were dealing with the wounded, you could hear firing with rounds going off in the background, along with various explosions and people shouting and on top of all this, we had fast air-support, too. I could hear over the net that Bri had been found and he was now just up ahead. I breathed a massive sigh of relief. I was told to stay alert and ensure the route out from the platoon house was kept clear. Within moments, the Company sergeant major was flying past us down the safe route on a small quad bike with the trailer on the back, heading up to where the platoon commander and sergeant were located. He was going that fast I thought he was going to flip it over. Things around us started to calm down a little, although everybody was still on edge covering their arcs of fire, we were exchanging messages and checking on each other, as well as redistributing ammo and chucking loaded mags of ammunition to anyone if they were running low. As the lull in the battle went on, snippets of unconfirmed information were getting thrown around between the blokes. I heard one of the guys say that Bri was unconscious after holding his section back to give him cover in fire, whilst he moved forward to attack a Taliban position and killed them all. At this point I didn't know any exact details of the incident, only what I had heard on the net, and what was loosely being passed on to each other through the midst of a firefight.

I then saw the sergeant major riding back down the safe route on the quad, this time he was driving very steadily indeed. I looked across and could see Bri lying on the back of the trailer with his arm hanging off the side and for a moment I stopped and looked at him as he went past. When I think of it now, it seems as if he went past in slow motion, probably because I didn't want that moment to be the last time I saw him.

Finally the whole platoon was back together and accounted for, and after Bri and the rest of the injured had been casevaced back to the platoon house, we all started to peel off and head back. I was one of the last guys back in to our compound, and I went through the gates and stood there with the rest of the platoon; we were all fucked from the extraction and looked exactly how you'd imagine everyone to look after yet another hard-fought day. I started to reload my magazines of ammunition and I tried to keep my mind busy and stay on top of things in the section. I was working out my section's ammunition state and tried to find out who in the platoon was injured and who was not. Then I saw one of the guys come out from the med area where Bri had been taken for treatment, he came over and said, 'Bri hasn't made it.'

Bri's actions that day and the way he led his men was inspirational and nothing short of heroic. I'm proud to have served with such an awesome Paratrooper. He was a true airborne warrior, as was everybody I served alongside.

*Corporal Charlie Curnow, 3 Para*

From the point where the firing started, I took my section forward to try and identify the Taliban firing points and start engaging them. As I did this, three casualties from Bryan's section came around the corner and clearly needed medical attention. Myself and Joe along with the patrol medic started to apply tourniquets, field dressings and morphine. I asked them what happened and where they had been attacked, which they explained was an ambush from a flank at very close quarters. They didn't know where Bri was, but saw him firing and charging towards the position and believed he had been hit. Joe then stayed with the casualties and I pushed forward with three other guys to try and locate Bri.

As we crept along a small river, we identified dead Taliban and could also hear them all around us and very close. As we then saw what we thought could be Bri's position in among Taliban dead, we were suddenly engaged by rifles and a heavy machine gun. How none of the four of us were killed is a miracle, as one guy had a direct hit in his body-armour plate, one took shrapnel in the arse and I took shrapnel in my leg. There was a real sense that we were seriously outnumbered, pretty much surrounded and that the enemy had the upper hand and was gaining momentum. We were really pinned down, so we called in 81mm mortar fire nearly on our own positions to help nullify the threat. Looking back, I felt from that point, if Brian hadn't taken out the initial Taliban position, they would have most certainly hit us again as we were by then very exposed and losing men. I knew I'd been hit, so I quickly extracted, as I couldn't feel or walk on my leg. I was taken back to the patrol base that was approximately 500 metres away and given treatment.

I was still listening to my radio and heard that Bri had been found, but was unconscious. I then saw him carried in on a stretcher, but recognised the familiar signs of a lifeless body. From then on, the base took accurate direct and indirect fire and it was going to be unlikely any form of casevac would happen. About one hour later we could hear the Chinooks, which must have gone against all orders to fly in, and I greatly appreciated the bravery of those pilots. As we were moving to the Chinooks, I could still hear fire and there was a great sense of urgency to get everyone on board. At this point I could only limp, but managed to grab a corner of the stretcher and get Bri onto the Chinook.

Guys sat anywhere they could while more vital ammunition, reinforcements and water was literally thrown off the back of the Chinook. I could still hear a lot of fighting in the background and as we took off, I was very much expecting an RPG to hit us. The mood on the Chinook was sombre and it seemed very silent as well, although I knew there was a lot going on with the treatment of casualties. I sat next to Bri in his body bag on the floor of the Chinook for the whole duration, firmly holding his shoulder and said goodbye and helped carry him off when we arrived in Bastion. I then attended his funeral and met his wife and brother. Sadly, I am the only corporal from our platoon involved in that incident alive today.

Bri was everything you expected of a commander in the Parachute Regiment and more. He was fearless.

**The citation for Corporal Bryan Budd's Victoria Cross reads:**

During July and August 2006, 'A' Company, 3rd Battalion, the Parachute Regiment were deployed in the District Centre at Sangin. They were constantly under sustained attack from a combination of Taliban small arms, rocket-propelled grenades, mortar and rocket fire.

On 27 July 2006, whilst on a routine patrol, Corporal Bryan Budd's section identified and engaged two enemy gunmen on the roof of a building in the centre of Sangin. During the ensuing fierce firefight, two of Corporal Budd's section were hit. One was seriously injured and collapsed in the open ground, where he remained exposed to enemy fire, with rounds striking the ground around him. Corporal Budd realised that he needed to regain the initiative and that the enemy needed to be driven back so that the casualty could be evacuated.

Under fire, he personally led the attack on the building where the enemy fire was heaviest, forcing the remaining fighters to flee across an open field where they were successfully engaged. This courageous and prompt action proved decisive in breaking the enemy and was undertaken at great

personal risk. Corporal Budd's decisive leadership and conspicuous gallantry allowed his wounded colleague to be evacuated
to safety where he subsequently received life-saving treatment.

On 20 August 2006, Corporal Budd was leading his section
on the right forward flank of a platoon clearance patrol near
Sangin District Centre. Another section was advancing with
a Land Rover fitted with a .50 calibre heavy machine gun on
the patrol's left flank. Pushing through thick vegetation,
Corporal Budd identified a number of enemy fighters 30 metres
ahead. Undetected, and in an attempt to surprise and destroy
the enemy, Corporal Budd initiated a flanking manoeuvre.
However, the enemy spotted the Land Rover on the left flank
and the element of surprise was lost for the whole platoon.

In order to regain the initiative, Corporal Budd decided to
assault the enemy and ordered his men to follow him. As
they moved forward the section came under a withering fire
that incapacitated three of his men. The continued enemy
fire and these losses forced the section to take cover. But,
Corporal Budd continued to assault on his own, knowing full
well the likely consequences of doing so without the close
support of his remaining men. He was wounded but continued
to move forward, attacking and killing the enemy as he rushed
their position.

Inspired by Corporal Budd's example, the rest of the platoon
reorganised and pushed forward their attack, eliminating more
of the enemy and eventually forcing their withdrawal. Corporal
Budd subsequently died of his wounds, and when his body
was later recovered it was found surrounded by three dead
Taliban.

Corporal Budd's conspicuous gallantry during these two
engagements saved the lives of many of his colleagues. He
acted in the full knowledge that the rest of his men had either
been struck down or had been forced to go to ground. His

determination to press home a single-handed assault against a superior enemy force despite his wounds stands out as a premeditated act of inspirational leadership and supreme valour. In recognition of this, Corporal Budd is awarded the Victoria Cross.


*Sergeant Major Andy Newell, Pathfinder Platoon*

Afghan came round for me in early 2006 and was to be called Op Herrick IV. We all got given the go-ahead to prepare and train for it, even though the politicians were officially saying, 'No, no, no,' we all thought it was eventually going to be a big, 'Yes, yes, yes.'

We started planning and training for the op, just in case we actually ended up going, then suddenly about halfway through the training the government said, 'Stop – we haven't said we're going yet.' There followed a six-week period where all the contracts for equipment like ballistic matting for the WMIK Land Rovers, more body armour, all the bits and pieces we'd need to go there, were stalled or stopped. The government was wobbling and making up their minds whether to go or not; by the time they'd reinstated the contracts, all the other nationalities had got their orders in ahead of us, so we deployed with hardly any kit. We were only allowed to deploy half the troops from the Brigade and even the Brigade HQ was split in half. They sent the Brigade Commander, Brigadier Ed Butler, up to Kabul as COMBRITFOR (Commander British Forces) and replaced him with a Colonel from the Guards, who was now in charge of the depleted Brigade.

We flew out to Afghanistan a couple of months before the rest of the Brigade deployed, which we were quite happy about. We loaded ourselves onto a couple of C17s with all our vehicles and equipment beside us and eventually arrived at Kandahar airbase. We then set about the task of endless in-theatre familiarisation training packages, intelligence briefings, equipping ourselves and our vehicles, topped off with lots of range work with the various weapon systems.

The Pathfinder Group (as we were known) consisted of a small HQ group (split between the Brigade HQ and Forward Operating Base (FOB) Price), thirty deployable troops, consisting of PF, Engineer Recce, specialist signallers and an interpreter. Our transport consisted of eight Land Rovers, two Pinzgauers, a few quad bikes and motorbikes. We modified the Pinzgauers by fitting a gun mount on the roll bar so we had weapons on every vehicle. We were given the call sign 'Mayhem' to use, which we thought was quite appropriate.

Due to the fact that we'd deployed before the rest of the brigade, we now came under the command of the in-theatre HQ known as 'Prelim Ops'. Once we felt we were ready, we moved forward to (FOB) Price near the town of Gereshk, which was built and occupied by American SF troops and also some UKSF. Once we were all safely in, we made ourselves as comfortable as we could. We were brought up to speed on 'the threat' by both the US and UKSF and conducted yet more training and range work as we prepared for our first live mission.

One of our early missions was to speak to the Chief of Police in a place called Now Zad to get some 'ground truth' about Taliban activity in his area. We asked the SF guys who'd been out there before us, 'When we go to these villages to meet the chief of police, what's the best way to go about it?' They said, 'Biggest thing, don't tell them you're coming. Go there at night, sit outside the village at a distance and phone up the chief of police in the morning and say, "Come out and meet me," never go straight into the village.

The PF Group deployed by vehicle to Now Zad, whilst I ran

the mission from the Ops room in FOB Price. As they approached Now Zad under cover of darkness, they came under quite severe fire from an unknown force using Russian heavy machine guns (DShK) and small arms. The PF returned fire quite spectacularly, because all ten vehicles were able to get both guns going straight away. The position they were attacked from was previously an old Russian trench position on a hill that became later known as ANP Hill, located just outside Now Zad.

As the PF extracted themselves from the threat, under heavy fire, using our practised vehicle contact drills, one of the Weapons Mount Installation Kit (WMIK) Land Rovers drove across a culvert, the ground gave way and it flopped onto its side. The three-man crew in the vehicle only just managed to get out of there. The vehicle commander couldn't get his weapon out, because it was jammed between the vehicle and the ground as was his day sack. The GPMG was still mounted on the vehicle but they had to leave it, grab what they could and bug out. The other wagons picked them up, still under fire, and pulled back to some high ground almost two kilometres away. At one stage, there were four different firing points firing at them, and then they started firing at each other.

A group of the enemy went towards the vehicle that still contained some mission-essential equipment, so we had to deny it to them by firing our Milan (anti-tank) missiles into it. They still managed to get away with the GPMG, a ruggedised laptop, a CWS and they even got the commander's SA 80, which he eventually ended up buying back from them for $5. The contact turned out to be a 'Green on Blue', where so-called friendly forces, in this case the ANP, fired on our troops by mistake.

One of our early missions was to deploy and observe Sangin to gain information about the place and the pattern of life, etc. At this point, no UK troops had set foot in Sangin. Three or four days later, on the way back to base, one of our WMIKs, containing the engineer recce team, set off an old Russian mine. They hadn't been driving on tracks, and there weren't any mine maps; if there were any, we didn't have them.

When the mine exploded, the rear gunner, who was in his early twenties, took the worst of the blast and ended up losing his leg. The vehicle commander got severe whiplash and was initially paralysed from the neck down, but can now walk again. He was later Medical Discharged from the army due to his injuries. The driver escaped with just cuts and bruises. One thing that could have lessened the injuries on the rear gunner was Kevlar ballistic matting, which we had not received. Within a week, I'd lost two of my vehicles and three of our men. That was quite a shock to the system, but we dealt with it, reconstituted and got on with doing the job in hand.

We carried out other missions, including foot patrols into Gereshk and one to conduct Tactical Landing Zone (TLZ) recces for locations that could be used for any future airborne re-supply operations. We were working in the middle of nowhere, when we heard Brigade HQ saying 'over to your east, Musa Qala is under contact. We're not sure if it's true or not.' So we drove over there and arrived at last light on the plateau overlooking the town.

The place was awash with tracer and explosions from RPGs going off. Very large groups of Taliban were attacking the ANP compound in the town and the ANP lost twenty guys that night. We weren't allowed to go and help, as we were still supposed to be just supporting them at that time. It was too dark for heli support, as the light levels weren't sufficient for NVG flying, so if we'd had any serious casualties in need of urgent casevac, we'd have been buggered, too. We had to sit there and watch it happen, which was very frustrating. It eventually finished during the night and the Taliban withdrew.

The next morning a 200-strong ANP/militia 'war party' met

us on top of the plateau and Brigade HQ tasked us with going along and helping them clear the Taliban out of the area, right up to the town of Baghran. Off we went with every type of vehicle you can imagine in this convoy, including motorbikes and a lot of Toyota Hiluxs with people jammed in the back of them. As we approached each village, we'd see the Taliban on their motorbikes, running for the hills; unbelievable. We still weren't allowed to engage them at that point. We continued right up to Baghran, where the Taliban had killed a load of ANP and taken over the town. We stayed outside the town, splitting our group in half, locating ourselves on top of two hills overlooking the town: I took command of one half and the boss took command of the other.

We were definitely not going to approach the town just yet, but we decided to announce our presence to the Taliban. We called for aerial support and an American B1 bomber turned up overhead, so we got him to fire a large JDAM bomb into the side of the steep cliffs a couple of kilometres outside the town to ensure no one was hurt. The explosion echoed throughout the valley, which made the Taliban instantly run off into the distance. That's how we cleared Baghran.

The ANP descended into the town and reinstated the chief of police; we stayed there overlooking the town for a few more days. I spent some of the daytime drinking tea with the deputy chief of police from Lashkar Gah, teaching him rudimentary English.

The Brigade HQ then told us we were to return to FOB Price now that the town had been cleared of Taliban and the ANP had been reinstated. We were all ready to go back via a different route, as per our Standard Operating Procedures (SOPs), but we were told we had to stay with the ANP/militia group, which meant we would have to drive back the exact same route we'd driven to get there. We were not happy, but we had no choice!

We were packed up and ready to leave. We decided to let the Afghans go first and then we cracked on back the way we'd come towards Musa Qala. In the process, we thwarted six IED attempts and an ambush. As we'd approach a village/town, the ICOM chatter would increase, and you'd hear the Taliban discussing how they were going to bomb us, relayed to us through our interpreters, who said, 'They are going to hit the third vehicle in the convoy.' They were not after the Afghan police; they wanted to hit us. I sat in my vehicle during one of these alerts and counted the vehicles in front of me, 'One, two, ah fuck, I'm third. It's me again!' At the time, you couldn't do anything else but laugh.

Then there was a prominent ambush area that we had to drive through and the Taliban were there again waiting to attack us. The Afghans went in to take them out, and there was a gun battle; again, we weren't allowed to be involved in a firefight at this point. Soon enough the casualties started coming. Ten ANP were injured, so we turned into an aid station and patched them up, unfortunately three of them died. We then had seven casualties. One ANP guy was shot through the shoulder, which didn't hit anything serious, so he went straight back into action. Another got shot through the calf, we patched him up and he went straight back in, too.

Then the boss decided he'd had enough sitting around, and he said, 'Sod this,' and he went forward with one of our Joint Tactical Air Controllers (JTAC) and a couple of snipers. The snipers shot a couple of Taliban and the JTAC brought in an American A-10 to finish the rest of them off. If you've never experienced an A-10 firing live, well, it can only be described as awesome. What was left of the Taliban retreated and the ANP returned to the convoy.

Brigade HQ were initially going to make the ANP take their own casualties with them, but I said, 'No way! They've got injured protecting us.' So I called in a casevac and an American Black Hawk turned up, and we only just managed to cram them all on board. The ANP tried to put their dead on there, but we said, 'No, you don't understand, you have to carry them back.' So they wrapped them up and put them on the back of one of their pick-ups and we drove back towards Musa Qala.

On the plateau above Musa Qala, we had another heli resupply. A Chinook landed and we started unloading these baskets of mangoes and bread and 5,000 cigarettes for the Afghan police, but before the Chinook had landed, the ANP had said, 'We've got go to and bury our dead,' and they just fucked off into the desert, so we were left with this huge pile of scoff. I stopped the loadmaster halfway through unloading, and I said, 'We can't take this,' but the crew wanted to get it off because they had another task. This big mountain of food was just left in the sun, but the cigarettes came in very handy and none of us had to buy any more for a couple of months.

We were now sat on this plateau above Musa Qala. We found out later that it was an old Russian minefield, and we'd just conducted a heli resupply on it! We were very lucky.

At the beginning of this patrol, we'd gone out at night watching Musa Qala getting shot up. As we were getting ready to head back to base, Brigade HQ came up on the net. 'Turn around; we want you go back into Musa Qala to the ANP compound to reinforce them.' We got the ANP to clear the route out to us from the compound, and then they walked us in. They did a fantastic job, I'll give them their due, clearing all the vulnerable points on the route. I must admit it was one of the scariest couple of hours of my life as we crawled very quietly down these narrow alleyways, under cover of darkness. We arrived in the compound whilst it was still dark and kept our heads down for a day or so. We could hear that the Taliban were totally surprised, as we listened to them talking on their radios and saying, 'How the hell did they get in here without us knowing?'

The whole place was also a complete shithole! There was a prison in the middle of the compound containing about thirty prisoners which included mostly Taliban, people who hadn't paid dowries, crooks and common criminals. The compound was about 200 metres by about 150 in a zigzag shape, right in the centre of the town. Outside the front gate was the town's square with a big obelisk in it, built by a previous chief of police, to honour fallen ANP. There were no real bunker or sangar positions around the place, everything they had was makeshift, even the front gate had no covering on it, and so you could see straight into the camp. So we got some old corrugated tin that we found lying around and covered the front gate.

I brought in several Chinooks to resupply us with food and water. We did a few town patrols and didn't really get bothered that much. Then a company-sized American unit with these monstrous lorries, all armoured up to the eyeballs, took over from us. We returned to FOB Price, carried out some more tasks for Brigade HQ and then started the R&R rotation.

Then 3 Para did an air assault mission into Sangin, which was a massive success – it caught the Taliban completely by surprise, but they stayed there too long. The 3 Para rifle company that was left in the town was supposed to take over from the Americans in Musa Qala, but were bogged down dealing with the Taliban and couldn't leave. The Americans were saying, 'We are leaving on this specific day, whether someone comes to relieve us or not!' Consequently, we got tasked to go and take over again from the Americans we'd handed over to a month before.

It was supposed to be a two- to four-day operation. We knew that wouldn't happen, as we'd been there a couple of weeks last time when were only supposed to be there a few days, so we took nearly double the ammo and supplies, because the Americans had had a few contacts. It was definitely hotting up, because Musa Qala town sits at the crossroads of the main supply routes (MSRs) between Sangin and the Bagni Valley, Now Zad and the hydroelectric dam at Kajaki. Now Zad was also hotting up and the Gurkhas were being attacked frequently and quite badly. We were to be the northernmost brigade unit, right at these crossroads.

We took over from the Americans during daylight this time and they left pretty quickly. The compound in Musa Qala by this time was a wreck, full of RPG and bullet holes. The whole place was stinking, it was filthy and the kitchen area was full of maggots and rats. It was like an open lean-to garage with a fire pit and that's where they cooked their scoff. We set up a routine, we went out on patrols, and searched a few houses that overlooked the compound. The longer we spent in Musa Qala, the more ICOM chatter we heard, and our electronic warfare (EW) signallers were telling us about the proximity of the Taliban. The boss and I held regular Shuras with the chief of police and the town elders. We even started training the Afghan policemen, trying to get them to march and do drill, which provided some light relief for the lads.

An American logistic/artillery unit moved into an area sixteen kilometres to our north to support their operations north of them. So we now had an artillery call sign within range of our compound. We used them quite a few times to assist us when we were getting contacted. The American artillery was extremely accurate; you'd see a couple of Taliban with weapons, so we'd call them in to take them out. It became like one shot, one kill. There was one incident during a contact, where we brought artillery fire onto a building used as a Taliban armoury; they gave it away on their radios, but it was also a local mosque.

This didn't please the Brigade HQ too much, but there wasn't a big outcry about it, so we must have got the right place.

There was another incident where we were in contact and a lorry load of the enemy were buggering off because we were getting the better of them. We brought an RAF Harrier in, but the pilot refused to fire on them. This really pissed us off. The pilot said, 'Are they Taliban or insurgents?' We said, 'How the fuck do we know, they don't wear uniforms? They've just been shooting at us; they're one or the other.' But he wouldn't fire and they escaped. I think he was a new pilot and he wasn't battle hardened yet.

Some Foreign and Commonwealth Office guys came in to have a nose around; but almost every time a helicopter with them or others on board came near Musa Qala, the Taliban started shooting and firing RPGs at them. This meant the RAF refused to fly anywhere near us. We were basically left on our own for weeks and ran out of food and Puritabs, so the $5,000 I'd been given for local projects had to be spent on food. We went downtown to the bazaar and bought a big gas cooker, a large cooking pot, anything that we could recognise that was tinned and lots of pasta. The best weight loss diet in Helmand province!

We had a local guy that we paid $5 to bring us ice every couple of days. The Taliban shot him within a week. One of our gun mounts was cracked, so we got a local guy to come in to weld it and the Taliban killed him as well. We had to drink unpurified water, so we just boiled it. The whole mood of the place was getting very unfriendly.

We decided to carry out a night ambush on the MSR that ran up the north/south wadi next to the town. Twelve of us were going to go out as the ambush party and the rest of us, on the two-storey building outside the compound, were going to be the fire support, because we could see directly over their heads into the wadi and the green zone opposite. The ambush party was on enforced rest and I was manning the sangar overlooking the main wadi with Aide, our VM, while they rested and then I was to stay there for the duration of the ambush.

About twenty minutes into my stag, we were scanning around the area with the thermal imager and saw one of the jingle (decorated) trucks came down the wadi and park up behind a copse, just out of sight to us. They stayed there about five or ten minutes then drove off. We couldn't see if anyone got on or off. I then saw a few people walking in a line down the wadi, but as it was dark we couldn't confirm if they had weapons or not. Five minutes later, scanning across to the right, there were two guys sat on a rooftop pointing in our direction. I said, 'Get the boss ready; something's going to happen.' A short time later we saw a flash as the first of many RPG rockets flew straight past us and exploded over the compound. The rest of the Taliban, about forty of them, opened up with small arms, all aimed at the two of us in the sangar.

The moon had risen, it was a clear night and we were totally silhouetted on the roof. They continued firing small arms and RPGs at us for about an hour. I was on the GPMG and the other guy was on the .50 cal, both rattling away. The RPGs were missing us, thank God, but the compound was getting showered with shrapnel. It's actually quite a spectacle when you see a big contact going on, flashes, bangs, flares, green and red tracer all over the place. Tony, an Australian SF guy attached to us, and two others came across the walkway to our building, whilst under fire, so we now had five of us up there. We had already pre-positioned weapons for the ambush, so we had two GPMGs, one .50-cal, a .338 sniper rifle and a 51mm mortar, our personal weapons and lots of ammunition.

We were all returning fire against the Taliban, when Tony asked to fire the 51mm mortar, as he'd never fired one before.

'OK, Tony, stick up a couple of illumination rounds and we'll see what's going on.' Up went the first two illumination rounds, no problems, and lit up the area. 'OK, Tony, here's your direction, this is your range, off you go, fire two or three High Explosive (HE) rounds.' Pop, went the first one, but there was no explosion. We thought it was a dud. He fired a second one. Pop, off it went, nothing again.

So I leant back in the middle of this contact and said, 'Tony, you did take the safety pin out of the mortar rounds, didn't you?' He replied, 'There's a safety pin in these things?' Someone shouted, 'You fucking knob' and we all ended up pissing ourselves laughing, in the middle of this contact. I ended up bringing in an artillery fire mission, which promptly ended the contact.

Listening to the Taliban radio chatter the following day, it turned out that the Taliban who'd attacked us weren't the normal Musa Qala ones, these had been down in Sangin fighting and losing against 3 Para. So they'd come back up the wadi to rest and regroup and thinking, there's only a few guys in Musa Qala, let's give them a go, which turned out to be a VERY big mistake for them!

A few weeks passed and we were getting rather thin, extremely low on ammo, on batteries, on absolutely bloody everything. But we weren't short of rats, bloody enormous rats roaming the compound. A couple of times Brigade HQ tried to resupply us by parachute, but both ended up missing and some stores landed in the main Taliban area, which was really annoying. An American relief convoy came up from the south, straight up the wadi, against our recommendations, and got absolutely pummelled by the Taliban. Once again, we had to bring in fast air to help them out. Luckily no one was killed, but it was a very close call.

A week later they sent a British convoy to relieve us, but the

Taliban also turned them back about five kilometres away from us. So we were sat there, thinking, this is not good! The Chief of Staff got on the sat-phone a couple of times and said, 'We know you're in the shit, just hang in there. We'll get to you.' All the time, Sangin was getting worse and worse.

We were saying, 'Come on, 3 Para, move your arse!' We came up with several options how we could be extracted from the place, which could have worked, but Sangin was their centre of focus. We were basically left to fend for ourselves. Eventually they got helicopters up to us and brought in some engineers and a doctor. They also brought in $25,000 so we could buy local materials to properly defend the compound.

We managed to get an R&R swap-over done at the same time, so some of the guys who had come in with the original group did get out while others came in. The boss, two guys and myself stayed in place for the duration.

We were then told a Danish recce squadron was going to come up and take over from us. This was approaching the end of the six-week point. We were all getting rather skinny now, money was rapidly running out, but we now had forty-five troops plus a couple of medics, so we were in reasonable shape, but still getting hit regularly. They said they needed one of us to come out and lead the Danish to Musa Qala, because they didn't know where they were going. So I said, 'I'll do it, not a problem.' A helicopter picked me up and brought in three Danish guys as an advance party. I flew back to Bastion, briefed them up on Musa Qala and the route we would need to take, and then led them in. It took over three days to fight our way back in.

We left in daylight, against my advice, so we got dicked straight away by Taliban on motorbikes. We were about forty-odd vehicles in this convoy, four big drops wagons with ISO containers on, three Danish, one English, several Humvees and the little Mercedes jeep version of our WMIKs. I was in the front wagon, follow me, and let's go.

We harboured up the first night, but the Taliban had already pinged us. The Danes had their own EW signallers with them, so they knew they were getting dicked the whole way. As soon as it turned dark, I made them move five kilometres to a new harbour area, but we didn't manage to lose them. A large group of Taliban in vehicles came to attack us that night. They parked up their vehicles in a long line and advanced in an extended line towards us. Using our thermal imagers we could easily see them and managed to dispatch most of them. Luckily there was an American bomber flying overhead and he took out most of their vehicles for us. After that it was quiet for the rest of the night.

The next night we had to cross two wadis to get into Musa Qala. We'd just driven through an area when one of the following Humvees, about seven vehicles behind us, hit a mine, right where we'd done the heli resupply weeks earlier. That was quite scary. We then had to get out and walk manually checking for mines, as we had no mine detectors. It was quite horrible listening to the injured guys who were still on comms, screaming and moaning in the Humvee. We had lost our element of surprise, but we pressed on once the injured had been extracted back to Bastion.

We went to the second wadi, where it gets channelled as you approach the green zone. To get through the green zone there is a 400-metre-long track and then you're out into the main wadi, with Musa Qala on the other side. Everyone who wasn't manning a gun or driving a vehicle was outside walking the vehicles in with me leading at the front. The PF could see us from the compound and we could see the compound as we were walking along, so we pressed on cautiously. Suddenly, out of this doorway, about thirty metres in front of me, jumped a figure in a burka, and I instinctively raised my weapon to engage it but then thought, it's a woman, so I hesitated.

What I didn't notice, partially due to the sun being in my eyes, was the RPG on the person's shoulder. All I saw was a black figure, which turned out to be a man. He fired the RPG straight past my head and it exploded behind me. I fired and a couple of others fired and that was him dead. Then there was a bit of a stalemate, shit, what do we do now? We then got the call that the PF in the compound could see Taliban lying in wait along the rooftops to ambush us, which made us withdraw a few hundred metres. Fortunately, the PF JTAC brought in a Harrier and sorted them out.

The Danes then decided they didn't have enough people to go on foot through the green zone. We'd held this place with thirty guys for nearly seven weeks and they were bringing in over eighty, with a large amount of vehicles! So during the next day we planned how we were going to get the convoy to Musa Qala the next night. It was now the third night we'd been trying to get there. We decided to head well out to the east, away from Musa Qala, and double back on ourselves under cover of darkness. We rested, planned and prepared for the evening's activities during the day and left our position after last light, slow speed, no lights, using NVG only to navigate.

The Danish EW signallers, listening to the Taliban radio chatter, had picked up that a large force was coming from the Bagni Valley to attack us that night. It was a really dark night, and we managed to give them the slip by heading east instead of south as they had expected. We eventually looped back towards Musa Qala. When we were a few kilometres outside, the first of several explosions rocked the valley. The grand plan, which we worked out with Brigade HQ and the PF during the day, was to attack known Taliban positions with fast air, to the west of the town, as a distraction, while we approached from the east. The convoy deliberately crawled along at snail's pace to ensure the noise was kept to a minimum, and so we didn't raise a large dust cloud. As the explosions continued periodically, we were constantly crawling closer. Then some Apaches came along and led us. Using their superior night-vision capability, they identified and fired on a couple of Taliban positions on the way in.

By now the guys in the compound were down to their last few magazines of ammo for their personal weapons, although they still had some GPMG and .50 cal ammo left. The thermal imaging and CWS batteries had all but gone, meaning they were almost blind at night, which was a really serious situation to be in. It was hugely important to get these batteries to the PF as soon as possible. My day sack was crammed full of them for just that reason. Once we reached the edge of the town, the Danes were now really hesitant about entering. I tried to persuade them that it would be okay, but they didn't seem to be listening. My worry was that they would abort the attempt to get into the compound, which would leave my guys in the shit for longer.

In the end, I just said, 'You lot, follow me, and I'll clear the way.' I left my day sack in the lead vehicle and went forward, wearing just my NVG. I led them up the street towards the town square, clearing every side street and stall as I walked. We reached a point halfway up the bazaar and met up with some of the Afghan police, who luckily recognised me and lined the route to the town square. When I arrived at the square, Afghan police had secured it with the Royal Engineers we'd had flown in previously. I stuck two of the wagons down the western bazaar facing the wadi, put two on the northern one, and I had the rest of the convoy behind me. On the eastern side was the compound, so I said, 'Right, it's time to breathe a bit easier now.' I was talking to my boss on our radio and started walking towards the front gates to check they were open when suddenly I thought, shit, I've left the thermal imager batteries in the vehicle, and started to turn around to get them.

The next thing I knew, I was lying on my front, NVG hanging off my head, left arm outstretched, right arm under my body, weapon gone somewhere. It took me a few seconds to think, What the fuck am I doing on the floor? What happened? Did I get hit by a wagon? Then I tried to move my right arm, which was feeling a bit weird, and the top half moved and the bottom half didn't, it hurt like hell, too. I thought, oh fuck, someone's shot me. I instantly thought it was a sniper. There was a commotion going on around me, vehicles moving and people shouting. I thought, fuck – if it's a sniper, he's got me in his sights, so he's obviously got night vision, because it was a really dark night. I thought, I'm not going to move or he'll shoot me again.

I lay there for a couple of minutes, thinking, is he going to shoot me in the head or the body? I lay there for a while, waiting, accepting my fate, and then I started to get dizzy from loss of blood. Apparently, my guys told me afterwards, because I don't remember this, I got on the radio and said, 'Hello, Zero Alpha, this is Alpha November, you won't believe this. Some fucker just shot me!' I thought, I ought to get inside the compound by now, so I picked myself up, put my goggles back on and walked towards the front gate. I just left my weapon, I didn't know where it was and it didn't concern me at the time. No bugger came to help me, which really pissed me off. I walked into the badly lit medic's room. There was no electricity in the camp at night, so we all used head-torches to see. Our South African medic started to sort me out until eventually Tariq the doctor arrived and put some morphine into me.

After a while, the blokes started popping their heads in to

see if I was okay. The morphine had really started to kick in now, but I was barking orders at them about thermal imager batteries and ammo. I was just giving them orders, and apparently I became even funnier the more the morphine took hold of me. I remember one of the blokes, called Gav, popping his head in; again it was dark apart from the head-torch, and all I saw was this set of grinning white teeth like the Cheshire cat out of *Alice in Wonderland*. I said, 'Get out you fucker. Stop laughing at me.' By this time he knew my injury wasn't life-threatening and replied, 'I can't help it, Andy.'

Then the boss came in to check up on me and let me know what had happened. It turned out that one of the ANP had actually shot me. His excuse was that he had fallen asleep on his stag and because he'd heard the vehicles and the movement outside, he'd woken up suddenly and just loosed off a burst of bullets. One bullet had caught me in the arm and managed to shatter my bone into over sixty-odd pieces. Meanwhile Tariq had strapped up my arm, he had one of these bracelet-strap watches on and as he leaned across he pulled his hand back and he caught a load of my chest hair and ripped it out. I protested, 'As if it's not bad enough being shot, you've got to pluck me as well!' They were all pissing themselves laughing.

A casevac request was sent to Brigade HQ, but the RAF refused to fly, God bless 'em. They were going to leave me until the morning and I'd probably have lost my arm if I'd had to wait until then to be picked up. Luckily a passing American Black Hawk helicopter came to casevac me. He landed in the compound on NVG, among all the high-tension wires and cables, which was really quite impressive. He flew me to the field hospital at Camp Bastion, where they operated, and a few days later I was casevaced back to the UK.

For me the tour was over.

*Sergeant Tom Blakey, Pathfinder Platoon*

During Op Herrick IV, the Pathfinders were deployed to Musa Qala in Helmand Province. We took over the defence of the police station compound at the District Centre of the town, which had recently been attacked and nearly overrun. We were told we were only going to be there for one or two days. However, this quickly changed when 3 Para battle group became entrenched in Sangin and other areas, and we ended up being in Musa Qala for nearly two months.

When we arrived at the compound, there was evidence of the recent fighting everywhere, from bullet holes in the wall to RPG strikes and partially burnt-out buildings. As we were supposed to be there as a quick stop-gap, we had no defence stores, such as HESCO bastions (collapsible wire-mesh walls), razor wire or even sandbags. We also had no mortars, apart from a couple of hand-held 51mm mortars (which are mainly used for smoke or illumination) and only personal weapons and the GPMGs and .50 cals from our WMIK Land Rovers. This was certainly not a Forward Operating Base (FOB) as most soldiers know it. We also had only twenty-one bodies to do a task that needed a company plus.

Facilities were virtually nil at the compound, and conditions were pretty harsh. We had no washing facilities other than a hose pipe, toilets consisted of a couple of cut-off oil drums and Operational Ration Packs (ORP) were all we had to eat. In fact, we actually ran out of rations several times, as resupply was deemed to be too risky after a certain point. Pasta and rice was bought from a local bazaar and a couple of goats were butchered to fill the gaps. Just about everyone went down with diarrhoea and vomiting at some point, but there was no realistic option of extracting people.

After an initially quiet period, the Taliban attacked on a

nearly daily basis, ranging from sniper shoots to indirect fire to full-on frontal attacks. The first time they attacked was at last light, and I had just started to get some head-down in my hammock. I woke to the sound of firing, so grabbed the GPMG and a box of link from the front of my WMIK Land Rover, and ran up the steps to the top of the central building, which had a commanding view of the area we were being attacked from. I didn't have time to get dressed properly, and was wearing only flip flops, shorts and my helmet.

We quickly identified the firing points and I spotted a fighter in the prone position and hammered him with a good burst from the GPMG, shouting, 'Fucking get some!' as I did so. He pretty quickly ceased to be a threat.

During one attack, we had an American B1 bomber on station to provide Close Air Support (CAS). Once the JTAC had given the details of the target to the pilot, he lined up for attack and released the weapon, a thousand-pound JDAM bomb. I was running up the stairs of the main building to get into some cover as I could hear the bomb incoming, however something wasn't right. Instead of the noise of the bomb coming from a flank or passing overhead, I could hear it getting louder and louder, as if it was screaming towards us. As I got to the top of the stairs the bomb impacted no more than a hundred metres from where I stood. It had hit a mosque directly opposite our compound, and this massive explosion went off right in front of me, with bits of 'wriggly tin' and walls flying up in the air.

My immediate thoughts were that we were definitely going to have some friendly force casualties, given the proximity of the impact to our compound. After carrying out a head check, I was amazed to find everyone was OK! Luckily the blast was contained by the sturdy ten-foot compound walls, or we would all have been killed. It was later found that the JTAC was not at fault (i.e. he had given the correct target coordinates to the pilot), but there was a fault with the weapon guidance system.

*Corporal Hugh Keir, 3 Para*

Went to Bastion, had a couple of small ops there on the reaction force, and then we heard that the Pathfinders had become stuck in Musa Qala, which was further up the Sangin valley than Sangin, further north than we had ever been. We moved as a battle group: there was B Company plus extras, snipers – fucking loads of us, anyone who was free or who wasn't on an operation, plus the Canadian cavalry with their LAVs. It was a multi-national big op, because Musa Qala is such a difficult place to secure.

Our aim was to secure the area around Musa Qala and enable a detachment of Royal Irish, part of 16 Brigade, to insert into the district compound (DC) allowing the Pathfinders, who had been stuck there for ages, to extract. We were extracting and got ambushed by the Taliban on our side of the wadi, further up in the green zone. There were only a couple of them, while we were moving through a marijuana field, but it wasn't too bad. I can think of worse places to get ambushed. Smelled lovely.

My opening impression of Musa Qala began before we even got there. On the brief, because it was a battle group op, we had a lot of time to prep and because I was running the sniper team, I was in with the planning team – the officers and other commanders like myself. And you could tell by looking at the map, doing a map appreciation, that it was not a great place to be at all in terms of defending the DC. Not great, because it was a typical Afghan rabbit warren town, all of those buildings . . . there are no wide roads, it's all alleyways and every building joins onto the next building. You could, in theory, go from one end of the town through the centre to the other end of the town by going through buildings and not ever being exposed. You wouldn't have to go on a walkway, because it's all interconnected. There were very few open spaces, very easy to keep yourself concealed. The town was unoccupied, because of all the fighting that was going on there, and it was only occupied by Taliban and us.

So, on the map appreciation you're thinking, if I was going to pick any spot in this town not to occupy, or to pick the worst spot, I would pick that spot, the DC, the epicentre of a very built-up town which affords freedom of movement to the enemy and that's very difficult to get out of. Easy to get in, difficult to get out. And then when you saw it on the ground, you saw the same thing. What was more challenging when you saw it on the ground from the DC in the centre was that there were a lot of high buildings, two storeys, three storeys high, so in terms of providing good vantage points for the enemy to engage the district compound, there were lots of good spots, dark and shady areas, making it very difficult to spot well-disciplined fighters, which is why it took a battle group to get a couple of platoons of Royal Irish in there.

We left there after the op and went back to Bastion and were involved in a couple of other ops, but the Danes and the Irish were struggling to maintain that position in Musa Qala. The enemy presence there was becoming significant. It had been identified by the Taliban that we'd spread ourselves too thin. A bridge too far, if you like. As a battle group we were already stretched, we were holding Sangin at that point. It was not a small area; we needed a lot of troops there. Sangin, Kajaki, Now Zad, Gereshk and now Musa Qala – and Musa Qala was the most remote, the most extreme. That was identified by the Taliban as being a bit far out. They could maybe tell purely by the fact that there was not much activity from us there. There weren't many helicopters coming in, because they couldn't afford to take the risk. So they upped the level of intensity in their engagements on the compound. And the decision was made that it would be bolstered by Para Reg OC Major Jowett and Company Sergeant Major Joe Scrivener, who were brought in to establish us as a company and not just two platoons and the Danish.

Myself and Jared Cleary were the snipers and we had an Intelligence Sergeant, Freddie Kruyer, and a Light Electronic Warfare Team (LEWT), which had the technical equipment to listen into enemy radio communication on the walkie talkies. We were there to augment them. There was a sniper threat there, and two men had been killed by head shots. Our brief was to go in and counter-snipe.

The Danish had their own snipers there, but at that point they hadn't been able to identify the sniper. Because again, that problem of the town, it's a three-hundred-and-sixty-degree battle, you need lots of pairs of eyes looking in all those windows and doorways, all at the same time to spot one round coming from one area. If you don't see it the first time, the odds are stacked so heavily against you. There was technology to identify shooting points through sonic/sound signatures/triangulation, but we didn't have it at the time. It was just grassroots warfare.

We flew in at dusk and landed and Jared and I got shown to a room, in a mud hut, next to the ops room where all the radio equipment was and that was where we were going to sleep. We had only been in there fifteen minutes when the fucking whole place erupted with the sound of gunfire. It was dark at this point. We didn't know what the compound layout was yet, so we just grabbed our weapons and went running outside. There was tracer flying everywhere, incoming, outgoing, enemy RPGs going off, it was the most intense bit of fighting

I'd ever experienced. The first ten minutes there was nothing like anything else I'd done on that tour. Everyone was firing and it was multiple firing points from outside, multiple flanks being attacked. The Taliban knew what they were doing. It was a complex attack with multiple weapon systems and multiple flanks making it as difficult as possible for us to defend. It went on and on and on. It was so difficult to spot the enemy. It was craziness. Ten minutes, twenty minutes . . . and then it was done. We came back in and carried on unpacking our kit and getting a grip on what was going on. I thought, welcome to Musa Qala.

I think two or three days later, there was another dawn attack and Lance Corporal Hetherington got killed. What became apparent was that the place was difficult to defend. You had to be conservative with your ammunition, your food and water. You had to think about the detailed things, like your energy expenditure. Those attacks, seven or eight times a day, were constant, though it died off during the night. But it was daytime, because as soon as you'd finished one, you'd come in and get some water and maybe you'd have half an hour to chill out and then you'd be fucking back out again.

Because we were the only two snipers there, we didn't give ourselves any rest. Because if we went into a guard rotation and thought we'd go and man this or that sangar, it meant at some point we'd be at rest for six hours and there was no sniper cover for those hours. So it was agreed that we wouldn't go on the rotation, but for every engagement, we'd go out on every single one. So Jared and I, daytime to night-time, every single contact we were out doing it, every single one. It was one of those situations where you didn't realise the impact it had on you until later on, even after the tour. I had sort of switched off emotionally. It was that intense that you couldn't afford to pay any attention from an emotional point of view, you needed to stay focused, because if you started worrying about things, you weren't going to operate properly and you'd get killed pretty damn quickly. And so it just became repetitive. I couldn't sleep during the night, couldn't sleep during the day. It was a fucking nightmare going on and on.

It was almost a stalemate from the start. We weren't getting anywhere, the Taliban weren't getting anywhere. We were killing them, they were killing us, injuring us – not as significantly as we were doing to them, but they could replenish themselves, all we could do was sort of cover and keep going. If the Taliban did breach the walls and take the compound, we'd all aim to get to a building we called the Alamo, as it was the only place big enough to hold all of us. The last stand, really. Jared and I used it quite regularly, as it was the highest point and we could see the majority of the town.

From where I was positioned I saw a civilian, who was blind but determined to walk from outside the town to the centre, tapping the walls with his stick. There he was, with all this action going on, heading for an old bread shop, which wasn't even operating. Every day he'd walk in and walk out. Mad man. He was as old as the hills, must have been about ninety.

From that firing point, I saw two guys moving. They showed up as green in our NVG. I knew the area they were in from seeing it in the daytime and they were 665 metres from where I was. They were moving from a firing point across and they were hunkered down behind some old burnt-out vehicles. Suddenly one went out of view and the other stayed crouched down behind it. He came up slowly and then went back down.

I hadn't identified a weapon at this point. Then, as he came up the third time, I saw a weapon. He's looking to see where he's going next or what he's going to shoot at. I can just see his head and his shoulders; he's static behind the vehicle looking over. He thinks he's safe. Six-hundred-odd metres is probably the limit you want to be firing at during the night and I had only done it in training. I went on the radio and told them I was engaging. I shot and his rifle went flying and he dropped behind the car and he didn't move again. That was the end of that one.

Jared had a good one. The Taliban were six or seven hundred metres away; they thought we couldn't see them in the trees. We saw the torch in the trees, in night vision you'd see it plain as day, even if you couldn't see it with the naked eye. We knew that they were coming towards a wall, so I gave Jared the data for where I thought they'd try and cross. We could see the torch, see the tree, but not the body. We're waiting for him to come out of the trees and towards the wall. He creeps up the wall, we see the flash of a weapon, Jared shoots, the torch goes flying into the air, you could see the beam, can't see the body, just the torch light swirling through the air. I reckon Jared got that one.

The Alamo. That one lasted for two or three weeks. They tried to change their tactics and had the luxury of being able to do just that. We didn't, we were stuck in that fucking compound. They then started to incorporate mortars into their attacks. The LEWT told us that Chechen mercenaries were firing the Taliban's mortars. Their accuracy and the skill indicated that they weren't Afghans anyway. They were very, very good; every time their mortars would land inside the DC. At the same time we had small-arms attacks, Chinese rocket attacks, RPGs, and they were throwing grenades over the walls. I had put up a Welsh flag inside my room to get some shade, but it soon became full of shrapnel holes.

Their mortar attacks were four or five times a day, three or four to eight, nine rounds at a time. Over twelve days, we took fifty-five casualties and three dead. That includes the ANA. It was just fucking crazy and the noise was amazing. Because the mortars were having such a significant impact on us in terms of casualties, the OC took the decision that you weren't allowed outside the buildings at any time. And if you were a sentry in one of the sangars, you had to stay in hard cover. In the event of a mortar attack, no one would deploy out, only myself and Jared with the intention of trying to find the mortar team, or more likely the mortar spotter, a single person away from the mortar, forward observing the target and reporting back.

It became quite a nerve-racking experience. When the mortars came in, Jared and I had to go out into this shit and find this guy. It became a ritual that on the face of it didn't have much significance. We would get our kit, go into the ops room and ask where the direction was and the watchkeeper would give us an indication. From that I'd choose where myself and Jared would go. We'd then go into a doorway, which was sandbagged up to stop the shrapnel coming in. It was the last safe point for us before going out into the open ground. Every time would be like the last. It would be like we were having a last conversation. We'd say, 'Are you ready?' 'Yeah, I'm ready.' Of course, we're ready. But this was more of an acknowledgment that yes, we're fucking doing this, and we may not come back through this door alive.

We'd go sprinting out across the open ground. In some places it was up to a hundred and fifty metres to wherever we wanted to go. We'd go to areas in the DC or one of the other buildings there, or high ground, so we'd get a good vantage point. On one occasion, I went into the ops room and the watchkeeper gave us the detail and I decided I would go in the Alamo. I'd always tell the watchkeeper in there, who was manning the radio, where we were going to go. So Jared and I sprinted out, got to the Alamo and something clicked in my head. I don't know what made me say it, not a sixth sense, just something unusual in me, I said, 'Get ready for this; we're going to have a drama up here.'

Went up the steps and I was coming through a hole and looked in and literally a yard away at head height, I was staring at the blood and body of a Royal Irish Ranger, a private called Draiva, a Fijian guy. A huge lad and he was laying there. All his clothes were torn to shreds. He'd been hit by the shrapnel from a mortar round. Jared shouted over the side of the building for medics. Everyone in the camp shouted the same thing, so that the medics got the message.

We started treating Draiva and I was thinking, where do I start? We're team medic-trained, but only in basic battlefield first aid, you go through your A, B, C . . . Is his airway clear? Then, thank God, two medics came and got straight on to him. As they took over, I remember looking behind me at this rubble and Frenchie, one of the medics, asked is there anyone else up here and as there was only one sentry up there normally, we said there wasn't. The rubble had been a mud sentry box, almost like the shape of a telephone box with a window in it.

I looked again and could see a pair of boots sticking out and I thought, fuck! Went over and started throwing off the rubble and found it was another Ranger, Lance Corporal Muirhead. He looked okay, but everywhere he didn't have body armour was peppered with cuts and shrapnel. We got him out of the rubble and because of the threat of the mortars and how close the med centre was, we decided to get them off the roof and straight down there.

We got to the med centre with Muirhead and as we went down a corridor, Draiva was there with a blanket over him, dead. Captain Stacey, who was the doctor, and Frenchie started working on Muirhead. While they were dealing with him, trying to work out what his injuries were, mine and Jared's job was to clean him up to stop the long-term effects of septicaemia and to help identify further injuries. Everywhere he had body armour, he seemed okay. After the medics had managed to stabilise him, a chopper came in and extracted him, but he died two days later in Oman.

It was about that time that the mine strike went off at Kajaki and I heard that Stu, who had been my number two in Now Zad, had lost his leg.

What had being going on at the same time was a dialogue between Major Jowett and the Taliban commander and elders in the area. There was to be a ceasefire and we were to leave Musa Qala, but it was a question of how that was to be done. On the logistics side of it, they were reining back on what they were doing – they had started shipping things back to the UK, which meant the resources were getting even more limited, which meant launching a battle group operation to get us out was impossible. You couldn't do it and the Marines coming in couldn't do it, because they weren't ready, so how the fuck do we get out, because the RAF weren't coming in to get us either. A ceasefire came and we stopped. Still ready for it, still manning positions, but no fighting. This for me was shit, because I still had insomnia and wasn't sleeping.

It gave us an opportunity to buy some flour. The local bread maker came back into the town and by the grace of God, although I'm not religious, the bread shop was right outside the front gate. We'd buy bread from him every day and we started buying flour as well. But the bread was full of weevils. The blind man never stopped, he was still coming in daily, but this time he was getting his bread. He was more battle hardened than I was and not a scratch, not a bloody scratch on him.

We were still on the ground and the battle group are going home. The Marines were in and we're still there. This was month seven for me from the day I deployed to Helmand. Fuck me, it was demoralising. So these weeks were going on and on and I was thinking, are we going to stay here forever? Can't get out, can't get water in or food, and can't live on potatoes for the rest of my life. I don't want to live the rest of my life in Musa Qala.

I still had my insomnia and was totally knackered. We were told, one night, to get all the kit packed and ready to move by 4 a.m. We were going. Don't tell a fucking soul. Don't tell the police. Packed the kit away and at 4 a.m. the front gates were opened and what we called jingle trucks start filing into the compound. They were the old stereotypical Middle Eastern cattle trucks. They drove into camp with an Afghan driver and co-driver, who were both civvies. I thought, who the fuck are these people? What the fuck's going on here? But that was how what had become known as Easy Company was getting out; on the back of these trucks. All of us, the whole company climbed on the back of these trucks like fucking cattle. A commander would get in the front of each truck, so I got in the front and what was happening was, the jingle trucks were driving us out, through the town and into the desert, through the dasht (the area of desert nearest the green zone).

It was quite nerve-racking, I'm in this cab now with this Afghan driver. Behind him, in this cubby hole, sat behind leaning over his shoulders, is another Afghan – his co-driver. Suddenly, I wanted to sleep, it's 4 a.m., I'm in this wagon, I get a pistol out of my holster and I put it under my right thigh in case of any trouble. Put a seatbelt on, because they're maniac drivers. My eyes start closing . . . eight weeks of not sleeping was catching up on me. I'm thinking, I can't go to sleep here, I can't.

We drive out, going through the town, and at intervals there would be a male of fighting age, a Taliban, as a show of faith. It was fucking surreal, but at the same time we didn't care – how else could we get out? All these people had died, been injured, we were leaving there and handing it back. It was this or we didn't leave, ever. We're still holding Sangin, still in Kajaki, let's make the strategic decision to get out and live to fight another day. But it's the Taliban extracting us, not the RAF, not our own people. Bizarre, absolutely bizarre. It was about a four-, five-hour journey to the takeover point and as we approached, an Apache came down and flew straight past us at about fifteen feet. It's like we were back in control.

There were a couple of Chinooks sat there in the desert. Royal Marines out in the desert were securing the HLS. We got off the lorries and stood around there waiting to be extracted and having a cigarette. There was no elation, just the sense of silent relief.

We got back to Bastion. The significance of being extracted by the Taliban didn't really resonate with me at the time. We got briefed that we were going to stop in Bastion and told not to talk to anyone about the extraction. We got the choppers to Bastion and all I could think about was the food. We looked like we'd done seven months of fighting. There are rules in Bastion: don't go in the cookhouse unless you're clean shaven and without weapons. We went in with our weapons; we were ragged, gaunt as fuck and had lost loads of weight. Went to the hot plate and no one batted a fucking eye.

# 9

# AFGHANISTAN
# 2006

## Kajaki

*Corporal Stuart Pearson, 3 Para*

On 6 September 2006, I was five months into a six-month tour in Helmand and for the previous four weeks had been based up on the Kajaki hilltops overlooking the Kajaki dam. The dam provides most of the electricity to the residents of Helmand, so if this was to fall into Taliban hands, it would cause a whole lot of problems. The hill I was on was known as 'Normandy' and I had nine soldiers under my command. About 800 metres to my east was the hill known as 'Athens' and this was the main Control Point with either a sergeant or captain in command. We had comms to Athens, but they had the main radio that could communicate with our HQ in Bastion; they also had around twenty soldiers, including two medics.

At around 1200 hours that day, one of my lance corporals, Stu Hale, left Normandy with Jarhead and Farrel, to head for a ridgeline 700 metres to our south, in order to set up a possible snipe against an illegal VCP manned by the Taliban, which had been seen during the night of the 5th and early hours of the 6th. Approximately fifteen minutes into the patrol I heard a loud bang and, although I'd never heard one before, I knew it was a mine. I gathered a further three soldiers and with our webbing and rifles we made our way down to the patrol, which we found 300 metres to our south in a dried-out riverbed. I stopped short of the casualty, who I realised was Stu Hale.

Jarhead briefed me as to what had happened and how he had applied a tourniquet and had administered morphine, both of which had been marked on Stu's face. I relayed what had happened to Athens via Normandy. We were quickly joined by a group of soldiers from Athens, including two medics, commanded by Corporal Mark Wright. I briefed Mark as to what was going on and we discussed what we felt we needed to do. He requested a helicopter with a winch; this was denied, for some reason. I knew I had to look for a possible HLS; I found an area and nominated a couple of soldiers to clear the path to the HLS. Once this was done, I then decided to clear a path to a secondary HLS, in case the first wasn't what the helicopter pilot wanted.

As I made my way back along what I thought was a cleared path, to Stu Hale, I stood on a mine and felt myself being flung up in the air. As I landed, I knew exactly what I had done, so lifted my left leg to see what the damage was and saw it was gone around ankle height as I still had the top lace of my boot attached to the remainder of my leg. I told everyone that no one was to move, but Andy Barlow came running over to me and I threw him a tourniquet from my medical pouch, so while he was working on my leg, I stabbed an ampoule of morphine into myself: although it never hurt, I knew it wouldn't be long until it did. Mark Wright and a medic, Alec Craig, came running over to me; Mark to get my details to relay to Athens and Alec to carry on with first aid.

I was told a helicopter would be with us soon, but the helicopter sent was a Chinook and Mark was shouting into the radio saying that's not what we wanted, as it didn't have a winch, but it came anyway. It landed around fifty metres from us, but the medics instructed it to come nearer. While this was happening, a third mine went off. This severely injured Mark, who was lying over me, protecting me from the downwash of the Chinook. He had injuries to his left arm, chest, neck and face; it also blasted my remaining right leg and hit Alec Craig in the chest. Tug Hartley, our medic, then made his way to Mark to administer much-needed first aid. Even though he was badly wounded, Mark was keeping us going, reassuring us.

While all this was happening, someone threw me a bottle of water, which I failed to catch. Andy Barlow, who was beside me, got up to get it, but stood straight on a mine and lost his left leg. This explosion injured Mark further and also my right leg again. Tug and Dave Prosser took some of it in the chest, too.

Amidst all this chaos, it turned out to be Dave Prosser's birthday, so Tug got everyone singing 'Happy Birthday' to him! Although this was a comical moment, it also gave Tug time to look around at all of us to see if we were all still 'with it' and responsive.

After what seemed an eternity, two American Black Hawks were released from Kandahar for us and these came in one at a time. We were winched up and Mark, who was the most severely wounded, and the rest of us were flown a mile or so to meet up with a Chinook, which had a MERT (Medical Emergency Response Team) on it with paramedics and numerous medical aids. I thought, thank fuck that's over. Then looked at Mark and the medics were giving him CPR, but it didn't register with me that he was so catastrophically injured. Later, when I came round, I looked again and Mark had actually died and had been placed in a body bag.

I can't remember much until ten days later in ICU in Selly Oak hospital in Birmingham.

In ICU I had numerous operations, mostly to save my badly injured right leg. After two weeks I was moved upstairs to the ward S4, where I stayed for another five weeks undergoing skin grafts. I was then transferred to Headley Court rehabilitation centre to start my long road to recovery.

*Lance Corporal Tug Hartley, Royal Army Medical Corps, 23 Air Assault Medical Squadron*

On 6 September 2006, I was stationed at one of the Kajaki outposts with 3 Para Mortars and Support Company. I was there to provide medical cover in case anything went wrong. Previously to that, I had been in Afghanistan since around April time and then I was spearheaded out of Afghan to go to Lebanon for the refugee crisis with Special Air Service. Came back from Lebanon, thought my desert tours were over, so I decided to marry my fiancée. We got married on a Saturday, honeymoon on the Sunday, and I got a phone call on Wednesday and deployed back to Afghan on the Friday.

I was sent to Kajaki. Being honest, I believed it was a bit of a resting post. My sergeant major trying to screw the nut for me, knowing that I'd worked my tits off previously while I was out in Afghanistan, being in Sangin, Gereshk and other areas. So he thought he'd send me down to Kajaki for a bit of R&R, because there wasn't much happening.

While I was there previous to 6 September, nothing much happened. We were looking down on the Taliban and we were pretty sound. The hardest thing for me was living with the notorious sex pests of 3 Para Mortars, but they were good guys.

I used to get up every morning at ten-thirty and go with a couple of boys, Lee and Nash and walk down to the dam, where we'd wash a bit of doby (laundry), bit of a swim and wash in the river. But for some reason, there was something inside that told me not to go that day. Obviously being a medic, I took a hail of abuse for being a minger and not bothering to wash, but luckily I didn't, because around eleven o'clock, Mark Wright came running into my little basher. There'd been a mine strike on the other hill. I remember grabbing my T-shirt, grabbing my webbing, med-kit and rifle and we set off.

It was about a k and a half down off our mountain and up their hill. Going up that hill was probably the most physical and demanding thing I've ever done. I did fall behind the rest of the pack. They were like machines knowing that one of their blokes was injured, but I was carrying a med Bergen, weighing about seventy pounds, rifle and webbing as well. I managed to keep up, though.

Then we went down the back of their hill and as we entered the wadi at the bottom, some of the guys had already set up cordons and safe areas. I could see Stu Hale had lost his leg and got damage to one of his fingers. Jarhead, one of the Para Reg Toms, did an excellent job with the tourniquets and, in my belief saved Stu Hale's life with his treatment. We went into the minefield, assessing Stu – it didn't look that serious: amputation of the finger and leg and I believe, a fracture to his good leg as well. Administered morphine to him, re-attached the tourniquets and I put some dressings on him.

The guys from 3 Para were amazing: Jay Davies, Paul Brown, Chris Conn – they were all assisting me and did a real good job. Meanwhile Mark Wright, Stu Pearson and Jarhead and the others were trying to make a plan. I was trying to get a cannula into Stu's arm to get some fluids into him and as I struggled to find a vein, I remember looking around and my experience of being a Sapper, I served in the Royal Engineers for six years, sprang into action and I saw anti-personnel mines some way on the surface, some partially dug in.

As I composed myself and continued with the treatment of

Stu, my good friend Alex Craig came running down the hill to assist me. What I wasn't aware of at the time was that Alex had heard the call on the radio with the Zap (army personal indentification) number for Stu, beginning with Hotel Alpha – Alex naturally thought it was myself, my last name being Hartley, and actually ran through a known minefield into an unknown minefield to assist us. To be honest, it was a weight lifted off my shoulders – once he came in, it was like having a wing man.

Between me and Alex, we got Stu all singing and dancing to the point I'd got a report written up and everything, got oxygen on him – the report was stuffed down the front of my shorts – and we were literally just waiting for a helicopter with a winch to come, because we'd trained in Oman prior to deployment with winches. That's what we thought we were going to get.

Time went on and more people started to notice the threat of the other mines. Between myself and Mark, we decided it would be best to move Stu to a safe location where we could easily winch him out with the downdraft not causing any further problems. Stu Pearson got a couple of guys to clear a safe path through. Took a while in the blistering heat, but we plodded away – there was no fear or emotion showing, the guys just got on with the job. Eventually, we were cleared and Stu Pearson walked back to make sure it was all safe and myself and some stretcher bearers picked up the stretcher and carried it across to where we believed was the safe location.

Once we got to the safe location, Mark and I decided that myself and four others would stay to load Stu Hale onto the winch and everyone else should pull out. A lot of the guys walked straight back across the marked path and Stu Pearson was the very last man to go across it and he got about ten to twenty metres away from us and he just detonated on the path.

As Stu detonated, I remember looking and thinking, I just walked from there! Alex Craig and Mark Wright jumped straight in to help Stu. I remember shouting across, 'Alex, do you need me to help?' He told me to stay where I was and he would manage Stu Pearson. Again, it worked – everything went well. Young Andy Barlow came down, a Fusilier kid started to give us assistance as well – it wasn't a bad situation. We had two guys who'd lost legs, but it wasn't the first time we'd dealt with these kinds of things. It was okay, it was alright, both guys were stable.

Time dragged on. I was shouting to Mark, 'Where is this helicopter?' We kept getting told, ten minutes . . . ten minutes . . . ten minutes . . . ten minutes turned into thirty minutes and thirty minutes turned into hours and hours just went on and on. Eventually, we could hear a helicopter in the distance – it was a big sigh of relief knowing that people were coming to assist us and hopefully we would get these guys out of there. As it came closer and closer, we started to realise it was a Chinook helicopter, not a Lynx. My actual perception was that it was the MERT, the Medical Emergency Response Team that was going to land and send some doctors in, or even bring air tour to clear a path.

The Chinook flew in over the top of us and round the back of the hill then came in a second time, came in low. It was seventy metres to my south, south-east when it started to touch down, landed on its back wheel and ramps. The load master came to the door and started waving to us to come on. I was standing up giving him the middle finger, 'Not a fucking chance!' Seeing two of the boys had got blown up, I'm not risking carrying the two casualties seventy, seventy-five metres through a minefield for anybody.

We started signalling about the mines as Will and I were doing the YMCA dance – the loader didn't have a clue and eventually, the helicopter took off. I don't know why, throughout my entire military career and working with the airborne forces, Chinooks have always nose-dived and gone forward. For some reason, this Chinook sort of bucked off over the top of us . . . a brown out, I couldn't see anything – eyes and mouth full of sand and dust. It turned into a scene from *Star Wars*, people were moving around protecting themselves from the dust and mines were going off.

Then I remember lifting my head up, covering Stu Hale and looking over to where Stu Pearson was and seeing a blast go off around waist height. And then it all went quiet. The dust settled and the helicopter disappeared. I remember seeing Alex and the colour had gone out of his skin, small wounds across his chest. I looked at Mark and he had a severe injury to his torso and a small injury to his face. I could see Stu Pearson had been hit again.

The shouting and screaming started then. People begging for help . . . I remember thinking, it's ten metres away, I can't go across there – it was the day before my son's first birthday. I remember looking down and seeing my rifle and bending down and feeling the coldness. The part of the rifle between the trigger housing and the magazine housing and for a split second, I was going to execute Alex Craig, Mark Wright, Stu Pearson . . . it was a split second, but it seemed like an eternity to make the decision, thankfully I never did. Stu Hale had got my med Bergen under his leg trying to elevate it. I remember grabbing it and thinking, fuck it, I've got to do something.

I threw it, it didn't go bang, so I jumped on it and slid it out from underneath my feet and I repeated this trying to cross the minefield to get to where they were. I remember falling off it at one point and everyone shitting themselves, nobody more than me. I stopped about halfway and was looking forward to where Stu, Alex and Mark were and looking back to where the stretcher bearers and Stu Hale were, thinking, what the hell am I doing? It's my birthday tomorrow, it's my son's birthday tomorrow, and I'm crossing a minefield in the middle of Afghan. Tempting fate, if I had gone backwards, I would have got hit. If I went forward, I was probably going to get hit, but I had to risk it for the boys. I pulled it out again and threw it; nothing went bang, so I jumped on it. I was about a metre, metre and half away.

Young Andy Barlow, the Fusilier kid, he was in there trying to give first aid. His head had gone; he had never seen anything like it. Someone from somewhere came with some water and threw it to Andy, and he caught it. Then he was thrown a second bottle, but he missed it and when he turned to pick it up, he stepped on a mine. Again that mine hit Mark – Alex had been pulled out of the minefield by then – and it hit Stu for a third time. It lifted me up and dumped me on my arse. Again a brown out, couldn't see anything and I thought, this is it, this is what it feels like to be dead. It's not that bad, there's no pain or anything just silence . . . not as bad as people make out. And all of a sudden, I had a burning pain in my chest and I sucked in a big breath and it hurt like fuck. And I knew I was alive.

I remember looking down and I was bleeding heavily from my left shoulder, my chest was killing me. But I was alive. At that point, I accepted that I was going to die and when you accept that you're going to die, things get easier for you. I could easily move around, it made me free. Because obviously, prior to that all I had was fear, but now I was free because I knew I was going to die. But if I was going to die, I was going to die doing the best I could for the other guys. I picked up my med Bergen and walked the remainder of the way.

Went straight to Mark, he was hammered – he'd took by far the most direct hits. Threw a tourniquet to Andy, told him how to put it on Mark. Gave Stu more morphine, checked his tourniquet. Grabbed a large bandage to try and dress the wound on Mark's chest – the bandage was too small but that was the largest I had, so I took my T-shirt off and had to pack it into the wound and tie a bandage around it. His arm was barely hanging on, from just above the wrist, the inside of his bicep, tricep had been blown away. His face was damaged, teeth partially gone, burns down his throat. I remember Andy screaming that the morphine wasn't working. Mark laughing and telling me I was going to get a VC for being crazy and crossing a minefield. Stu was calling Irn-bru, Irn-bru and morphine, that's all he wanted.

Once I got to him, we were in a makeshift triangular shape – it was bizarre how everyone had landed. Head by someone's feet and then head by someone's feet into a triangle and I was in the middle with Mark's body slouched up against my knees. Time dragged, time went on. I kept shouting, 'Where's this helicopter?' Ten minutes, ten minutes . . . ten minutes never came. Seemed like a lifetime, with the pain in my chest and the blood I was losing from my arm and my shoulder. Kept wanting to pass out and every time I wanted to pass out, the boys who had left Stuart Hale kept shouting, stimulating me to keep me awake.

Snoop, I think it was, came halfway down the hill – he was asking for the Zap numbers again, I was trying to shout the Zap numbers to him, but the burn in the chest was really, really hard. He kept asking me to repeat myself, 'Say it again, say it again.' Till the point where I got frustrated and ended up shouting, 'If the helicopter doesn't come soon, we're all going to die.' But all my shouting got me nowhere.

Time, again, seemed to go on and on. Mark said some inspirational things, you wouldn't believe someone with that severity of injuries could come up with it . . . but he did it, to keep everyone else stimulated and keep everybody else awake. Dave Prosser, the young lad, spoke with me – he'd already come in to give us some help and he'd caught a little bit on the chest earlier on. He went on about it being his birthday, so I had to get the boys to sing 'Happy Birthday' to Dave, for me to check people's levels of consciousness. And then Mark was saying about getting married, so we talked about him getting married to Gillian: what it cost, will she still recognise him, things like that. Stu Pearson was shouting that he wanted more morphine. It got to a point where I'd run out of morphine, I'd run out of medical kit. There were no tourniquets; I'd run out of everything. Mark started to complain he was thirsty, but I'd got nothing. The water that had been thrown in had been blown up with Andy.

I remember looking down and seeing an old bag of fluids, saline that was used to put into people. It's not the best thing to drink, but I moistened his lips a bit, got rid of some of the sand and shit inside his mouth. I remember cutting the corner off and pouring it into his mouth. As I watched it pour into his mouth, I watched it come out the side of his neck. I think he saw my face. He saw my reaction and I think he knew. But he didn't give in. He kept cracking on with his jokes, making inspirational comments and things – keeping everybody motivated.

Eventually we were told there was a helicopter coming in ten minutes again. Within two minutes we could hear the rotor blades of a Black Hawk coming in. There were two of them; again they flew past us and around the hill. I was shouting at the hill, to the guys that were in communication with them, telling them to look for the fat bloke in the blue shorts, meaning myself. Then I started signalling to them which casualties needed to go first.

The Black Hawk came in, and one of the Pararescuemen (PJs), Cameron Highstead, American Air Force, fast roped down with a six-foot stretcher. Everyone was shouting at him: 'It's a minefield, it's a minefield.' And he just gave us a thumbs up. He said he was sorry he didn't have a stretcher, but he had a strop. He couldn't get Mark in the strop. So he ran across and I believe he took Stu Hale first. Then he came down with a stretcher and started to take the boys out. Mark grabbed my hand, saying to me, 'If I die, please tell me Mum, Dad and Gillian that I love them. Tell my uncle, who is Regiment Sergeant Major in Special Air Service; tell them I died being a good soldier, and a good paratrooper.'

He made me promise. I told him not to be silly, I was going to see him again and he made me promise him I would come and see him back at Bastion. So I did. As they winched him up, I remember our hands separating as he got hoisted in the air and as he got up into the air, I remember being rained on with his blood.

Everyone else got taken out of the minefield, me being the last one there. There were bits of med kit, bits of clothing, and a rifle; there was a day sack – all sorts of shit lying around. I was thinking to myself, I'm still going to die. I'm lying there trying to cover up as much bits of equipment as I could to stop the downdraft of the helicopter from blowing any of it onto a mine.

It got the point where the strop came down for me and I put my arms through it, thinking, when they lift me up, I'm going to be on a mine and I'm going to bring this helicopter down with me, but at least I knew I'd done my best.

Thankfully as I went up, nothing went off. I remember getting into the back of the Black Hawk; some of the boys were in there. Smudge was slumped against the side door, I remember walking over to him, sat down beside him and he gave me a bottle of frozen water that the PJs had given him. We just put our arms around each other and no one spoke, no one said a word. I remember a tear rolling down my cheek. Tears rolling down the other boys' cheeks. Still, no one said a word.

Got back to the HLS and the boys all got off. I needed to go back up the hill to sort my kit out, make sure everybody was okay. Went to climb in the back of a stripped-down Land Rover and as I grabbed onto the frame to pull myself, blood squirted out some of the little holes that I had, but nothing massive. Had an adrenalin downer, threw my guts up. I remember getting picked up by the scruff of my neck and getting thrown on the Black Hawk with this bloke shouting to the guys to take me to Bastion.

When I landed, it was very, very surreal. I don't think they were aware there was another helicopter coming in. I remember getting off the Black Hawk and getting an oxygen mask on. I was burnt, I was dirty, I was bleeding. I remember there was an ambulance driving away from the HLS and it stopped and it came back. A guy jumped out the front, he happened to be one of my best friends at the time, Gary Lawrence. One of the best medics I've ever known or worked with. He scooped me up, put me in the back of the ambulance and drove me to the field hospital. He didn't take me to the ambulance entrance; he took me to the front entrance. There was like a big gang of people; there'd been another incident in Musa Qala and Sangin the same day, same time. There were all these officers and senior NCOs stood there in a big gang and as I walked, it was like the waves parted. And no one spoke to me; they just looked at me with disbelief. They let me walk straight through.

I walked into the hospital and in my hand I had a T-shirt that I had pulled from the minefield. The reason I had pulled it from the minefield was that the wings on the T-shirt were different from what the Para Reg wore. I knew it belonged to Alex Craig, one of my best friends who'd come to assist me on the minefield. I walked to the ward and I could hear Alex screaming. As I walked in, they were putting a chest drain into him and I pushed them all away and I gave him his T-shirt. He just threw his arms around me; I put my arms around him. Again without saying a word, we shed a few tears.

I walked across to the other ward to see Stu Pearson lying there. He'd been made unconscious, tubes hanging out of him. There was a bed sheeted off and I could hear someone shouting and screaming. I pulled the curtain back and it was Dave Prosser. Dave was shouting, 'He's dead, he's dead.' I said, 'Who's dead?' He said, 'Mark's dead.'

That feeling left me empty. Like my whole life had been sucked out of me. If anyone was going to die that day, it was going to be me. But it wasn't: I was alive and Mark was dead. I promised him I'd see him back at Bastion. I had failed my promise.

I was admitted to the hospital and treated for my wounds. Nothing too serious. One of the medics who I'd served with, Steven Parsons, came into see me. He explained the reason why no one had spoken to me when I walked in. It was because it had come across the radio that someone had died; they believed it was one of the medics. Alex Craig had come in, thirty, forty minutes before me, so everyone had presumed I was dead. So when I walked in, they all thought they had seen a ghost.

But it was Mark who was dead. He'd gone unconscious on the Black Hawk and they revived him. And once he was on the Chinook with MERT, he asked if everyone was on. Doctors said yes. And he just closed his eyes. He timed his death to perfection. He made sure everyone was saved.

It's my belief and without doubt that Mark Wright is by far one of the most heroic men I've ever served with. His determination, his selfless sacrifice, his sense of humour is what kept everybody else alive that day.

Alex Craig risked his life to come into a minefield to assist me. Unbelievable. Jarhead saved Stu Hale's life, no doubt about it. Andy Barlow, an eighteen-year-old drummer from the Fusiliers, came into that minefield knowing the risks that were there, still came into assist. Stu Pearson and the boys that cleared the route knew what might happen, but still did it.

We've always had banter about the Crap Hats and whatever else, but there was none that day. As the Paras say, every man is an emperor. Every man who was in Kajaki was an emperor that day and more people should have been recognised for the service that they gave. Because of Mark's leadership and dedication and heroism, I wanted to make true the promise that I made him that I'd see him back at Bastion. So when the Chinook came in to take the boys back to the UK and take Mark's coffin back, I spoke to a few friends and pulled a few strings and managed to ride in the ambulance with Mark's body to the Chinook for the ramp parade.

I remember lifting the lid of the coffin and putting my hand on his chest and thanking him. It was a day I will never ever forget for many, many reasons. I know I probably sound a little bit emotional right now telling it, but I'm not emotional thinking of the badness, the horror or anything like that. I'm emotional because of the heroism, the dedication, brotherhood and bond that was formed that day. I thank all of them for what I witnessed, what they demonstrated, what I saw. Young boys became men in that minefield and men became legends in that minefield and that will live with me forever. Absolutely forever. I was and I am 25067964, Corporal Hartley P, Royal Army Medical Corps, 23 Air Assault Medical Squadron, George Medal recipient.

Mark received the George Cross posthumously and his citation read: 'Despite this horrific situation and the serious injuries he had himself sustained, Cpl Wright continued to command and control the incident. He remained conscious for the majority of the time, continually shouting encouragement to those around, maintaining morale and calm amongst the many wounded men.'


*Colonel Peter Hill, Royal Army Medical Corps*

I specialised in orthopaedic surgery practising at Frimley Park Hospital and had done very little in the way of any military operational tours other than six months on the green line in Cyprus and a three-month period just prior to going to Frimley as part of the military hospital up in Basra during the second Gulf War. It therefore came as rather a surprise to be called, whilst in the States, to be told by my boss in military ortho-paedics, 'Peter, I need you to be in Afghanistan in two weeks' time.'

My first impression on arriving in Afghanistan was that it was a very mountainous country and, of course, the heat was oppressive during the middle of the day. I flew from Kabul to Helmand province in a C130 Hercules to Camp Bastian. Camp Bastian in those days was a very rudimentary camp with minimal perimeter fence and was a collection of canvas build-ings and with very much an expeditionary type of set up. I was familiar with the hospital organisation as it was identical to the one I had experienced in Basra. There was a long, central spine concrete base and off this were the wards.

I didn't know the 16 personnel Med Reg, but I was soon made to feel at home. The general surgeon was in the TA and some of the anaesthetists I had met earlier on in my career when we were in training. The orthopaedic surgeon, who I was replacing, had left the day before. Not surprisingly his depart-ure had been delayed, due to his replacement injuring himself and having to find me to come out at short notice. Our accommodation was fairly rudimentary, but quite comfortable: we had six men to a pod and we all had our individual cots surrounded with mosquito nets. Luckily we had proper toilets and showers and didn't have to put up with field latrines or trenches. Although it was hot, the air was dry and when you sweated, you did cool down. Food was very good as it always tends to be, as morale is always maintained with having a full belly and adequate provisions.

There was the usual BFBS entertainment package with radio and television, although at this time in Camp Bastian Wi-Fi did not exist, although there was a computer terminal in the hospital which allowed you to send emails back to the UK.

We didn't really know how busy we were going to be. John Reid, the Secretary of State for Defence, had said we were going to go into Afghanistan, not a shot would be fired. And indeed when I arrived at the hospital it had been very quiet, although it had only just opened. There was a lot of downtime, which was spent going to the gym, reading books, playing volleyball and watching films in the evening. The British troops were stationed in various towns in what was known as the green zone, which was the irrigated land either side of the Helmand River. Camp Bastian was fairly inaccessible by road and the main form of transport was by helicopter and fixed-wing aircraft. At this time, Camp Bastian didn't have a dedicated airfield and had just a dirt strip, which meant the only aircraft that could land were the C130s.

I soon got into a routine of phys in the morning, breakfast, going to the hospital checking my equipment and waiting for patients to arrive. A lot of the patients were homegrown from people who'd sprained their ankles and hurt their thumbs playing volleyball, so we didn't have a lot in the way of casualties in my first couple of weeks. Having said there were no insects, we did have the odd camel spider, which were quite scary but harmless. On one occasion, one entered our accommodation, but was quickly dispatched by my general surgical colleague with his boot.

The entrance to the hospital was an A&E-type department, where casualties were initially assessed. Those that were seriously injured were taken straight through to the operating theatre, which was in the next tent and consisted of a McVickers table, the standard military operating table that was very uncomfortable and difficult to use. It had been swapped for a modern operating table from a mobile operating theatre that we also had attached to the hospital. This was a big white elephant and had been procured at great cost, but was entirely useless for use in the desert environment. The air-conditioning didn't work and there was no room inside to manoeuvre, but it did have an operating table. The anaesthetic equipment was a standard military anaesthetic machine, which was very robust and mobile. Surgical implements you would expect to use in any modern hospital and these were sterilised on site, in the building next door, by the operating theatre technicians. We had scrub nurses as you would do in a normal hospital and theatre technicians.

Further along the spine of the hospital there were the wards, administration cell, physiotherapy department and an X-ray department. X-rays were fairly rudimentary and had to be taken using photographic film and then developed in a dark room. This was all very low tech but effective and in subsequent years would be replaced by electronic X-ray machines, which could produce images instantaneously.

Reflecting back on my time in Afghanistan in 2006, we all worked together as a very close-knit unit and the camaraderie was excellent.

Various cases stand out: there was a little boy I inherited

from the previous orthopaedic surgeon; he was the son of a local policeman. He had been injured, I can't remember precisely how, but it was probably an improvised explosive device. He had sustained an injury to his foot. He had lost quite a large amount of skin around his heel and this was being allowed to heal. He required a lot of visits to theatre to clean the wound and dress it. We made a rudimentary section dressing to encourage healing and placed a skin graft over the wound, which healed up successfully. He must've been in the hospital for about five weeks while we treated him and his father used to visit once a week. During this period he learned some rudimentary English. My lasting memory of him is him riding off into the distance with his dad on the back of his motorbike with a large watermelon balanced between them.

As a military hospital we weren't meant to treat locals, although there was a very 'hearts and minds' aspect to what we did. There was quite a strict protocol for who could or could not be treated in the hospital. The local Afghan police and soldiers were treated along with the occasional child, especially if they had been injured by coalition forces. The treatment of the locals often posed problems, because we couldn't provide the same standard of treatment as we could have done in the UK. This meant you had to adopt a pragmatic attitude to the injuries where you might try and preserve a limb in a UK soldier, but you may end up amputating the limb of an Afghan; purely because local medical facilities were very limited and you needed to provide a definitive operation that would not require further treatment. There was a limb-fitting centre in the local town where people could be offered a prosthetic.

In 2006, the evacuation chain for coalition forces was quite long-winded and this posed some problems in getting the severely injured UK troops back to the UK. It involved a trip on a Hercules helicopter back to either Kandahar or Kabul, and then a further trip back to the UK in a jet aircraft. Theoretically it was possible to have an injured soldier in Camp Bastian and then back in Birmingham, the receiving hospital, within twenty-four hours. As time progressed, the number of casualties increased; this was partly because what was known as the 'fighting season' had begun. Although we were meant to be controlling the heroin crop, once the poppies had been harvested, the locals were then available to fight. Also, during the period of Ramadan it was much quieter.

Casualties tended to arrive every two to three days, we would have a busy spell and then the workload would quieten off. The nature of military wounds is that they are debrided, cleaned but never closed and therefore the patient arriving on one day would need subsequent days of surgery and debridement in order to maintain a clean wound. With two surgeons and a couple of anaesthetists, there was more than enough work to keep us busy, but we always managed to sleep through the night and wake refreshed in the morning.

We did have one particular very busy forty-eight-hour period when a group of Paras were caught in a legacy minefield left over by the Russians near the Kajaki dam. I think we had five seriously injured patients . . . we had a variety of injuries. Some of the soldiers had trodden on land mines, which had resulted in traumatic amputations of the leg. The people standing near them were then peppered in shrapnel and flesh. We were lucky that the medics on the ground were especially good and well-trained and because of their early actions a lot of patients who may have succumbed within the first hour were saved.

When the soldiers were injured, they were collected by their Medical Emergency Response Team (MERT) and on the whole they were brought to hospital within an hour of injury. The MERT consisted of an anaesthetist and the paramedic team. Very seriously injured patients could be anaesthetised on the aircraft, which preserved their airways and that was the best way of giving them adequate analgesia. I'd never seen these kinds of injuries before, but soon got used to treating them. For the blast and land-mine injuries, the tissue was often flailed away from the underlying bone and the amazing thing was the amount of dirt and debris and stones driven up into the tissues which had to be removed. I was lucky that I was working with a very experienced vascular surgeon, who had the skills to stop the bleeding, if required. For the UK troops we try to preserve as much length as possible and allow the surgeons back in Birmingham to decide how high an amputation should be. With the locals, we were much more aggressive and amputated back to clean tissue, as we knew then the wound would heal.

I remember a trooper who was very severely burnt. He had seventy-per-cent burns to his body, including his arms and legs. One area that wasn't burnt was around his head, where his helmet was, and around his chest, where his body armour was. The skin when burnt becomes like leather and has to be incised to allow the swelling to be released, otherwise the underlying muscle dies. The burnt skin is called eschar and the operation to relieve it is an escharotomy. His arms and hands were so severely burnt that pulling off the skin was almost like pulling off a piece of clothing, revealing a mixture of pink and white patches underneath. The white patches were where the skin was completely dead and the pink patches where it was still living. He was very quickly flown back to the UK after we had done all we could.

The cases that required temporary fixation of the fracture required a device called an external fixator. This is when we screw pins into the bone and then attach the pins with a bar and tighten up the bolts, and this allows the fracture to be held rigidly. Most fractures could be treated with a plaster of Paris and more complex ones with surrounding soft-tissue injury, such as the burns patients I just described, were best treated with the external fixator. Burns patients had to be dressed with a special burns dressing, which consisted of an antiseptic cream called Flamazine surrounded by a gel net and Gamgee dressing. Following the dressing, the patients often looked like the Michelin man from the tyre advert.

Two years after returning from Afghanistan, I saw a Channel 4 documentary on this trooper and it made me reflect on what we did, as he was walking normally and had settled down and married his fiancée, despite his life-changing, disfiguring injuries. It seemed to make it all worthwhile what we were doing. Other patients who stand out were a group of five children who were all burnt when they threw a bomb into a campfire, which then exploded. I remember them arriving. The local doctor had painted them all in gentian violet, so we had these bright purple children. They took up a considerable amount of time as they required burns dressings twice a day for about two weeks and eventually we managed to discharge them to a humanitarian hospital in Lashkar Gah.

Another notable patient was an Afghan female who had half of her face blown away by a bomb which landed on her house. She attended the hospital, but there was really nothing we could do for her as her injuries must've been many weeks old and even in the UK her treatment would have been a challenge. I think her family was after blood money, which was duly paid, and then she disappeared, but I wondered what happened to her. We had a couple of Afghan policeman who decided to shoot themselves in the foot to get out of their military service. Somehow they managed to have food brought to them on the ward and they had bread provided that was full of cannabis and made them as high as a kite, which made them amusing from the ward discipline point of view.

The other notable case was a young corporal who was injured

by an improvised explosive device. The medics on the ground gave him a surgical airway and he was brought to the hospital. He appeared to have brain damage and both his legs were severely injured with fractures below the knees and debris and mud blasted up into the thighs. We had to do above-the-knee amputations on him and also remove his spleen due to internal bleeding. He illustrated a problem that we had in that we didn't have any way of imaging what was going on inside the brain. In 2006 we required a CT scanner and this was only available at Kandahar and he had to be evacuated there for a brain scan. He was subsequently flown to the UK and survived his injuries.

We had a couple of patients who had severe brain injuries and a soldier who was shot through the head and arrived in the emergency department with his brain exposed. Unfortunately, he passed away. We had another soldier who had a penetrating head injury and he had to be flown to Pakistan for scanning and treatment there.

A few patients with chest trauma required a thoracotomy, where the chest is opened to try and stop the bleeding. We had a couple of cases of what is known as clamshell thoracotomies, where the whole chest is opened up from the front and also the abdomen in order to control the major blood vessel, the aorta, as it leaves the heart. This is fairly heroic surgery and not something I had experienced in the UK. In my three months there, I think we must have performed clamshell thoracotomies on two occasions, but neither time did the patient survive.

I left Afghanistan in the autumn of 2006. Overall it was a very positive experience and a pleasure to work in such a close-knit team, despite the austere environment; we managed to provide a high level of care and maintain our own health and the workload was not too heavy apart from the odd spike. It was manageable.

I returned to Afghanistan on three other occasions in 2009,

2012 and 2014. In 2014, I went out as the Medical Director mentoring the Afghan surgeons in the local hospital. The facilities were very rudimentary, but in true Afghan style, we managed to get on and provide a reasonable standard of care for their own soldiers. I left the army in the summer of 2016 having soldiered for twenty-nine years since I started as a medical cadet. I can always remember my tour in 2006 as being the most memorable and the most satisfying. We had a small group of people who provided an excellent standard of care, which we could be rightly proud of, and this was the time before the Taliban insurgency was at its height in Helmand province.

Once back in the UK, I was privileged to work at Headley Court, which was the Defence Medical Rehabilitation Centre near Leatherhead, and often saw and treated patients in the recovery phase following their life-changing injuries, a few of whom I had been the surgeon first treating them.

*Private Luke Hardy, 3 Para*

Towards the back end of the tour, we were about to hand over to the Royal Marines, who were going to fly in and take over Sangin district centre. My sniper section, at this point, was attached to C Company. It had been the same as everyone else's experience: very hard, full on, tiring, getting contacted two or three times a day. Our minds were still very much on the task in front of us, but you couldn't help naturally thinking about home. There was myself, the sniper commander, Kyle Deerans, Warren Nixon and Steven Llewellyn.

For the last couple of days, we had been talking to the commander about having our photograph taken on the rooftop where all the action takes place when the compound is attacked. We'd all run up to the rooftop and fight from there. As snipers, we had our own little sangar on the rooftop due to it being a high point. The boss is a very straight, down-the-line Paratrooper, as he should be, he's the commander, but we'd been dropping hints that we wanted to have this sniper section photograph on the rooftop and we wanted it with our maroon berets on. He didn't want to know, but we managed to come to a compromise and break him down. He said, 'Right, we'll have a quick photograph, but not berets; we'll quickly take our helmets off, body armour still on, weapons up: photograph taken.'

Went up to the rooftop and found someone who was happy to take the photograph. Quickly whipped the helmets off, all stood there, quick pose, and I can remember the second the photograph was taken there was a flash, which I assumed was the camera, but it was an RPG came flying over our heads and an AK-47 round splattered all around us. I remember it as a bit of a film moment, because I dived through towards the back end of the sangar and as I was in the air, I looked to the left and in slow motion I could see the boss and Warren Nixon dive into the other sangar on the left-hand side.

As they dived inside, an RPG made a direct hit on their sangar and I thought, they're dead, they're fucking dead. I was in a ball in the back end of the sangar, but Steven ran out and grabbed me into the sangar and as the commotion died down, I popped my head out and I saw Warren pop his head out of their sangar. We looked and in all the smoke we saw that the RPG was a direct hit, but it had lodged itself in between the sandbags at the top of the sangar and the roof.

So, as we were all settling down a bit, adrenalin running, I could see his face like, what the fuck have we done here, how are we going to explain this? And we were just laughing, talking about and picturing those Taliban soldiers waiting outside our FOB, waiting for the right moment, and seeing these five idiots stood there and taking off their helmets. You can imagine them chatting to each other, saying, 'Here we go, get them now!'

But we got the perfect picture and the Taliban didn't get us.

# 10

# AFGHANISTAN
## 2007–2008

**Operation Herrick VIII**

On 1 April 2008, 16 Air Assault Brigade was back in Afghanistan with 23 Regiment (Air Assault) RE, 13 Air Assault Support Regiment RLC, 7 Para RHA, and 3 and 2 Para – a force of over 1,150 men. The Pathfinders formed the major component of 16 Air Assault's Brigade Reconnaissance Force.

2 Para operated as Battle Group North operating from five Forward Operating Bases (FOBs) in the Upper Sangin Valley. These were situated in the area of the 'Green Zone' fertile farmland stretching one kilometre either side of the Helmand River. They operated in temperatures of over 40 degrees centigrade, in humid conditions, scrambling across ditches and streams that irrigate the area, carrying 60lb equipment weights on patrol and wearing body armour. The fighting was intense. At FOB 'Gibraltar', C Company came under attack thirty-six times, were bombed twenty-two times and were involved in twenty-nine firefights – five men were killed and forty-four wounded, but this for the loss of some 150 Taliban.

3 Para conducted both combat and 'hearts and minds' operations with Regional Battle Group (South). They ranged across a spectrum of terrain varying from the irrigated humid conditions of the Green Zone to the harsh and arid desert in Helmand and Kandahar Province; from the mountains of Zabul near the Pakistan border to close street confines in Kandahar City.

In August, the 3 Para Battle Group provided security for the delivery of a massive new hydroelectrical turbine to the Kajaki Dam in northern Helmand. This was conducted through known Taliban strongholds while the enemy was distracted by diversions or cleared from the convoy route. The turbine was delivered with no British fatalities, discrediting the opposition and delivering a much-sought material success for ISAF and the Afghan government. The tour ended on 1 October 2008.

*Corporal David 'Goth' Baillie, 2 Para*

The morning of 8 June 2008 was just like every other morning in Helmand. Get up at 2.30 a.m. and get your shit squared for the patrol. As a Section Commander of 4 Platoon, B Company, I would confirm my guys knew the mission details, where we were going and what we were going to do when we got there. Al Farmer, my second in command, would double-check ammunition, radios and batteries were sorted. My section lived in a HESCO bastion bunker, in FOB Inkerman, that we had affectionately named 'The Command Post.' Before each patrol we would have some music playing, normally the soundtrack from a war film from the sixties. It was all a bit tongue in cheek, but it gave us a boost to our morale.

Little things about that day stick in my mind – things that would change the course of lives just a few hours later.

Dave Murray was a young guy with bags of potential, a great Paratrooper in the making. That morning I decided to swap him out of the normal order of march for my section and put him as my point man. As the first guy in my section, he would lead us to where we needed to go. The point man is referred to as 'the sandbag man', the guy who will be hit first if anything happens, allowing the section commander the chance to react and take the fight to the enemy. I don't know why I decided to change him that day, but I did.

I also remember Jason Hallem, normally my point man, asking if I wanted to take his med kit as he had to swap it out for a radio, since he was changing position. I said no. It was extra kit and he was already carrying over 80lb. He put it down and carried on putting on his body armour and webbing. I remember looking at the med kit for what felt like an age before my training and professionalism won over. I took my daysack off and reluctantly put in the med kit. Better to have it and not need it, than need it and not have it.

The patrol itself was uneventful, the company pushed out deep into the green zone. The overall aim of the mission was to interdict the Taliban and to mingle with the local population to win hearts and minds. We were out for hours before we began heading back to our FOB. Each platoon rotated through being the point platoon of the company snake. On the way back to the FOB, 4 Platoon were to lead the company. The platoon rotated sections through point section in order to ensure everyone was rested, as being the point section could be very hard work, finding routes, crossing rivers and being on constant alert for the enemy.

My section was leading the company when we were told over the radio to 'go firm', meaning stop and find cover and firing positions. There were people who needed to take a break and drink some water. Not really surprising, considering how hot it was, the weight we were carrying and how long we had been out. Whilst we took a quick break, I took a look at my map and decided to move through the outskirts of a small village, instead of moving across the open ground. We were a couple of kilometres from the FOB, which I could see on the high ground in the distance. I called Dave over and briefed him on the route that I wanted to take. It would provide us with cover from view and cover from fire, as well as giving the company some much-needed shade.

With the new route confirmed, we began to lead the company into the village. We were walking down an alleyway with tall compound walls either side about fifty metres long with a T-junction at the end. As we got to the T-junction, Dave went right and I went left, ensuring we were covering our arcs. I knelt down, took up a firing position and started scanning the open ground to my front for threats. I remember Dave saying, 'Goth, I am just going to check this bloke.'

The right path led deeper into the village and Dave must have seen a local to the right as I was securing the left. Dan Gamble, the third man in our order of march, had passed behind me to join Dave as he was the platoon's Pashto speaker. I started to turn my head to check what was going on, but before I was even able to look over my shoulder, there was a massive explosion. I don't remember the explosion, I didn't see it, I can't recall hearing it. Maybe I blacked out for a second or maybe my mind refused to register what happened. Either way, Dave said he was going to check someone and the next thing I remember I was lying in a ditch facing the opposite direction. No bang, no flash, just instantly thrown upside down into a ditch.

I picked myself up, trying to figure out what had happened; somehow my daysack had come off one shoulder and I couldn't see out of my right eye. There was dust everywhere. I placed my hand to my eye and my hand came away covered in blood. Shit, I thought, I have lost an eye! I then heard Dan scream, 'Somebody give me some morphine.' Then everything became very real.

As I climbed out of the ditch, Jason ran past me towards where Dave and Dan were laying. I moved towards their bodies, Dave was slumped against the side of a compound and Dan was a few feet back from him; it looked like he had been folded in half. Dave was covered in blood, the bright red in stark contrast to everything else which was covered in dust.

Jason was already working on administering first aid to one of them, I think it was Dan, so I moved past their bodies further down the path. A horrible decision to have to make, but one you are trained to do. I could have stopped to give first aid but we didn't know what had happened, we could be under RPG attack and our right flank was now exposed. I hate myself for walking past their bodies, but I know it was the right choice. I had to secure the area and ensure there was no danger to the rest of the section.

As I moved forwards, I slipped on something and almost lost my footing. It felt like when you step on a banana peel, but when I looked down to see what it was, I saw a lump of meat and gristle. Next to it, lying on the ground was a foot and the lower half of someone's leg. I got on to my radio and signalled Wayne Sykes, the platoon sergeant. 'Contact, suicide bomber.' I sent the message even as I was thinking, no way, there is no way this has just happened, this happens to other people, not me.

I moved further down the alley out of the dust; there was a local standing there, a youngish looking male dressed like a farmer. He didn't seem at all phased by the fact that there had just been a massive explosion. I quickly knelt down, took aim and placed my finger on the trigger. Every instinct in my body wanted to kill him, to drop him where he stood: he could have been a threat, he could have been another suicide bomber, or he could have just been a local farmer in the wrong place at the wrong time. He posed no immediate threat, but I still wanted to kill him. Again my training took over, we don't kill people who are unarmed, and we don't kill civilians. I screamed at him to 'fuck off' and he quickly moved back into his compound.

Martin Wilson, the Snipers Platoon sergeant, moved up to

my position and took over from me. I moved back towards the incident, which was when I saw the third and fourth casualties. A medic was working on someone who had been behind me, Wayne was knelt next to him. I remember asking who it was, I couldn't tell whoever it was, as they were grey. Wayne told me it was 'Cuthy' (Nathan Cuthbertson) and my heart sank.

Someone told me to relax and move into one of the smaller compounds. At this stage, the whole platoon had taken control of the incident, all-round defence was out and our medics were working on the injured. I moved into the compound and joined the rest of the platoon; they were working on the fourth man, an engineer from 9 Squadron, who was attached to our platoon. His arm was a mess and he was lying on a stretcher with M for morphine written on his forehead.

My face was still covered in blood, although I was able to see out of my right eye now. I must have been in shock, because I didn't register the fact that I had been peppered with shrapnel until later that night. The casevac of the guys was carried out at great risk, as we used vehicles from the FOB which chose to drive down an unproven route to help with the evacuation. We carried additional kit from the guys who had been evacuated. I carried Nathan's GPMG as we moved the last few kilometres back to Inkerman. When we got to the FOB, 7RHA, the artillery unit in our FOB, were waiting to help us in and taking kit and equipment off us, and getting water to people who were physically and emotionally exhausted. They told us that the explosion had been so strong it had shaken the compound.

The rest of the day was a blur. I finally discovered that I had been hit at least five times, including a piece of shrapnel that had hit me about a centimetre above my right eye. I also picked lumps of flesh from my webbing and took them to the MP who was working with the company group. I hoped that it could be used to help identify the attacker, although I wasn't sure whose body it might have come from.

I knew what was coming when the platoon commander called us in for a brief later that night; he confirmed that Dan, Dave and Nathan had not survived their injuries. I buried my face in my maroon T-shirt and broke down in tears. Most of the guys did, but we rallied around each other as only the Paras can. I can't describe how, it's something you can only experience. A band of warriors who would and had given their lives for each other.

The next day I was evacuated to Bastion camp where doctors took X-rays (which, against the rules, they let me keep). I was flown back to the UK about a week later, as I had contracted a virus from the blood, dust and shrapnel from the explosion.

One of the hardest things I had to do when I was home was explain to my family that I was speaking to the Battalion staff left in Colchester, to find out when they could get me back to Inkerman. I explained to them that if the Battalion wouldn't let me go then that was fine, but I couldn't stay in England whilst my section was still fighting on without me. I couldn't live with myself, if I didn't try. The look on the guys' faces and the greeting I received the day I got back to Inkerman was worth it. I spent another couple of months fighting the Taliban with some of the best soldiers in the world, before finally leaving Afghanistan for good.

I remember 8 June 2008 as if it was yesterday, I have the date and the names tattooed on my back as a constant reminder that better men than I died so that I may be here to tell this story. I have no doubt that the actions carried out by Dan and Dave saved many lives that day. They carried out the correct drills and stopped the suicide bomber from getting any further. If he had got around the T-junction, he would have killed most of my section.

My point man died, my third man died, my fourth man died and my fifth man was severely injured in the explosion, yet I walked away from it. I am positive that Dan and Dave shielded me from the blast with their bodies and that will stay with me for the rest of my life.

*Private Reuben Bennett, 2 Para*

It was the morning of 8 June, my twentieth birthday; we had a very early start leaving the gates about 4 a.m. before morning prayers had started. Our patrol was supposed to last five to six hours, some of my section gave me shit little birthday presents, but they said we'd celebrate when we got back in. I'd only been in country for a month and had just passed out of basic training. I was the newest bloke in the company and been given the heaviest kit, the ECM blue receiver, with extra batteries, which I could barely lift off the floor.

Our mission was to go to a village we had not yet visited and see if there was anything we could do for them; we patrolled out and were in position about 6 a.m. at the village. We asked about for the village elder, but the locals seemed a bit reserved about talking to us. An elderly man who must have been in his sixties, but looked in his nineties due to the harsh conditions they live in, came out and spoke to the OC, Major Lewis MC, and said that the village could use a water pump and the OC was happy and there were handshakes all around. We carried on patrolling around the village, but by now we were all tongues hanging out due to the 50 degrees midday heat.

I was in 2 Section and we were leading the patrol back in and were about to cut down an alleyway when our GPMG gunner began having dramas with his sling and weapon. We took a knee while he sorted himself out and 1 Section leapfrogged in front

212

of us and down the alleyway. We covered them by going into a sort of vineyard next to the alleyway. Out of sight to us, the elderly man from before suddenly appeared in the alleyway in front of 1 Section, and waved. Dave Murray and Dan Gamble, who could speak Pashto, walked forward to greet him. There was then an almighty explosion and what sounded to me like bullets whizzing by my head.

Suddenly calls of 'Mortars!!!' and 'IEDs!!!' rang around 2 and 3 Sections, but nothing was heard from 1. Goth Baillie, who had been blown about ten feet from where he was standing, got on the net and told them that we had been hit by a suicide bomber and there were casualties. We secured the area and moved in on 1 Section's position, which looked like the opening scene of *Saving Private Ryan*: bodies were strewn across the ground and there was loads of screaming. By now everything was moving in slow motion and as I came to grips with what had happened, being a brand-new soldier who had basic trauma skills, I was told to secure a perimeter. I could see our team medics frantically ripping bags open and using all sorts of med kit on the blokes.

Military information support teams (MISTs) were sent and we waited for a MERT to come and save these critically wounded four lads. We waited and waited. The guys helping the wounded were having to lie to them, saying the heli is inbound and coming any minute now mate, just hang on! But the Chinook never came. The OC went to plan B and called for a convoy from the FOB to pick up the injured and move them to Inkerman and the relatively safe HLS where they were carried by Chinook to Bastion, but all three died.

The engineer survived, though he lost an arm. We patrolled back to camp, but we were all in shock. We had been out on the ground for hours longer than we were meant to and by the time we got into camp I was on my last legs, mentally I was fucked. I was shell shocked and had to be walked back to my pit by one of the sergeants, as I couldn't even work out where the hell I was! We flew out to Bastion to carry the coffins onto the Hercs. When I got into Bastion, I found an email from my girlfriend at the time, effectively telling me she didn't want to be with me any more. I went out to the perimeter of Bastion far away from everyone and sat there staring into the desert for hours, truly the lowest point in my life and the worst birthday I could ever imagine.

We returned to the bomb site a few days later, so that the investigation team could check the scene. There were bits of the suicide bomber's face hanging off a tree and we recovered a leg. I went to the spot where I was when the explosion happened and there were metal ball bearings in the tree. That was the noise I heard that sounded like gunfire.

*Lieutenant Wes Smart, 3 Para*

I arrived at 3 Para right after the Battalion had got back from the Herrick 4 tour in Sangin, which was very well publicised. So we were right old newbies and were treated as such. But very, very quickly you get into it. It's not a learning curve, it's a wall you hit and start to scramble up.

C Company, 3 Para was split in two and my platoon was sent to go with B Company, 2 Para for the pre-deployment and OPTAG training in the build up to the tour. For the tour we were a platoon in B Company, 2 Para. As a 3 Para platoon, there was a great debate when we first went across about whether we would wear blue DZ (Drop Zone) flashes or green DZ flashes and CO, I think, in the end left it to the blokes all to decide, the 2 Para lads as well. They all said they're a 3 Para platoon, let them all wear green. So B Company had two platoons with blue patches and one platoon with green.

Herrick 8. It was my first operational tour, I turned twenty-six out there, and those seven months still define much of my character.

I was on the advance party for B Company with the first few taking over from the Marines that were at Inkerman at that point. I had heard the stories at Bastion about Inkerman being nicknamed 'incoming'. I had only been in the FOB a couple of hours and was being shown around the platoon accommodation by a Marine sergeant when I heard this faint boom and looked at him and he looked back at me, as if 'What the . . . ?' Then we heard the whistle of the Chinese rocket coming in and he shouted, 'Everyone take cover!' I remember hitting the deck and crawling under the canvas camp bed next to me and thinking to myself, what bloody good is this going to do?

The next day it rained, it was the only time I saw rain out there and it was what I imagined the Somme must have been like, because the desert literally turned to mud everywhere, like knee-deep, waist-deep stuff – it was crazy. I never saw rain again until I returned to England.

I remember after the first set of patrol orders I gave, feeling all the energy from the blokes, everyone was really keyed up, you hear all the stories, you train really hard and do you know what, the first few patrols we went on . . . nothing. It was like walking the range. They were obviously sussing us out. But once it came, it never stopped, and you knew every time you stepped out the door, there would be a contact. It was just a question of where, when and who was in the lead.

Inkerman is sat on a big rock edge, overlooking the main route up to Kajaki, the 611. Literally the road was outside and it divided green farming from desert. It's a good dominating position. Living there was hard, and everyone got D&V at some point. I'm talking not knowing which end to point towards the plywood hole (the toilet) type of sick here.

We had been briefed specifically as part of the bigger plan that Inkerman to the north and Gibraltar to the south were the two FOBS that were meant to go out and be the focal points for kinetic action, so that Sangin district centre had some breathing space, to allow for the reconstruction of Sangin to bring in some economic prosperity. In brief, we were to 'go out and get in amongst it.'

I had a Pashto speaker, a Private Spink from 2 Para, no special unit or anything, he had simply shown aptitude and had spent a year learning Pashto. Some of the faces of the locals when he spoke Pashto were something to see! Him speaking Pashto was like how the Queen pronounces English, but he quickly learned to adapt to the dialect.

I remember now how inexperienced we were as a platoon in our first contact compared to our last. The first contact we had, we went out on a platoon patrol and the suspense kept building and building because on our radios we could hear what the enemy were saying. We were paralleling a road in the green zone coming back towards the FOB, still within the footprint of the larger-calibre weapons mounted at the FOB, and on the ICOM you could tell the enemy were getting excited. 'They're nearly there, they're nearly at the crossing.'

They were using code words as well – 'Get the big thing ready' – and you could feel the suspense, the knot in your stomach getting tighter and tighter. My platoon sergeant, Sergeant Marshall, said on our radio as we were paralleling along, 'Boss, you might want to think about a dog leg.' That was a good idea, so we did a right turn into the inside tree line, then turned left to carry on in the same direction and that's when they let off a few rounds at us.

We had created a bigger distance and they were not great shots, the whole platoon was shooting back at them . . . the FOB then opened up and the call came back that we had been contacted right instead. We hadn't, it was very confusing at the time, but everyone learned and learned quick. My rifle got a stoppage in that contact, typical, only time in the whole tour. We all thought, okay, everyone's been shot at, everyone's shot back, we've learned a lot about situational awareness. Sergeant Marshall's suggestion saved us from a very close-quarter ambush that day and for me I learned not to feed everything from ICOM down to the blokes; you learned what the pertinent information was, that the guys need to know.

Everything revolved around farming in the green zone. One day you're in poppy fields looking out some 200 metres for the enemy, the next day you're in fields of maize and you turn a corner and there the enemy is. We all learned with the locals to ask, 'Who are you? What's your job?' They'd say, 'I'm a farmer'. First thing you say is, 'Well, let me see your hands'. If they've been farmers since the age of eight or twelve, their hands are going to be hard and callused and if they're not . . . 'Why are you lying to me?' You quickly learn reading people, the blokes were brilliant at it, we also learned to estimate our own wealth in cows so the locals could understand!

Once we got into May, fighting season began and it didn't stop until October. The contact that stands out the most was a company patrol on Sunday 8 June, when 4 Platoon were hit by a suicide bomber. My platoon had led that patrol when setting out from Inkerman quite far up into the green zone and as the day wore on, Major Lewis said let's head back in and the platoon behind us took over the lead. We were heading back to the FOB and less than a couple of kilometres away from the FOB, the suicide bomber had come around a corner, approached Lt David True's platoon, detonated and that's when we lost Murray, Gamble and Cutherbertson. That was pretty vivid. If we had been in the lead, it would have been my platoon.

On 24 July the company lost Lance Corporal Rowe (Veterinary

Corps) and his search dog Sasha. That was on a company patrol, where there was a sustained firefight. After recovering his body, one of the platoons went back out to recover the body of the dog.

The one battle group operation that sticks out most in my memory was into the Musa Qala wadi. We took Chinooks, it was a night flight and my platoon went in first, and as we ran off the back of the Chinook there was tracer going off into the sky, and as the Chinook took off it fired its flares . . . and I thought, it's like in the movies here, this was proper Paratrooper stuff. Once we had the second wave and the company group was together, we had to take the high ground before first light and we advanced with two sections up with Corporal Sterling and Corporal Hawthorne at the front.

The platoon had some jungle training before the tour and we used that tactic at night so that we had the maximum amount of firepower, no matter which direction we were contacted from. On NVGs with no artillery or mortar illumination, we fought for the high ground. The sections were firing and manoeuvring towards an enemy position uphill with little or no cover available. An Apache attack helicopter came into position dangerously close under the OC's control – that felt great and in the morning, when the sun came up, we thought, we just did a night attack on an enemy position, and captured a command and control point. I felt good about that one.

From the patrols around Inkerman, there was one when we did a night move north through the desert before sweeping into the green zone. We started on the way back and it was just after dawn and we were moving along the tree lines. There were people in the fields in front of us, women and kids all quietly going about their business, and suddenly everyone started running – I've never seen a woman run across a ploughed field so fast and sweep a kid up in her arms without breaking stride. Everyone shouted, 'Stop, get down.' One of my sections fired a mini flare to mark his position and then the whole world erupted. That was a proper ambush.

It was a constant game that you played as an officer with your command group of corporals and your sergeant in planning the routes to try to set the Taliban up and avoid getting set up yourself. You'd try and set a route the enemy would see and then change it suddenly, you were trying to set them up. Sometimes they got an ambush in and that happened this time. They were behind a mini wall near a compound and we were behind an irrigation ditch.

If I had realised at the time that it was an 'L' shaped ambush, and not the usual linear-type ambush, I perhaps wouldn't have run across the bloody ploughed field with a section of eight men led by Lance Corporal Reynolds behind me. No one was hit, but you learn very quickly that crack and thump becomes whizz when it's close, and when you see it pepper potting around your feet you go, 'Oh shit', but you're committed. You've no choice; you have got to keep going. It did mean we won the firefight, however, and broke the ambush.

Cpl Kennedy was wounded in the leg on that patrol and Cpl Hawthorne was Mentioned in Despatches for his actions in keeping the enemy at bay.

In August, 3 Para came and set up a patrol base at what was called Emerald. It was about three kilometres further up the road from Inkerman. Another great position overlooking the road and green zone, the compound had the look of a fortress from the road. It started as a company house and then D Coy 3 Para moved off and the OC, Major Lewis, decided that he wanted to keep that position, so it became a platoon house and I was the first platoon to go up there. I waved goodbye to 3 Para and then there were thirty-two of us and as a young platoon commander, it was brilliant.

By this time we had Sergeant Stephanie Vella, a female medic, with us for two months. There was a political debate back then, it is different today, should women be on the front line? However, she was there, and she saw contact. She was only metres away from it. I'll be honest, when you're a twenty-something, young Para Reg Platoon Commander, and you get given a female medic, in your head, you're thinking – is she going to last, has she got the stamina? And she did. She stuck it out with us for those two months. She patrolled, she was truly part of the platoon. It was an interesting dynamic.

We had one guy who was hit when he was back-filling another platoon for a patrol. He was Lance Corporal Dipnall. He was lying prone, when the round went through past his collar bone and down his body. He really was a popular guy, really good bloke. The FSG (Fire Support Group) which had the old type WMIK Land Rovers, casevaced him back. They bombed straight out of Inkerman and didn't do the mine-sweeping clearance bit, because they knew how important it was to get Dipnall.

When they got him back, the three section commanders and I met him at the HLS site. The FOB doctor who worked on him was saying, 'There's nothing more I can do, he's got a drip in, he's in pain . . .' I remember putting him on a Chinook and giving the big thumbs up to him and thinking, the Chinook's here, he's alive, great – you're going to get medical care. From his point of wounding, he was back in Bastian in an hour and two minutes. I was told that Dipnall died on the Chinook and twice on the surgical table in Bastion, but he wasn't ready to go and eventually recovered. I think he lost his kidney and a bit of his spleen. He's alive and has kids now. That was the only serious injury the platoon took.

I remember having an interview with Lt Col Williams (CO 3 Para) when we got back to 3 Para. The first thing I said was that I was glad I had brought everyone back alive and he said,

'Yes, you're right to say that, but you all also did every job that was asked of you.'

*Sergeant Stephanie Vella, Royal Army Medical Corps*

This was my second time in Afghanistan, as I was initially there in 2006 but rarely deployed out of Camp Bastion. I arrived in FOB Inkerman a day after three soldiers had been killed by a suicide bomber. As expected, the mood was very low. I had been in the Army for twelve years and was a sergeant at this point and nothing in my Army career had prepared me for the madness that I was going to endure for the next four months.

These guys were and are the bravest, strongest guys I have ever had the fortune to meet and know. Tiny moments mainly stick in my mind, like the look on an eighteen-year-old's face as he ran to a contact. Faces staring out from a drainage ditch after a casualty had been evacuated asking, 'Is he OK?'; chatting in a makeshift gym about general rubbish, a fleeting look of worry about an injection after he'd nearly been blown up by a grenade, arguments over whose turn it was to make the brew.

Conditions were austere, fresh food was virtually non-existent and family and friends would send out food parcels; I lost two stone in weight over that four-month period, some soldiers looked like they had stepped out of a concentration camp by the end of the tour. There was a constant battle to control the diarrhoea and vomiting outbreaks and a random fever that would affect some soldiers and not others with no explanation as to what was causing it. Conditions were hard.

At the beginning of my time in FOB Inkerman there was no fridge, but we eventually managed to get one for the medical detachment to at least be able to store items at a stable temperature. The freezer compartment managed to over-freeze, so the doctor decided to defrost it . . . with a knife . . . and punctured the freezer compartment, which in turn released all the gas and left it inoperable. He called me over, still with a knife in his hand, and told me that he thought he'd 'broken the freezer'. He continued to explain, whilst I looked at him and tried not to shove him in the freezer compartment, thinking, how can a man that is so clever, wonderful and such an amazing doctor be so ridiculously stupid. That was the end of the medical detachment fridge freezer.

There was no particular need to wash that often, everybody smelt, whether they'd showered or not. There were a few competitions on who could go the longest without washing, there were some particularly impressive lengths of time. One went so long that when he ended up stuck in the FOB I was in on our next tour, I checked when the last time he washed was before I lent him my spare doss bag.

I was sitting by the medical detachment one evening and laughed as I could see the silhouette of a lance corporal from the platoon that I went out on patrol with a majority of the time. I knew it was him, as his hair was sticking up on end, but there was a golden glow around him from the kitchen light. A few days later, he was severely injured from a gunshot wound to the chest; I thought he was going to die. Once he was evacuated, we patrolled on and as we pushed on, other soldiers from his platoon were asking whether he was going to be OK; all I could do was say, 'Yes,' and just pray he was.

On our return to the FOB, the other female medic who had evacuated him to the FOB with the FSG told me the MERT had got him back to Bastion alive and he was on the operating table. There are no words to describe how I felt, however, I see pictures of him now with his family and know that whoever was looking after him that day is truly good.

Although at times they were the most annoying individuals ever, I knew they would look after me and I knew that they knew I would look after them. I loved those guys and still do, probably more than my family. If I had to go through it all again, wondering if today was the day I'd get it and die; I would one thousand times over. They were the best, worst and funniest days in such an awful place and I'm grateful I had them.

*Captain Levison Wood, 3 Para*

Before I joined the Paras, I had hitchhiked through Afghanistan, Pakistan and Iran. But getting the maroon beret in 2006 was probably the proudest moment of my life.

I was introduced to my blokes by my predecessor, Chris Hitchins, and he was like, 'There's the platoon. Say hello.' And I'd not prepped anything, you know the usual subbie – didn't know what to say. So I said, 'Looking forward to working with you all.' Then Crabtree, the senior corporal at the time, said, 'Can I tell you a joke?' and I was like, 'Yeah, course.' He said, 'How many Sangin vets does it take to change a light bulb?' And I was like, 'I've got no idea.' And he replied, 'Of course you've got no idea, you weren't there!' Brilliant. We got on like a house on fire after that.

That was my intro to the Paras. But I loved it. When I took the blokes out in 2008, they were all fresh faces and I'd only got about two people who'd actually been to Afghanistan. There's such a high turnover. A lot of people left after that. So it was a platoon of twenty-seven novices basically. I had the best time of my life.

We were doing a lot of stabilisation ops. We were based in Kandahar airfield, but we'd go out on the ground for a couple of weeks here, a month there, so we weren't stuck in a FOB, which was good in that it was a very varied role. We were digging wells, building schools, plus kicking doors down. A lot of the stuff we were doing was the hearts and minds. I felt, we were doing a positive thing. We went into the area known as Maiwand. There we built and refurbished a school and helped to rebuild a police station.

We were overseeing the contractors, but it was hands-on in the sense that we were seen to be doing stuff. We were shopping in the local market, little things like that. Ultimately, it's what the war should have been about, you know – getting the people on side. But some people were too concerned about getting rounds down and that was a mistake. We did see a lot of action, but not as much as the guys in the FOBs, because we were the ones dishing it out, rather than receiving. We got ambushed. We did lots of patrols in Helmand and all around the south really. So, it was interesting.

The second op we did was just north of Gereshk. We were on the edge of the green zone and we'd seen a mine strike, one of the vehicles had been blown up and the blokes had been lucky, they were all fine, they'd been blown clear of the vehicle. So we went in and rescued them and got them into another vehicle and were about to do a three-point turn in this mine-field, so they overtook us and unbelievably were blown up again. They were all fine. Amazing.

So we got them all back out of the minefield. I was basically looking after the guys that we'd just rescued effectively, and my vehicle then had to go with another team back onto the hill. It wasn't a Taliban field, it was an old Russian minefield, so we had my vehicle and we were going back to knacker the vehicles and blow them up so the Taliban couldn't use the radios and things. Then my vehicle, as it was going back up, bang and that went up. The driver was fine, the team in the back were fine, the only seat that wasn't was the one I would have been in, and had been in all day, it was obliterated.

I remember an occasion we were down near a place called Nalgham, near the Arghandab Valley near to Kandahar, we had been on patrol, it was a strike op actually, it was an airborne, heli drop-off into someone's back garden to arrest a bomb maker. Almost immediately it went kinetic and it was a huge ambush and it was about ten hours of fighting. Yeah, it was a long old day – literally it was shoot and scoot. We'd chase after them to the next village and then they'd open up again and we'd go to the next village, going around in circles, of course. We didn't get the guy.

I remember another occasion we went down this narrow alleyway in this village, I was sort of second bloke and I saw this arm pop over the wall with an AK and it sprayed the whole road from about ten metres away. He just opened . . . and whether you call it luck, call it chance, call it fate, nobody got hit. But everyone ran into this irrigation ditch, we dived for cover. I looked down and there was a bloody mine between my feet. They had obviously planted these mines in the ditches so you'd get blown up. So again, very lucky.

We were commanded by Lt Col Stuart Tootal before we deployed to Afghanistan (Lt Col Huw Williams took us to Afghanistan). He was a passionate man and a good commander. He was in tears when he left. He gave a very impassioned speech. All the blokes were taking the piss, of course. He loved it, he loved the Paras and I think it was genuine love.

I'll never forget the last jump I ever did. It was a families' day up at Catterick and it was a fun one. I had been on the piss the night before and I don't know where I'd stayed, it wasn't in my own bed. I rang up my sergeant, Chris Wright, who was a joker, and asked him if he would bring my uniform and Bergen to where we were doing the jump. So I turned up at the airport and he said, 'Your Bergen's there in the corner.' So I quickly got changed, but using all my strength, I could only just about pick up my Bergen. And I think I was the last off and first down. Where I landed was about a kilometre to the RV point where all the families were waiting and I had this bloody Bergen. When I eventually arrived, all the families were asking why I was so slow. Chris Wright was just pissing himself. I emptied my Bergen and he had put in two crates of Carlsberg, a toaster, a laminator machine and a load of dumbbells – a pack full of shit.

What did I learn from my time with the Paras? You can't even think about giving up, you don't entertain the thought, because when you do, you will. It's not even an option to fail. So it was like that for me really. The Paras are given that self-belief. When you passed P Company, you're bullet proof, you can do anything. And I think that was the kind of mentality you had to have to survive.

# 11

# AFGHANISTAN
## 2009–2010

*Private Jaco van Gass, 1 Para*

It would have been almost a year from when we joined the battalion to going out to Afghanistan. By that point the blokes were frustrated as we'd been training hard. We'd joined up to do this, but it wasn't such a bad time really, because it gave us time to pick up some experience. We were prepared by 1 Para, who had already been out there.

We were on field exercise when our Colour Sergeant came up to me and said, 'Van Gass, pack your stuff and get ready, because that Land Rover's going to take you back to camp – you're off to Afghanistan.' I thought this was a joke and started to laugh. He said, 'Stop laughing, I'm dead serious. One of the guys dropped out and you've been chosen to go. So you want to go?' This was after three months with the battalion – my wings were still wet and I hadn't even tasted any clouds or had any desert kit issued. So I replied, 'Do I not want to go!' It was 110 mph from then on. I got everything ready, issued and packed, and off I went. We flew with the RAF from Brize Norton, landing at Kandahar and then to Bastion.

Being South African helped me adjust to the climate – your body, whatever you put it through, adapts to it. I was used to the cold weather and I would say I acclimatised quicker than the other guys. We were teaching the Afghan National Army (ANA) from five in the morning to early evening, six days a week, with one day's rest.

We were not just committed to training the ANA, we went out on patrols with them, which was an awesome learning curve. The biggest thing was the language barrier. It was a big problem, because you were shouting instructions and giving lessons with the 'terp' (interpreter) not putting that message over with the aggression it needed. We had to give them time off for their prayers at first light and last light. The length of patrols would vary, depending on the op and how far we needed to go, and the information we had. Some would be a couple of hours and others a day or two. On the patrols, they'd usually go out to a quiet spot on the side for their prayers. When we were in the vehicles it was up to them, but we were not going to stop in a danger zone for them to say a prayer.

After we had two weeks' leave, our first action was a night one. We got the information on this guy and we knew exactly where he was and what we had to do. So into the helicopter with our kit and after an hour or so we got dropped off about ten miles from where the target was. We did a covert op working with the Afghan forces, teaching them to do certain ops in order that they could take over. It was the whole of our platoon and a company strength of the ANA.

It was the middle of the night, so we had the element of surprise and the advantage of the technology to see at night with the NVGs. We walked in as silent as we could for ten miles up to the target. We knew the guy was there – the bravo. He had a couple of bodyguards – he was quite a high player – and it all kicked off the moment we crossed the compound and blew a massive hole through the wall to get in. This was our first experience of exchanging fire, so it was a big adrenaline thing: should I shoot – should I take cover. But the moment that first shot fires, everything calms down and your training kicks in. It was amazing. There were no casualties and we captured the guy we needed to take and it was a very successful op. Then it rolled on with similar operations. We performed an important task in Afghanistan and whatever came our way, we adapted to it. Whatever we needed to do, we did it.

There was fiercer fighting than that a day or two before I was due for my R&R. We went out on a big NATO operation. The target was to push the Taliban out of a certain area. There were about ten Chinooks involved, dropping us in various different areas in the region, and we worked our way together with other forces, pushing the Taliban out from one point and advancing forward to a certain area and keeping that ground. We covered miles – and we had the advantage of fighting at night. We'd push through and take over a compound, then keep that area during the day. We'd get our rest as much as we could in the day, even though we'd get attacked and mortared. That was a three-day op and it was one of the hardest, because we needed to carry our three days' water and rations as well as our kit.

It does sometimes come down to personal skills and drills. There was some fierce fighting going on, sometimes a couple of metres away. We'd be firing rockets and there were RPGs flying over your head and tracer everywhere. I was carrying a rifle and an underslung grenade launcher (UGL). We'd trained to fire whatever weapon you had with you. I also carried a couple of 66s and hand and smoke grenades, but no white phos.

At the end of three days you come back and it's a great relief that there have been no major casualties. You've done good work and the op went according to plan – you can't ask for better. It was very strange for me, because that was one of the bigger firefights I'd had up to that point, yet three days later I was on a plane back to South Africa for ten days' R&R.

You go from an environment where your life is on the line and everywhere it's dust and you're living on the bare minimum

– to the lush green and booze. I hadn't had a drink for three and a half months and suddenly there was proper food and chicks everywhere. But after two days, all I was thinking about was the lads back in Afghanistan. All I wanted to do was get back and go help my muckers. On my return, I volunteered to not take my R&R so that some of the married men could get more leave and see their family and children. After a fight we got that agreed, but circumstances changed so we still had to take our leave.

We were fairly busy that summer – which was great. It made everything go faster. If you do nothing, time drags. The busier you are, the faster the time goes. Once again we volunteered, the three of us, to stay on longer to do an extra couple of months to assist with the hand-over rotation for the next platoon coming in. We'd hand over the ops and equipment and volunteer to go on a couple of ops with them to show them the ropes. I had two weeks left of the six months tour and my belongings were packed, so I was living out of a box. All I had left was the stuff I needed – my first kit, ops kit – that's it.

We went on to the op against the bravos, captured them, chained them together and set off to our primary Helicopter Landing Site (HLS). After a few minutes walking, it came over the net that the primary HLS was a no-go. The choppers didn't want to land in that area – they didn't feel right. It came over the net that we were to move to the secondary HLS, which was actually closer. As we got nearer we could see two bravos moving, so we called in a Spectre gunship to have a closer look. They couldn't see any weapons on the two guys, so we moved closer. We sent one of the Afghan sections with one of our guys forward with an interpreter to approach them.

As he closed on them, the interpreter twice gave the command for the two of them to put their hands in the air and sit down.

They didn't respond – they just went on with what they were doing. He repeated the command – nothing. So our guy fired a couple of warning shots. One of their guys sprinted off into a building, came back out and gave a massive burst with an AK-47. That was probably the worst decision he'd made in his life, because the moment he pulled that trigger, all hell broke loose. But there were others well dug in and over the net we heard that four guys were running towards the back of this mound, trying to right-flank us. We confirmed that we had this area covered and that we were waiting for them.

They came around and we opened fire with warning shots. They responded with a massive burst, but as this was the middle of the night, they hadn't got a clue where we were. We had NVG and fired back and killed them. The Spectre gunship came in and reported that they saw more movement, so we got them to fire on these positions. They were pretty close to us, but it was necessary to get those guys out of there. The Spectre came in – everybody on their belt buckle, heads covered, while the Spectre ripped into this place. He shot the shit out of those trenches. They were cleared and everyone was back on to their positions, covering our arcs of fire. Some more bursts of fire came from various places and we fired back.

As this was going on, we were walking literally twelve o'clock towards the buildings and by the time we pushed out, I was facing two o'clock and we were covering that area. At my ten o'clock area, I saw two RPGs fired in our direction. The first one went way right and exploded far in the distance. The second one was fired low and just bounced on the ground. But the RPG needs a point of impact to explode and this was bouncing all over the place on the floor. I was on my belt buckle by this time, but we all got up on our knees to observe our arcs. I heard this massive sound and the next thing I saw was this red glow coming towards me. All I thought was, please don't hit me. I turned away and the moment I turned my head, there was a massive explosion.

I could still hear the blokes firing – the confusion was unbelievable. I got my senses working and I tried to get up. As I looked down, I could see I was burning. My clothes were on fire – I thought, my God, what's happened? I tried to pat with my left hand, because I still had my rifle in my right hand. But when I looked, I thought, bloody hell, I've got no arm, my left arm's gone. In my mind I thought, bollocks, that's not good. I remember it clear as daylight. I was still on fire, so I put my weapon down and was patting myself – but it still didn't sink in that I'd lost my arm. I thought I had to get back into the firefight. I got hold of my rifle again and sat up.

I was attached to one of the snipers, so I was carrying an aluminium ladder on my back. I think that saved my life, because when I was on my knees before it struck me, I turned and faced the ladder toward the rocket. The RPG clipped the ladder and ricocheted off into my arm. When it hit the solid bone in my arm, it was hard enough to initiate the switch and to explode. That's why all the injuries were on my left-hand side. That's how it almost took my leg away. I didn't have any facial damage. Imagine how I would have been – I'd have been single all my life!

I woke up a couple of metres from where I was and had no idea what happened. I saw my arm and thought, bollocks, I'll sort that out later – don't worry. I tried to get up but couldn't, so I rolled on to my right-hand side and sat up on my bum. All the while, I was still firing with one hand in the general direction where the other blokes were firing. My leg was starting to hurt now, but I was looking around as I fired and saw that my sniper partner had been hit as well – he'd got a bit of shrapnel in the back of his calf. He was screaming and holding his leg and trying to self-aid. I looked around and there were the other boys – there was stuff burning all over them from the phos from the explosion of the rocket.

I realised what had happened, but by now the pain in my leg was unbelievable and it started getting worse and worse. I thought, all right, you carry a tourniquet and a self-help first-aid kit on you at all times. My tourniquet was right in the front of my chest, so I put my rifle down, lay back down on my back and started applying my tourniquet to my right arm. But you need to ramp that thing up to get the blood to stop flowing. I was doing this and at the same time looking over at Reeves, who was in the RAF regiment and attached to us. He was behind me and I shouted, 'Reeves! Reeves!' But he couldn't hear a thing because of the explosion and all the firing going on.

Eventually when he heard, me he crawled over – saw my arm and I will never forget this. He said, 'Fuck, Jaco. You've lost your arm!' I said, 'No shit!' It's not like I didn't notice . . . I shouted at him to put my tourniquet on. He cranked it up all the way, which helped me. My radio got blown up and I had no comms, so he shouted at the top of his lungs for a medic, who came pretty quickly and started treating me. A couple of morphine lollies got down into the right arm. I had no idea about my leg, and all I was saying was that I thought I'd broken my ankle. I've never experienced pain like that in my life and I thought I'd lost my leg, it was so painful. I didn't feel my arm at all. The medic was saying, 'Your leg is fine – it's still there.' I said, 'I can't lift it, don't worry about my arm. I can't move my leg.'

They calmed me down, but by this time the firefight was getting heavier and heavier. We called the gunship in again and he let rip and flattened everything – all the buildings, everything he could see. We called in the helicopters – they were rapid and I think I was out of there in just over half an hour. Two

Afghans got decked trying to carry me on their stretcher. Someone was shouting, 'Three helicopters are going to land. Put this one on number one.' The helicopters nearly landed on top of us – a couple of metres away. They picked me up and ran with me, but I was bouncing all over the place and fell off. They actually dropped me! I've never seen so many guys go mental. The White-Eyes, the British guys – nearly knocked them out. They got me back on the stretcher and into the helicopter. Then as the wounded Afghans were coming in, one of them stepped on my leg. I was in agony. I was screaming, 'My leg – it's in bits and someone's stepped on it!' I was going mental. I was screaming, 'Let's go – choppers off!' There was a doctor on board and I got looped off as priority number one – I was the worst casualty.

The medics were working on me in the helicopter, but I had run out of adrenaline and was getting really tired and all I wanted to do was sleep, but they were trying to keep me awake. Blood was pissing out of me everywhere. I didn't know about my leg. It was the back of my calf, but I thought my ankle was in a rag. I lost consciousness, but I can remember landing and stretcher-bearers picking me up again. As they were running with me, off the helicopter – would you believe it – I fell off again. They might as well have dragged me by my helmet strap to the ambulance. I was screwed and nuts – the second time. They got me back on and into the ambulance and I was in and out of consciousness. I remember bits and bobs and them cutting off my boots and some of my clothes. By then I was just spaced out.

When I woke, I was in an American field hospital. The other boys all got checked over – everyone was OK and my sniper partner came and went straight to theatre. Some of the others had little bits in their arse or arm, which the staff could just pick out. The choppers came in and took them back to camp.

My sergeant, my best mate Stefan and one of the medics stayed behind with me. I was in surgery for a long time. I had internal injuries, because I got shrapnel through the side, which punctured my stomach and various other bits of my internal organs. I got cut open – they told me everything got taken out, washed off, fixed and put back in and stitched up.

After the operation, I regained consciousness and saw my boss and my platoon sergeant. All I wanted to do was say something – but I couldn't speak. I was too drugged up. I wanted to write something and they gave me a notebook and a pen and I was just scribbling. To this day I can't remember what I wrote; all I wanted to let them know was what I felt about leaving them. They were saying, 'You going to be all right?' And I was saying, 'Yeah, don't worry.' And I was giving them thumbs up. Then I drifted off.

The next thing, I woke up in Selly Oak Hospital. My mum and dad and my sister and her husband were there – and I found it very confusing. It was great to see my family, but it was a massive shock. I thought it was a field hospital in Afghanistan, as I could still hear 50-cals going down and rockets; every time I closed my eyes, I was back in Afghanistan. I refused to believe I was back in England. One moment I was fighting alongside my muckers and, all of a sudden, I'm in a bed in Birmingham. All the action, the noise, the smells and then you wake up and there's your family, and it's all quiet. You can't move and you're in so much pain.

I'm glad that it was me that was injured– not the man next to me on my left or right. I'd volunteered to stay on three months extra, because I had no roots. The guy to my left was engaged, and the guy to my right had his whole family in England, as well as a little sister just eight years old. He was my roommate and every single week she sent him a letter about how proud she was of her brother and a packet of sweets and a little drawing: 'My brother's in the army. My brother's in Afghanistan.'

If it should have happened to them and there was nothing I could do, I would have felt guilty. It might sound weird, but I'd rather me than anyone else on that whole battlefield. Life goes on. The achievement – everything I've done since that day – has opened other pathways and you've got to follow them. You look ahead and stay positive.

There's no turning back now, and you do everything to the best of your potential. *Utrinque Paratus* – ready for anything, and that means 'anything'.

# 12

# AFGHANISTAN
# 2010–2011

## Operation Herrick XIII

16 Air Assault Brigade formally took over as the lead formation of Task Force Helmand from 4th Mechanised Brigade on Sunday 10 October 2010. They were in theatre until April 2011. To mark the change, which signified the start of Operation Herrick XIII, a 'friendship feast' was held at the headquarters of the Helmand Provincial Reconstruction Team (PRT) in Lashkar Gah, which was attended by Afghan and British dignitaries.

The event was attended by the Governor of Helmand Province, Gulab Mangal, the Deputy Commander of 3/215 Brigade of the Afghan National Army, Colonel Amin Jhan, and the Helmand Chief of Police. A number of commanders from ISAF headquarters, Regional Command (South), Regional Command (South West) and the American-led Task Force Leatherneck were also in attendance. On Sunday 14 November 2010, Prince William flew into Camp Bastion and spoke with members of 16 Air Assault Brigade whilst attending the Remembrance Service.

On 12 December 2010, after completing deployment training at Camp Bastion, operations into the settlement of Tor Ghai in Nahr-e Saraj district were undertaken, led by 2 Para with support from 3 Para. After advancing on foot through ice-cold irrigation ditches, across undulating terrain and over ten-foot-high compound walls through the night, carrying kit weighing around 50kg, the troops were ready in position before first light. As the sun rose and the visibility from a sandstorm cleared, the advance into Tor Ghai commenced. The advance was led on the ground by Commanding Officer 2 Para, Lieutenant Colonel Andrew Harrison.

As soon as the village was secured, the soldiers engaged in a shura (traditional Afghan meeting) with the influential elders of the village. During this time, the local nationals were handed Afghanistan flags by the Afghan National Army and the following message was broadcast by loudspeaker:

> 'The Afghan National Army and ISAF are here to stay, so we can provide security for the development that is coming to your village. You can come out now. This is a new time in your lives, please stay and support your village elders who are working to bring you the many benefits of governance.'

16 Air Assault Brigade units worked towards the objective of beginning the handover of security responsibilities to Afghan forces during 2011. They achieved this through strong tactics, initiative and persistence in operations in areas including, amongst others, Nad-e-Ali, Nahr-e-Saraj, Showal Bazaar and Char Coucha, restoring confidence and security. The Afghan Army, for the first time, was also able to plan and lead their own operations due to the training provided and the improving situation.

*Sergeant Tom Blakey, Pathfinder Platoon*

During Herrick 13, the Pathfinders were deployed as the Brigade Reconnaissance Force (BRF). The role of the BRF was to conduct reconnaissance and patrol in areas of Helmand Province that weren't covered by the Forward Operating Bases.

The BRF was organised into three small platoons and

operated in both dismounted (foot) and mounted (vehicle) patrols, the latter using Jackal vehicles. During one of our dismounted patrols, my platoon came under contact from a tree line. We had an AH64 Apache gunship in support, so our JTAC brought in the Apache on a gun run as we prepared to assault. It was amazing to see the blokes assaulting forward as the 20mm rounds from the Apache smashed the hell out of the tree line just in front of them. Ally as fuck! However, the enemy had extracted themselves before our lads got there, and our sections came under contact from in-depth positions.

As our lead section was in contact with the enemy, I moved my platoon sergeant's group forward and provided support with our 60mm mortar. My mortar guy, Shaun, was from 3 Para Mortar Platoon, and knew his stuff with the mortar. He put a couple of rounds right into the positions indicated to me by the lead section. Then I got a shout over the radio of 'Man down!' It turned out to be my lead section commander, John, who had been shot through the hand and arm. I moved forward to extract him. He was in a relatively good way, considering he'd just been shot. He had been firing his rifle when a round had entered his hand, travelled up his arm, breaking his wrist and arm, and opening up his lower arm. He had already self-applied a tourniquet to his arm to stop the bleeding and was in a lot of pain, but didn't want to have any morphine, saying that he wanted to stay 'with it' until he got back to a FOB. What a bloke.

I sent the Casualty Report to the sergeant major and started to move John to a point where he could be extracted to the FOB. He was capable of moving on his own, but couldn't operate a weapon, for obvious reasons. The rest of the platoon was still in contact, and only one guy could be spared to help provide security for the move back, so we were quite vulnerable. We could have come under contact at any point, and there were only two of us who could fight. Even though we were supposed to hand the casualty over to a flanking platoon, things didn't work out that way, as is often the case when the shit goes down. I ended up taking John all the way back to the FOB, some two and a half kilometres, all the time thinking, if we come under contact here we're a bit fucked.

Luckily we got back to the FOB without further incident, and were met by a grumpy looking Tom at the front gate (he had probably been disturbed from his afternoon nap), who had no idea that we had a casualty. After putting this fella straight, I got John to the Medical Room at the FOB and he could at last get some much-needed care.

*Colour Sergeant George Scott, 3 Para*

On 10 November 2010 during Operation Herrick XIII, a composite platoon from B Coy 3 Para operating in the Nad-e-Ali district of Helmand Province conducted a complex fighting patrol into a heavily contested Taliban stronghold. The patrol achieved complete mission success in the area of operations and the enemy's dominance was completely removed. The epitome of mission command and a Private soldier's initiative was displayed that day. The Officer Commanding B Company's ISTAR assets had tracked eight heavily armed insurgent fighters to a compound a short distance north of Check Point (CP) Washiran, where there was also a large Taliban presence converging ready to attack ISAF. In response to this threat, the OC co-ordinated a 500lb satellite-guided JDAM strike onto the insurgents' compound and followed this with a fighting patrol to assault the compound and clear north to a pre-determined grid.

As commander on the ground, Lt Sam Whitlam faced an extremely complex situation, with dire options concerning his course of action, which would place his platoon at immediate and considerable risk. Because of his concern for his men, during the planning phase in the Ops Room, he turned to his commanders and asked for suggestions; the majority looked at the floor.

The problem was that between CP Washiran and the objective were two main supply routes riddled with improvised explosive devices, ruling out the option of a left- or right-flanking assault. Between these routes, running perpendicular to our axis of advance, were four prominent walls approximately eight feet in height. These walls were scalable by ladder, but this would have been extremely time-consuming and would have broadcast our intent to the enemy. The situation was destined to fail if the patrol didn't rapidly deploy, as we were under significant time pressure due to the insurgent activity, which was escalating.

While all this critical planning was going on, our Company HQ were constantly demanding an update. Private Ben Cunningham was loitering at the entrance to the Ops Room and had been listening intently throughout. He piped up, 'Boss, this is a no-brainer. Stick a Mastiff armoured vehicle on each junction providing "eyes on" each route as protection, place explosive charges at the base of each wall, then smash a Mastiff through the gap and stack the blokes up behind it. Simple.' After briefly consulting his commanders on their opinions of the feasibility of success, all agreed; it could work. So Lt Whitlam nodded and said, 'That is exactly what we'll do.'

A sense of purpose and focus now consumed the camp; last-minute checks were conducted whilst the section commanders gathered round Whitlam's map for final control measures and direction. Within a tense, short period of time, the platoon patrolled out of the gates of CP Washiran and began to advance north.

During our advance to contact, the Taliban opened up on us as soon as we came into view and we were met with a determined and aggressive response. Two 7.62 machine guns opened up on us from the tree line north of the objective and a number of RPGs came in, momentarily pinning us down under this heavy weight of sustained fire. Incoming rounds struck and ricocheted off the armoured vehicle we were trudging behind. It was slow progress, because we were knee deep and moving slowly as they stitched the mud in front of us, while we were putting rounds down on the enemy's positions.

As a section commander having spent much time in contact during the early stages of the tour, I was now used to operating in a highly kinetic environment. But the intensity of the Taliban's fire that morning was bordering on overwhelming. We were banging on the door of their safe haven. On the final stages of our approach, at the point where I needed to lead my section away from the relative safety of the Mastiffs (which by now had become a bullet magnet), a forty-metre sprint across a vast stretch of open ground was required. This directly exposed us to the line of fire of two insurgent firing points and it was purely speed and aggression that allowed us to gain that initial foothold into the target compound.

We regained momentum when a hole was punched in the first of four compound walls by engineers using an anti-tank mine, which meant that now we were on dry ground, we could swiftly assault the entrance to the compound and begin systematically to clear along our axis. We were heavily engaged in fighting into the night, but by eight o'clock we had consolidated on our position. A section of eight out-of-area fighters was spotted patrolling in our direction from the north and we called in air support. Four passes by an American A10 tank-buster aircraft destroyed them all and in doing so sent a message.

This single day of decisive battle destroyed the rule and

reputation of the Taliban. We achieved total dominance in the area, which meant that local villagers were able to begin farming their fields again for the first time in months and the children were able to return to school. November 10th was a hugely successful day in terms of output, but the mission command and trust placed in the soldiers by Lt Whitlam was exemplary. He showed confidence in his team, where other leaders could have been too proud and baulked at accepting advice from a Private soldier.

This humility of command is born from the culture of the Regiment and a relationship based on shared hardships. This action highlighted the tremendous talent, intuition and tactical ability at the Private soldier level. For Ben Cunningham to be able to think outside the box and offer a solution to a problem that an officer, SNCO and a handful of JNCOs were struggling with was highly impressive and exemplified the standard of the airborne soldier.

We were all pleased to see that the *Daily Telegraph* dubbed the patrol action 'The Battle of Washiran'.


*Private Luke Hardy, 3 Para*


This was my third tour of Afghanistan. I was still a member of the sniper platoon, but had managed to get a place on the CMT (combat medic technician) course. I'd been up to Keogh barracks and completed my six-months' course there. It is the same course and qualification as a soldier that is joining the army to become a medic.

Myself and Lance Corporal Danny Carter were attached to a B Company platoon in a FOB called Talanda, stationed in the district of the north of Nad Ali. 3 Para were mostly in platoon strength units posted in FOBs in villages throughout the district, so we actually lived amongst the locals and oper-ated out of those areas on a daily basis for the whole tour. The locals would go about their day, while we would patrol and have shura (meetings) with the village elders as much as we could. The children would hang around and you got to recog-nise who was who and watch them go about their daily business; as snipers, we would always be observing and writing up 'a pattern of life'.

When we first arrived, it was planting time and re-seeding time for the next year of crops, so they would be digging up the entire field and sowing the seeds. They did this with very basic tools and lots of hard graft. It was like you had gone back a hundred years and more. You'd see the kids on a daily basis, running around helping their families out. We'd give them bits of chocolate, out of the ration packs – you'd try to be as friendly and nice as possible.

At the end of the day they're stuck between a rock and a hard place. They don't want the Taliban there, they don't want us there. We have been placed there for tactical purposes, because intelligence has said that Taliban have been seen or known to operate from that area. You have to look back on the local people and feel sorry for them, because if they say no to the Taliban, then they're in the shit, they've got no option. They do not want them there as they use the local people's water sources and consume their food. They also cannot come forward to us and give us information, because they know the consequences of that action.

Back in 2006, the Taliban apparently said, 'The west have the watches, but we have the time.' Meaning that they know they are there forever, it is their land, we will eventually have to leave and they will still be there. And we can see today, as they have also been in the past, they were exactly right.

I was both medic and sniper on this tour. On this account,

244

I'd been away on my R&R and had flown back to Talanda that night from Bastion, absolutely shattered. I was in my doss bag, fast asleep. I woke up to a loud bang, which I presumed was a dream, so I just got my head back down to sleep. Seconds later, one of the blokes came running to my bunk and said, 'Luke. Incident outside, someone's done an IED, looks like it's a civilian as no patrols are out.' So in my dreamy haze, putting my combats and boots on, I ran out to the med hut; we'd converted one of the rooms in our compound into a medical hut with all the kit and a stretcher in there, all ready to receive patients when needed. I came stumbling in and saw a few blokes in there along with our other medic, Private Todd Owen.

My first image was of a small, young boy lying down on the stretcher with his father and Todd over him. He looked around three years old. His large intestines were hanging out and there was another laceration in the lower part of his stomach where part of his lower intestines were also exposed. His right testicle was also missing, as was his right hand. The child's skin was pepper-potted with shrapnel and bits of stone that had blown into him with the blast. For whatever reason, how your brain works, when you're suddenly given this vision, I saw that attached to his big toe on his left foot was a piece of straw that had gone through his toe nail, through the skin, and was hanging out of both sides of the toe. I touched it, it was a proper piece of straw. I've no idea how something like that had managed to do that and why I always think of that when this incident comes to mind.

After having a couple of seconds to take all this in and think quickly, the training kicks in. I told everyone else to get out apart from myself, Todd and 2nd Lt Bowen, while Sgt Cook went to sort out the medic extraction. The father stayed as well. At this point it was about keeping this child alive until we could have him extracted by air and taken to a proper medical facility with far more qualified and experienced people than ourselves. He was alive; he hardly cried or made much of a noise: I remember him just staring at us. I'll never forget his eyes, the blackness of his pupils. We tourniqueted his arm as much as we could, this small, tiny boy. Abdominal bandages were placed over his intestines, so as not to push the intestines back, and soaked in water. We worked on him as much as we could.

Fifteen minutes later, two Pedros turned up – which are the American Blackhawks converted into their Casevac helicopters. One of them flew low over the base ready to rain down fire on anyone that would attempt to fire upon the choppers from the wood line just outside our base. I picked the young boy up in my arms and ran out to the Blackhawk and did my handover to the American medic, who wasn't really interested in what I had to say, because he just wanted the child on the chopper and to get out of there before anyone could attack them.

They flew off. And then you have your moments of reflection with each other . . . did that really happen? Thinking about everything that had gone on, what we could have done better. In all fairness, we weren't really kitted out to deal with a three-year-old child. I do look back and think, now I'm a paramedic with the London ambulance service, if only I had the information and experience I have now in what I could have done right there. But at the time we didn't know much about children as patients; it wasn't something we spent much time at all on in our training. We found out a couple of days later that the little boy didn't make it, he passed away.

I can't really remember being depressed about it. It was obviously very sad and shows you directly what the cost of war can be and is. This is the side of war that politicians and those in positions of power and responsibility never to get to witness first hand. If they did, they would think longer and harder before making these decisions. This was my third tour and we had a lot of new and young lads with us on that tour. It was a case of: it's done, put it to one side and carry on. It was the same when Tom Beckett got killed, or any of the blokes. It's happened and it's shit, really shit, but we're still out there and have to stay switched on and carry on and do so with confidence, so the new lads can see this and follow and gain the experience from you that they need now, and to carry on with their task.

We had a whiteboard, which was next to the Ops room. Because the AO (area of operations) was relatively small, you could hear when the surrounding FOBS were in contact. If people had been injured or killed that day, their names would go on the whiteboard, along with the first four digits of their military number. I remember with Tom Beckett, I had returned back from a patrol and Cookie, who was the acting sergeant, took me to one side, and I saw over his shoulder the whiteboard with 'Sgt Maj Beckett' and he said, 'Bad news, Luke – Tom's been killed.' That was one of the big hits for me on this tour. He was such a big man in the Regiment and he'd had a lot to do with my career to an extent.

When I first joined 3 Para, he was my platoon sergeant in C Company; I moved across to snipers for my first tour and was attached to his company during the start of Herrick 6. Then when I went back to the UK, he came to be the Sergeant Major D Company, which snipers were a part of. I had been on a couple of sailing trips he had organised, he was a good guy. He was a hard man and old school, a proper Paratrooper, someone you would do no wrong by looking up to and fol-lowing in his example. I also knew his partner was expecting their first child at home. So when I heard his name . . . it did definitely knock me back.

We had a little service for him and I read a verse from the

Bible: 'Yes, though I walk through the valley of the shadow of death . . .' And that was it, we carried on and went back out on patrol.

## Check Point Quadrat

Regarded as the most dangerous check point in Nad-e Ali District, Check Point Quadrat lay in an open, isolated and highly contested position on the edge of the green zone. More than half of the soldiers in the Battle Group who suffered from gunshot wounds did so in the vicinity of Quadrat. Every other day, reports showed that Quadrat or the patrols that left from it had been attacked, often repeatedly. The attacks were heavy, accurate and well-coordinated and usually from multiple locations. The enemy firing points were often defended by Improvised Explosive Devices (IEDs). Furthermore an experienced and skilled insurgent sharpshooter operated in the area.

*Private Chris Crabtree, 3 Para*

I started Para depot in November 2009. Did my training, not a problem, and ended up getting into 3 Para at the start of August 2010. We finished Para depot on Friday, had our passing out parade and turned up on Monday morning, got there and the whole fucking battalion had gone on leave!

So we went on leave and came back and I found myself lined up in the corridor, waiting. The company sergeant major went straight down the line and said, 'Ten of you, two platoon, ten of you, one platoon.' And that was it. He then said, 'If you're new here, stick your hand up.' Ten of us stuck our hands up. And he went, 'Right, you've got to do four days training in Lydd tomorrow, cause you're deploying to Afghan with us.' Well, I thought, they're not hanging around.

In the training depot at Catterick we were fighting the 'Russians' – running about the woods, digging shell scrapes – stuff like that. Now we were being taught how to fight the Taliban. After the training, we all went to the office a few days later, where the sergeant said, 'Right, I need four volunteers.' And being a new bloke, I stuck my hand up. So there was me, Private Greenwood, John Beswick and another bloke. The sergeant said, 'Right, you're going to a different check point to everyone in here; there's a new checkpoint that's just been made called Quadrat – go two doors down that way to meet all the people you'll be serving with in Afghan.' I thought, this is fucking great, isn't it? I've turned up ready to go to Afghan with a bunch of people I don't know and now there will be more people I don't bloody know.

We went into the room and there was Second Lieutenant McDonald, who was brand new, just out of Sandhurst. Then we had four Para blokes, TA blokes, blokes from Royal Lancs, including a private in his forties, blokes from machine guns and blokes from mortars. Proper last minute . . . I always called us the twenty-first-century Dad's Army, because that's what we were.

We were going to this checkpoint called Quadrat and everyone was like, nothing is going to happen there. Where one platoon was actually going, there were three checkpoints quite close together and it was called Three Ways. In summer, the Duke of Lancs regiment had been there and had had lots of contacts, to the point where when they knew they were coming home, they stopped patrolling because they didn't want to risk anyone getting hit. When we got there, it was pretty much bullets flying from day one.

They didn't have the rifles in Colchester to send out. It was like, right, what we got left? Here's your SA80 and you can have a UGL, an Underslung Grenade Launcher as well. So I had one of those. Turned around to the boss and said, 'I'm pretty tasty with these.' He said, 'I hope so, I'm giving it to you because you're going to be our point man out the front,' and I was like, 'Fucking great!' Straight out the depot and the first bloke to get shot is me. Thought, alright, I'll give it my best.

We flew into Kandahar. As we were coming into land, we got the call, 'Right, everyone get your helmets and body armour on.' This was because as the plane was coming down, the Taliban might start shooting at it. That was the first realisation like, shit, this is a fucking war zone.

We landed, and jumped on a Herc to Bastion. Got all our kit, went to our quarters and then we had to do the RSOY package, which is a ten-days-long acclimatisation package. You need that time to zero your weapons, get to know people, get used to the temperature. We were on the Winter tour, so it wasn't so hot. We were going through the drill that we'd done at Lydd and that's when I really started getting into my job as the point man. I started realising what I had been entrusted with, looking out for these bombs, recognising the ground signs if bombs or IEDs had been laid in the ground, really paying attention to what I was doing. After that, we would just sit about Camp Bastion. You could go over to Camp Leatherneck, the American side, and get all the pizzas you wanted. They had Mountain Dew and Coke and Fanta – you could help yourself. They had ice-cream; we were like kids in a candy store.

We finished that package and that night we were told to deploy and got all our kit packed up. The Bergen I had was so heavy, so full of kit, ammunition . . . I could barely pick the thing up off the floor. Easily 150 pounds, the heaviest thing I've ever had to carry. Well over my own body weight and I'm built like a rake. I had to lay the Bergen on the floor and get myself in, roll myself up and over onto my knees, then get someone to give me an arm so that I could get up. We were quite lucky we had a Merlin take us in, one of the new ones that the Navy were using. Sixty seconds out and we were flying into the pitch black.

It was really weird seeing the light of Camp Bastion going away in the distance, and you're thinking it can't be that much further, and before you know it you're looking at this very faint amber dot on the horizon. As we were landing, the load masters were at the doors saying, 'You've got 120 seconds to get all these blokes off, all these bags off, everything – you've got 120 seconds and then we're off!' As we were getting lower, the moonlight was showing the area we were in. I remember coming into the field and seeing the walls of the compound. I remember the tailgate dropping and some guy was standing there shouting, 'Don't get killed, get your crap off, get fucking going.' I didn't realise it was actually Dean Walton who was saying it. He had been sent into Quadrat before us to lay the ground; he was one of the fort screws there. Really good bloke and probably the best soldier I've ever worked with.

We all came charging off the back, grabbing bags and kit. We were running like dogs, getting all this stuff off. In the end, we got it all on the floor and let the chopper go. We got our heads down in our doss bags and waited for the morning. It was pretty daunting. Just pure silence.

When we got into the compound, the generators were working, so there were a few lights on. Nothing compared to what you'd expect anywhere in the world. It's worse than pagan. Never known anything like it in my life, I've never been to a place where there's just so little.

I remember the very first patrol we did, we had our ECN (Emergency Communications Network), and our Electronic Countermeasures kit. Check Point Quadrat was about twenty miles out of Bastion. The River Neptune runs through Helmand

Province and where we were located was a gap in the river with a dirt bridge over it. To the north of us, there were maybe two miles of other compounds and areas and then open desert and Camp Bastion. And then behind us was the green zone of Helmand Province, where most of the fighting was taking place.

During the summer, when the Duke of Lancs were out there on Herrick 12, they were constantly attacked by the Taliban. When the winter bites, the Taliban make their way up and out of the desert and have to go through the gap in the river, where we were. We got up north, because that's where the Taliban were hiding. They had done their poppies, done their harvest and then they'd go out into the desert and do what they had to do. We got them as they were coming out for the winter and then when they were coming back for the summer, so we were constantly in action. This made our checkpoint the most contacted checkpoint in the whole of 3 Para's area of operations.

No one thought Quadrat was going to be what it was. Everyone thought the action was going to take place in Three Ways, Kumar, places like that. With only fifteen men, we were seriously undermanned and Corporal Dean 'Waldo' Walton was constantly on the radio to the Command back at PV Kumar. At some point we were doing four hours on stag, two hours off. Then we'd have long patrols in-between that time. That went on for about two weeks and it broke a lot of us. If we got into a big contact, we'd be out on the ground for nine hours.

I remember the first time I was actually shot at. It was a really strange feeling, because you don't expect it. I was used to the one-way ranges, firing down with nothing coming back, so when I actually started firing and someone was firing back at me, you get that feeling that you're going to crap yourself or you're going to stay strong. Luckily for me, I stayed strong.

On another patrol, we were looking for a Mastiff (armoured vehicle) that had just been blown up, when suddenly rounds were coming in, but it didn't register in my head some were coming my way, including our own machine-gunner Beswick, who had got a bit out of control. All the ground behind me was coming up with dust and I was thinking, fucking hell! And by now we're in major contact and I'm being shot at from the front, and shot at from behind. I was like, fucking leave me alone! Waldo saw that and ran up behind Beswick and gave him a good clout on the helmet. I'm there in the middle of contact trying to get this fire down. Waldo shouted, 'Everyone peel into the compound over there!' I was the last man in, as I was sending fire back from all these rounds that were flying at us. Then I had a hundred-metre dash over open ground under fire. As I came peeling in, I thought, fucking hell that was close.

Waldo got me in and I looked about and it turned out to be the local toilet. There was shit everywhere on the floor. I was like, 'Mate, you could have picked any building to run into and you pick the fucking shitter.' Waldo realised that there wouldn't be any IODs in there! We were up on the walls of the bloody shitter having a full-on firefight. We were taking shit, giving shit, standing in shit – it was a shit day. That firefight lasted for a good couple of hours, because we had to wait for the resupply that was coming down. We had to see those lads through. We went out early morning and didn't come back till after dark and we stank!

All came back unscathed. Really was a baptism of fire. Back at the compound, everyone was walking about looking very pleased. Waldo came up to me and he said, 'Good job today what you did, you're a new bloke, you've been out on the ground for seven days. Keep up the good work.' I was still as green as anything. He had been to Afghan every single time 3 Para had been out there, so for him to come up to me and say that was a great morale boost.

The situation was so confusing, kind of weird, but the

training kicks in automatically and you don't think about what you're doing, you act. And that muscle memory they put into you in depot. Like when you're getting shot at, take it to the knee, two rounds down then go, run for cover.

The one patrol that sticks out the most was the day that Greenwood got shot. We went out on patrol to the north-east area, and like with all the compounds, there's a little rat run. This was a fighting patrol; we went out looking for a fight. We went out, patrolling through the compounds, we had the I-Comm chat coming in from the interpreter – we had the best interpreter out there, he was called Hamid. He used to work for Dutch Special Forces, so he really knew his stuff. He was fully kitted up with plates and AK-47s and stuff like that and he was the only interpreter in 3 Para that was allowed to carry a weapon.

We turned up to a bit of open ground and a round came in and hit Greenwood. The round got lodged in the side of his front plate, but it's like getting punched in the sternum. It wasn't really a laughing matter at the time, but he was the first one to shout, 'Man doooown!' as he was hitting the floor. We got him up and the medic ran over and checked, put his hand behind him, but there was no blood, no exit wound, no entry wound. From then on, we were shooting at anything that moved, because we had no idea where the round had come from. We were just putting down cover fire until the medic saw to Greenwood. That was that. That was a good one. We got him up, got him back and we realised all he had was a bruise. He was lucky.

A lot of the time we were out there, there was a sniper who was going about for the Taliban. The media actually knew about him and called him the Nad-e Ali sniper. When the sniper came, the engineers ended up coming to Quadrat to bolster up our defences. We were getting contacted that much and all we had were mud walls around us. They had to stick Hescos (wire-mesh blast walls) all around. We went through a period of twenty-two days when we were contacted every single day. Most of the time, they would tend not to attack in the early hours of the morning, because we were already awake. They normally got us when we went on patrol, around about tea time, then maybe at eleven or twelve at night.

I remember being in bed at night and the compound was getting contacted and it looked like a scene from *Star Wars*, because we had green tracer fire coming over from them, then there was red tracer fire going back from us, so it looked like the goodies and the baddies. We ended up getting contacted from three different places; it was a coordinated attack on us. I remember I chucked my body armour on and was running about; I had my Underslung Grenade Launcher and my bag with all my bombs in it. The guys were calling, 'There's contact over here!' and I would run over just in body armour, flip-flops and my pyjama shorts, and I'd be firing these bombs off over the wall. Something like that at night could last for anything from a minute to twenty, twenty-five minutes.

During the day were the most intense ones. The longest one I had was nine hours, but it wasn't a constant bang-bang-bang; we couldn't carry that much ammo. The big loss for me and all the rest of us was Warrant Officer Colin Beckett. I saw the explosion happen in the distance.

The boss came up to me one morning and said you're going on a patrol and you're going to be near the back, so obviously I had the electronic countermeasure thing on, a big blue one which weighed about eighty pounds. Heat was about 25/30 degrees. The area we were going into was like a rat run and I thought there were a lot of blokes going into a small area. I didn't say anything. Even though I had been out there a while, it was still very much a case of listen to your peers. If the boss was a mate down the pub back in Essex, I probably would have said something, but here he was still the boss.

I remember getting ten metres out of the gate and having to take a knee in the middle of an open wadi, because we'd already bunched up that much. So we were going around the rat runs. The point man was leading and Conrad Lewis, a Reservist with 4 Para, was his cover man. The point man had been sent to us a few days before the patrol as extra manpower. He was a really good kid.

We were on the radio to the boss, and he was saying head here, head there, whatever. Then we came to this wall in the shape of an L. He was coming around and he had to stop and jump over the wall and walk down. There were compounds in the distance. So basically the lads were walking up, one hops over the wall, one covers and then one gets down and covers while the other hops over, so we were doing that, all fine, everyone had got over. Then it came to my turn and as I was going over the wall, next thing I knew the wall exploded in front of me and I fell back on my arse. Everyone was like, 'What the fuck, is it contact? Man down.' And I was like, 'No, no, I'm fine.' I heard the second shot come in and didn't realise what had happened. Then I heard, 'Man down, man down!'

Basically, the Nadi Ali sniper was the one that was shooting at us and he had hit both the point man and Conrad Lewis. We were protecting these two, if a tree blew in the wind we were going to shoot it. We had two lads down; we were fucking pissed off at this point. They crashed the Jackal armoured vehicle out from Quadrat. The crew didn't give a fuck about the bombs or anything, they just got the two lads up the road to Quadrat and got them on the MERT.

We had a new bloke from the Afghan Tiger team with an RPG so the boss came up to me and told me to show him the best way to use high explosives. If you've got someone shooting at you, you don't necessarily aim at the person, you aim for a tree, aim for a building – you try and create shrapnel to hit the fucker. I noticed that somewhere over in the distance there was a murder hole in the wall, I thought that's where the sniper could be, so I thought, fuck it, I'm going to send a couple of rounds and a UGL into that compound, just in case.

I got my first shot away and on the second one I noticed this Tiger bloke was watching where I was shooting and I could see the rear of his RPG out the corner of my eye. I sent my second round away, when suddenly the rear of this Afghan Tiger's RPG went bang. Next thing I knew, I was on the floor and I had blood coming from my ears, blood coming from my mouth – basically he'd set the RPG off in my face. I caught the whole back blast. And the back blast from the RPG is phenomenal, so I had taken the whole thing to the side of my face. At the time, it blew out my left ear completely.

I came round, came to and tried to sit myself up, pure ringing in my ears – proper like in a daze, so I sat and thought, fuck that hurt. Then Duncan Armstrong came running up to me and said, 'You alright, you alright?' and I was looking at his mouth and replied, 'I think I'm okay, can't hear shit,' but I was watching his mouth and he was telling me that that we had to run and catch up with the Jackal vehicle. The Jackal was already speeding off. I got my kit on and as I was running past, I grabbed the point man's daysack, because all their kit was still on the ground.

People were popping smoke to cover the extraction and I was running, just like pure running, running back in these tyre marks behind this Jackal and I saw the MERT come in. I thought, sweet, I'm near the gate now, just get back in! I was running across in no-man's land and I remember looking up to the super-sanger, which was in an elevated position. And Jamie Law of 4 Para, who was firing his GMPG, was hanging out, screaming, 'Get the fuck back in now!'

I looked down, not realising that the ground beneath me was going pffft, pffft, pffft. Someone was shooting at me and

Jamie was trying to suppress whoever it was. Luckily enough I got back in and literally I remember getting into the compound, putting my head around the corner and seeing them being put into the helicopter. I saw them go and that was it, I never saw them again.

I collapsed into a heap after that and the medic came over to me. All the other lads were back by then. I had a few burns, the blood, stone and dirt had sprayed up my side but I was okay, I knew in my head I was fine. I unloaded my weapon, put my shit down and cleaned myself up right away. Sat through the debrief right up the front near the boss, but one ear was fucked, talking about what had happened from leaving the gate to the debrief about the patrol and loss of our lads. It was just so unlucky.

We got back and the medic, Tim Dymitt, came up to me a couple of hours later. He stuck things in my ear and told me I had no tympanic membrane to protect my eardrum and that there was a lot of spotting and blood in there and I would have to go back to Bastion. I felt horrible with what had just happened and them losing another bloke as well on 12 February. I stayed in Bastion as long as I could to see if I could go back out on the ground, but in the end they turned around and said your time's finished now, you've got to go back home.

Went to Peterborough, the specialist ENT unit up there, to try and sort me out. The ear drum was ruptured but not beyond repair, so it took time to heal. I really wanted to get back to Afghanistan as everyone had been very complimentary about my patrolling. That was not to be, as I was medically downgraded and discharged. I'm on full war pension now.

**Lt Jamie McDonald, Cpl Jamie Law and Pte Conrad Lewis each received Mention in Dispatches for their bravery at CP Quadrat.**

# 13

# AFGHANISTAN
## 2012–2013

**Combined UK/US assault led by the United States
Marine Corps into a Taliban stronghold to disrupt
a key insurgent group.**

For his actions in this Operation, Lance Corporal Joshua Leaky
was awarded a Victoria Cross and the citation reads:

> Between May and December 2013, Lance Corporal Leakey
> was deployed in Afghanistan as a member of a Task Force
> conducting operations to disrupt insurgent safe-havens and
> protect the main operating base in Helmand province. The
> majority of operations took place in daylight in non-permissive
> areas, attracting significant risk. On the 22nd August 2013,
> Lance Corporal Leakey deployed on a combined UK/US assault
> led by the United States Marine Corps into a Taliban strong-
> hold to disrupt a key insurgent group.
>
> After dismounting from their helicopters, the force came
> under accurate machine gun and rocket-propelled grenade
> fire resulting in the Command Group being pinned down
> on the exposed forward slope of a hill. The team attempted
> to extract from the killing zone for an hour, their efforts
> resulting in a Marine Corps Captain being shot and wounded
> and their communications being put out of action. Lance
> Corporal Leakey, positioned on the lee of the hill, realising
> the seriousness of the situation and with complete disregard
> for his own safety, dashed across a large area of barren

hillside which was now being raked with machine gun fire. As he crested the hill, the full severity of the situation became apparent: approximately twenty enemy had surrounded two friendly machine gun teams and a mortar section rendering their critical fire support ineffective.

Undeterred by the very clear and present danger, Lance Corporal Leakey moved down the forward slope of the hill, and gave first aid to the wounded officer. Despite being the most junior commander in the area, Lance Corporal Leakey took control of the situation and initiated the casualty evacuation. Realising that the initiative was still in the hands of the enemy, he set off back up the hill, still under enemy fire, to get one of the suppressed machine guns into action. On reaching it, and with rounds impacting on the frame of the gun itself, he moved it to another position and began engaging the enemy.

This courageous action spurred those around him back into the fight; nonetheless, the weight of enemy fire continued. For the third time and with full knowledge of the extant dangers, Lance Corporal Leakey exposed himself to enemy fire once more. Weighed down by over 60lbs of equipment, he ran to the bottom of the hill, picked up the second machine gun and climbed back up the hill again: a round trip of more than 200 metres on steep terrain. Drawing the majority of the enemy fire, with rounds splashing around him, Lance Corporal Leakey overcame his fatigue to re-site the gun and return fire. This proved to be the turning point. Inspired by Lance Corporal Leakey's actions, and with a heavy weight of fire now at their disposal, the force began to fight back with renewed ferocity. Having regained the initiative, Lance Corporal Leakey handed over the machine gun and led the extraction of the wounded officer to a point from which he could be safely evacuated.

During this assault 11 insurgents were killed and 4 wounded, but the weight of enemy fire had effectively pinned down the command team. Displaying gritty leadership well above that expected of his rank, Lance Corporal Leakey's actions single-handedly regained the initiative and prevented considerable loss of life, allowing a wounded US Marine officer to be evacuated. For this act of valour, Lance Corporal Leakey is highly deserving of significant national recognition.

# ACKNOWLEDGEMENTS

I would like to thank all serving and former members of the Airborne Forces, who told me of their personal experiences and who, throughout the writing of this book, gave me their utmost support and co-operation. Sadly, a place could not be found for every person's story, but all of them deserved one. I would also like to thank those closely connected with the Airborne Forces, in particular the families and wives whom I met, whose stories should also be told. At Parachute Regimental HQ, Lt Col Paul Rogers and in particular Adam Jowett were extremely helpful throughout the writing of this book.

I am indebted to Major General Chip Chapman, not only for his help with the brief history of each operation, but for his excellent introduction and valuable suggestions, all of which have enhanced the book.

I would also like to put on record the sterling work of Andy Newell, his brothers Jim and Eddie Newell, Tom Blakey and Stuart Cardy, all of whom seemed to have an extraordinary insight, for not only finding the right person to tell their story of a particular operation, but to ensure that even the most reluctant (due to modesty) got that story to me.

From the beginning, I had the pleasure of working with Rupert Lancaster at Hodder, who has been highly supportive and very patient, as was my editor, Barry Johnston. My agent, Gordon Wise of Curtis Brown, has been at the top of his game throughout the writing of *The Paras* and I thank him. Lynsey

# ACKNOWLEDGEMENTS

Murdoch brought rich humour and support on the many occasions that we worked late into the night. I am indebted to her.

As always, my work was enhanced by the love and support of Don and Liz McClen, Deborah Moggach, Susan Jeffries, Lucia Corti and my dear friend Ruth Cowen.

# PICTURE ACKNOWLEDGEMENTS

# INDEX

# INDEX

# INDEX